Natural Disasters

Books in the **Contemporary World Issues** series address vital issues in today's society such as genetic engineering, pollution, and biodiversity. Written by professional writers, scholars, and nonacademic experts, these books are authoritative, clearly written, up-to-date, and objective. They provide a good starting point for research by high school and college students, scholars, and general readers as well as by legislators, businesspeople, activists, and others.

Each book, carefully organized and easy to use, contains an overview of the subject, a detailed chronology, biographical sketches, facts and data and/or documents and other primary source material, a forum of authoritative perspective essays, annotated lists of print and nonprint resources, and an index.

Readers of books in the Contemporary World Issues series will find the information they need in order to have a better understanding of the social, political, environmental, and economic issues facing the world today.

Natural Disasters

A REFERENCE HANDBOOK

David E. Newton

ABC-CLIO ™

An Imprint of ABC-CLIO, LLC
Santa Barbara, California • Denver, Colorado

Library of Congress Cataloging in Publication Control Number: 2019940817

ISBN: 978-1-4408-6761-3 (print)
        978-1-4408-6762-0 (ebook)

23 22 21 20 19   1 2 3 4 5

This book is also available as an eBook.

ABC-CLIO
An Imprint of ABC-CLIO, LLC

ABC-CLIO, LLC
147 Castilian Drive
Santa Barbara, California 93117
www.abc-clio.com

This book is printed on acid-free paper ∞

Manufactured in the United States of America

Contents

Preface

By the middle of 2018, the following events occurred:

- More than 100 wildfires destroyed an estimated 1.6 million acres of vegetation in the American West.
- Heavy rains in Japan—more than three times the normal amounts—produced flooding, landslides, and mudslides that killed more than 100 people and forced the relocation of more than 2 million individuals.
- The eruption of Mount Fuego in Guatemala directly affected the lives of an estimated 2 million people, including at least 33 deaths.
- An effusive (nonexplosive) volcanic eruption occurred on the Big Island of Hawaii on May 3. The event was followed by 2 major earthquakes and more than 500 minor earthquakes in the succeeding months.
- The first tropical storm of the year hit the Florida Panhandle, resulting in two deaths, the loss of power for more than 20,000 homes, and flash flooding in North Carolina.
- Dust storms in northern and western India resulted in more than 125 deaths and uncounted numbers of livestock, along with the destruction of homes and electrical generating facilities.
- An earthquake in Hualien, Taiwan, caused $21 million in property damage.

- Heavy windstorms across Northern and Western Europe caused more than 13 deaths, caused extensive property damage, and interrupted normal transportation systems.

- Mudslides caused by heavy forest fire damage the previous year resulted in 21 deaths, the destruction of 129 homes, and damage to 307 additional structures. (All examples are from Lauren Slocum. 2018. "The Worst Natural Disasters of 2018." Ranker. https://www.ranker.com/list/worst-natural-disasters-2018/lauren-slocum. Accessed on August 6, 2018.)

Reports of natural disasters exist as far back as human history has existed. Earthquakes; volcanic eruptions; tsunamis; tornadoes, hurricanes, typhoons, and cyclones; flooding; forest fires; landslides and mudslides, and other types of mass wasting; drought; limnic eruptions; sinkholes; and extreme weather have killed untold numbers of people, caused injuries and the displacement of even more individuals, resulted in unmeasurable amounts of property damage, and even changed the physical structure of land and water systems. Many of these events, in spite of their tragic features, have achieved a popularity among the general public that is unmatched by few other topics in geography and the environment. It is perhaps no surprise that the topic of natural disasters is one of the most popular topics of books written for children and young adults.

This book begins with a general description of the major types of natural disasters. The descriptions usually relate "the first," "the worst," "the most destructive," "most severe," or otherwise "most important" event of its kind. For a number of reasons, readers should use caution in noting such rankings. For one thing, records of natural disasters, especially before the 20th century, may be incomplete or inaccurate. Also, experts may use different criteria for determining "the most something" for any event. Nonetheless, the examples selected for this book of such events have been chosen because of some extreme aspect of their occurrence or some special interest they may have for the general public.

The impact of natural disasters on human lives and property is, of course, a major interest to government officials, public health workers, infrastructure and transportation companies, energy suppliers, and individuals and the communities in which they live. Although relatively little can be done to prevent most natural disasters, other mitigating steps can be taken. For example, natural disasters that are, at least in part, caused by human activities can be managed by the use of laws and regulations and other actions limiting the role played by humans. Probably the most action that societies can take with regard to natural disasters is education. Any number of programs that help individuals, organizations, and communities understand what they need to do before, during, and after a natural disaster exist. With this information, the worst effects of a natural disaster can often be averted or ameliorated.

Chapter 1 of this book is devoted to a brief overview of the history of major natural disasters and the mechanisms by which they occur. This background is designed to be of help to readers who want to know enough about a particular event to start their own research on the topic. This general introduction should be complemented, of course, by more detailed study of any one type of event, an activity for which very large additional resources are available.

Chapter 2 discusses current issues relating to natural disasters, such as the ways in which each type of natural disaster affects human life, and efforts that have been and are being made to prepare for and recover such events. Chapter 3 is of special interest because it consists of essays by individuals who have some special point of view about natural disasters, such as one who is making a career of studying such events or who has been personally affected by a natural disaster.

Chapter 4 is the first of the resource chapters in the book, providing brief introductions to individuals and organizations with some special place in the study of natural disasters. Chapter 5 consists of data about natural disasters and excerpts from laws, regulations, and case law about various aspects of natural disasters and their effects on humans. Chapter 6 is an annotated bibliography of relevant books, articles, reports, and Internet resources on natural disasters. (The reader is advised to pay special attention to the extensive notes provided at the end of both Chapters 1 and 2 for additional resources to which one can turn for further information on specific aspects of the topic of natural disasters.) Chapter 7 is a chronology of important events in the history of natural disasters. The chapter should provide hints about not only topics that are discussed in Chapters 1 and 2 but also additional subjects in which the reader may be interested. Finally, the glossary provides definitions not only for terms used in this book itself but also for words that one might encounter in one's further research on the topic of natural disasters.

Natural Disasters

1 Background and History

Farther up the coast in what is now Washington, Thunderbird and Whale had a terrible fight, making the mountains shake and uprooting the trees, said the Quileute and the Hoh people; they said the ocean rose up and covered the whole land. Farther north still, on Vancouver Island, dwarfs who lived in a mountain invited a person to dance around their drum; the person accidentally kicked the drum and got earthquake-foot, said the Nuu-chah-nulth people, and after that every step he took caused an earthquake. (Finkbeiner 2015)

For as long as humans have existed on Earth, they have tried to understand the world around them and changes that take place in the world. The earliest humans, for example, were interested in question such as the following: How do people become ill? How does a woman become pregnant? What causes someone to die? Lacking any other way to answer those questions, early humans created answers that seemed to make sense to them. For example, many early tribes decided that illness was caused when an unfriendly enemy cast spells on a person. The person would survive only if he or she could have that spell removed. (Some ancient beliefs, it should be noted, survive in the modern world.)

The ruins of Pompeii, Italy, with a view of Mount Vesuvius, a once deadly volcano. (Frenta/Dreamstime.com)

3

Natural events were also experiences of interest and concern. What was it, early humans wondered, that causes the sun and moon to rise and set every day on such a regular pattern? And what causes less common events, such a solar or lunar eclipse? Again, humans used their imagination and reasoning powers to come up with an answer. For example, eclipses were often explained by the action of some evil creature's attempt to swallow the moon or sun. This explanation was reinforced by the observation that eclipses always begin with a small chunk of the moon or sun disappearing from view (Grady 2017).

Among the most puzzling of all natural events are those that occur without warning and, generally, with disastrous effects on humans and the world around them. Such disasters include avalanches; blizzards; cyclones, hurricanes, and typhoons; earthquakes; floods; landslides; limnic eruptions (the sudden release of gases from a lake or other body of water); sinkholes; thunderstorms; tsunamis; volcanic eruptions; and wildfires. In the following sections, some of the many explanations invented by early humans for the most common of these events are discussed.

Natural Disasters in Human History

Untold numbers of devastating natural disasters have occurred throughout human history. No single book can discuss in any detail even a fraction of those events. It is possible, however, to offer some examples of such incidents.

Perhaps the earliest of all known such occasions occurred about 66 million years ago, when an asteroid from outer space crashed into Earth's surface near the modern-day town of Chicxulub, in the Yucatan Peninsula of Mexico. One could reasonably ask how anyone in the 21st century could know anything about an event that occurred so far in the past, long before humans even existed on Earth. The answer is that scientists from a number of disciplines have found geological and other data that provide a surprisingly detailed description of the impact.

Research on the Chicxulub occurrence can be dated to 1978, when scientists from the Mexican state-owned oil company Petróleos Mexicanos (Pemex) began a study of the Yucatan as a potential source of oil and gas. During this research, geophysicists Antonio Camargo and Glen Penfield discovered a nearly circular crater in Earth's crust that underlies the peninsula. An explanation for the crater's existence was offered only two years later by father and son geological research team of Luis Walter and Walter Alvarez. They hypothesized that, at some distant past, an asteroid collided with Earth in the region of Chicxulub. That impact produced the 150-kilometer (90 miles) diameter, 20-kilometer (12 miles) deep crater that exists today. The relatively clear features on the Chicxulub crater have made it a fruitful source for research on this earliest of all natural disasters. Today researchers know a great deal not only about the physical features of the crater but also about the devastation the asteroid impact had on Earth.

Perhaps the most striking of those consequences was the extinction of not only the dominant life form at the time, the dinosaurs, but also up to three quarters of *all* plant and animal species in existence at the time. Extinction has been attributed to enormous tsunami waves more than 100 meters (300 feet) high for hundreds of miles beyond the Yucatan, as well as clouds of gas and smoke released by the impact. Some researchers believe that atmospheric conditions were so dramatically altered for up to a decade that only a few plant and animal species were able to survive (Shonting and Ezrailson 2017).

No other disaster in history is known to have had such profound effects as the Chicxulub asteroid impact, but recorded history includes many examples of earthquakes, hurricanes, wildfires, flooding, tornadoes, tsunamis, volcanic eruptions, and other such catastrophes. A review of some of the most important of these events follows.

Earthquakes

Generally, earthquakes and other natural disasters prior to the 17th century were attributed by almost all human societies to the actions of a god, goddess, or other supernatural being who had special control over an event. In the case of early Mesopotamia civilizations (5000–3500 BCE), for example, the goddess of healing Gula (also known as Ninkarrak) was thought to be responsible for earthquakes and other disasters. She was said to have a violent temper and caused the earth to tremble and the heavens to storm when she became angry (Avalos 1995, 106–107). In the ancient Greek pantheon of gods and goddesses, it was Poseidon, god of the sea, who was also thought to be responsible for earthquakes, as well as other disasters, such as floods and storms at sea (Poseidon [Earthshaker, Dark-Haired One, Neptune] 2018). Throughout early Christianity also, earthquakes were attributed to a supernatural being, God, or Yahweh in the Hebrew tradition. Such events were almost always explained as the actions by God to punish humans for evil behavior or, on the other hand, to bring about an event desired by God (such as the opening of Jesus's tomb) (Chester 2018).

The first earthquake for which a written record exists is one that struck Mount Tai, in China, in 1831 BCE. The event is described in the *Bamboo Annals* (Zhúshu Jìnián), an encyclopedia of Chinese history from its earliest days (about 2600 BCE) to 299 BCE. Few details are provided, and no deaths are said to have occurred as a result of the incident.

Significant Earthquakes in History

One of the first earthquakes for which detailed (if somewhat contradictory) information is available occurred in 17 CE in the kingdom of Lydia. The kingdom occupied about half of the western portion of modern-day Turkey. The earthquake was reported and described by a number of contemporary authors, including the Roman historians Tacitus and Pliny the Elder and the Greek historians Strabo and Eusebius. Pliny alluded to the event as "the greatest earthquake in human history" (Ambraseys 2009, 106). According to these reviews, up to 15 cities and towns were destroyed in the quake. The Roman emperor Tiberius sent large amounts of money and other aid to the damaged cities, an act for which he was memorialized by a number of statues, commemorative coins, and other honors by the affected communities (Bulman 2012).

Earthquakes have always occurred in every part of the planet—albeit in some regions more commonly than others—with severity that ranges from the very mild to the very severe. In the former, the ground may shake so little that a person may hardly notice the change. In the latter, shaking may be so great as to open long segments of the earth, swallowing animals, plants, humans, cars, and buildings. The severity of an earthquake can be measured by different means. One of the most common scales for measuring earthquake intensity is the Richter scale, invented by American seismologist Charles Francis Richter and German -American seismologist Beno Gutenberg in 1935. The scale is a logarithmic scale ranging from 1 (least severe) to 10 (most severe). The term *logarithmic* means that each unit is 10 times greater than the previous unit. Thus, an earthquake that has a Richter number of 2 is 10 times as severe as one with a Richter number of 1. And one with a Richter number of 3 is 100 times as severe as a Richter 1 quake.

Another way of measuring the effects of an earthquake is the Mercalli scale that measures the severity of earthquakes with numbers from I to XII (always using Roman numerals). This system was developed by Italian vulcanologist and priest Giuseppe Mercalli between 1884 and 1906. This scale measures not only the severity of an earthquake (how much the ground shakes) but also the effects of the earthquake on humans and objects in the environment. A level IV earthquake ("mild"), for example, is defined as one that is "felt indoors by many, outdoors by few during the day. At night, some awakened.

Dishes, windows, doors disturbed; walls make cracking sound. Sensation like heavy truck striking building. Standing motor cars rocked noticeably" (The Modified Mercalli Intensity Scale 2018).

Throughout human history, untold numbers of earthquakes have been reported everywhere on Earth, with degrees of intensity ranging from close to 0 to almost 10. A few of these earthquakes have been so severe as to have earned a special place in the history of human civilization. One such event that has sometimes been called "the deadliest earthquake on record" occurred in Shaanxi Province, China, on January 23, 1556. The earthquake is also called the Huxian earthquake, for the district in which it occurred. Effects of the event were felt as far as 500 kilometers (310 miles) from the epicenter (the point on the earth's surface that is directly above the point underground at which the earthquake occurs). In some places, a crack in the ground up to 20 meters (70 yards) deep opened up.

A number of towns in the region were completely destroyed, with no survivors at all. The quake was damaging especially to people living in yaodongs, caves dug into a mountainside, sites that were also completely swept away by the earthquake. Overall, an estimated 830,000 people are thought to have been killed by the quake (Shaanxi Earthquake 1556 [Worst Death Toll] 2018).

Another famous earthquake occurred on November 1, 1755, in the southern portion of the Iberian Peninsula (Spain and Portugal) and northern Morocco. The epicenter of the earthquake is thought to have been on the seafloor of the Atlantic Ocean, about 200 kilometers (120 miles) from the Portuguese shoreline. A tsunami triggered by the earthquake, along with shaking of the earth and fires set by the quake, is thought to have killed as many as 40,000 people in Portugal and 10,000 more in Morocco. Descriptions of the earthquake suggest that the metropolis of Lisbon was "almost totally destroyed," while the town of Algiers, 1,100 kilometers (680 miles) east of Lisbon, was completely destroyed (1755 The Great Lisbon Earthquake and Tsunami, Portugal, 2018). For a list of tsunamis with highest water height in recorded history, see Table 5.3.

Important Earthquakes in U.S. History

Information about earthquakes in North America is relatively sparse, compared to that from the rest of the world. One reason is that native peoples on the continent tended to rely on oral histories, rather than written records, as a way of remembering early events. Thus, the first earthquake of which we have almost any information at all is one that struck the Pacific Northwest on January 26, 1700, the so-called Cascadia earthquake. One source of information about that event consists of Japanese records of a tsunami that struck Japanese shores a few days after the Cascadia event that cannot be explained by any other known phenomena. Another major source of information about the quake consists of evidence obtained by modern geologists about Earth movements that correspond to such an earthquake.

The earthquake is thought to have had an intensity of about 8.7–9.2 on the Richter scale and covered a 1,000-kilometer (600 miles) area ranging from Vancouver Island in the north to northern California in the south. It qualifies as one of the two most devastating earthquakes in the history of continental North America (the other being the Alaska earthquake of 1964). The average horizontal Earth movement along this region was about 20 meters (60 feet). Observers of the earthquake attributed the event to a battle between Thunderbird and Whale, two animals of supernatural size and strength. These animals were also thought to be responsible for other natural phenomena, such as winds and storms (Ludwin et al. 2005).

The frequency with which earthquakes occur around the world, or, for that matter, in the United States, differs widely from region to region. In the United States, about 90 percent of all earthquakes throughout history have occurred west of the Mississippi River. (The reason for this pattern is explained later in this chapter.) For example, consider the statistics for 2010–2012. We select this period because, after that time, certain human activities dramatically changed natural, historic patterns (again for reasons that are discussed later in the chapter). As Table 1.1 shows, by far the greatest number of quakes occurred in Alaska, California, Nevada, and Wyoming. Hardly any such events occurred in eastern states, such as Alabama, Connecticut, Florida, Michigan, and New Jersey.

An intense series of earthquakes near the town of New Madrid in the Louisiana Territory (the modern state of Missouri) occurring between December 1811 and February 1812 are of special interest, then, because they are now recognized as the most destructive earthquakes east of the Mississippi in U.S.

Table 1.1   Frequency of Earthquakes in Selected States, 2010–2012

State	2010	2011	2012
Alabama	1	1	0
Alaska	2,245	1,409	1,166
Arizona	6	7	4
Arkansas	15	44	4
California	546	195	243
Hawaii	17	34	40
Mississippi	0	0	0
Missour	2	3	2
Montana	7	11	9
Nebraska	2	0	1
Nevada	38	86	22
Oklahoma	41	63	34
Utah	17	16	16
Vermont	0	0	0
Virginia	1	7	4
Washington	5	14	6
Wyoming	43	6	9

Source: "Earthquake Counts by State 2010–2015 (M3+). Counts Are as of March 10, 2016." U.S. Geological Survey. https://earthquake.usgs.gov/earthquakes/browse/stats.php. Accessed on April 16, 2018.

history. The first quake occurred on the evening of December 16, 1811. The event was thought to have had a rating of 7.2–8.1 on the Richter scale. Relatively modest damage occurred as a result of the quake, largely because the region was sparsely settled. The incident was noted, however, as far away as Memphis, Tennessee, a distance of 230 kilometers (120 miles) from New Madrid. A second quake (aftershock) followed about four hours later, with an approximately equal intensity.

On January 26, 1812, a third earthquake occurred in the same general area as that of the 1811 quakes. It is commonly thought to be the least intense of the four quakes that hit the area. The fourth quake in the series occurred about two weeks later, on February 7, 1812. This event resulted in the total destruction of the town of New Madrid and subsidence (sinking) of the ground by amounts of up to 5 meters (16 feet). Contemporary accounts note that general shaking and warping of the ground occurred, along with ejections of gases, fissuring in Earth's surface, severe landslides, collapse of stream banks, and tsunami-like waves on the Mississippi River. The loss of one life and destruction of log cabins and other small buildings were reported from a number of locations as far away as St. Louis, Missouri (260 kilometers; 160 miles) and Cincinnati, Ohio (640 kilometers; 400 miles) (1811–1812 New Madrid, Missouri Earthquakes 2018).

Mention of the word *earthquake* in the United States almost always calls to mind the most severe such event to occur in American history: the San Francisco earthquake of 1906. The quake began at 5:12 A.M. on April 18, 1906, and lasted about a minute. Its intensity has been estimated to be about 7.9 on the Richter scale and XI on the Mercalli scale, the highest possible rating on that scale. The incident is of special interest to seismologists and the general public because so much has been written about the event. It may well be one of the most thoroughly studied earthquakes in U.S. history up to the late 20th century.

The impact on the city of San Francisco was a result of not only the earthquake itself, which resulted in the collapse and/or destruction of up to 80 percent of the city's structures, but also fires that broke out and burned through most of the city. An estimated 3,000 people are thought to have lost their lives, either directly or indirectly from the earthquake. Another 225,000 are thought to have become homeless, more than 60 percent of the city's population of 400,000. About 28,000 buildings were destroyed, resulting in a monetary loss of $400 million in 1906 dollars ($10.5 billion in 2018 dollars). The quake caused significant damage in cities and towns as distant as Eureka, near the Oregon border; 102 deaths were reported in San Jose and 64 deaths in Santa Rosa (these numbers are probably gross underestimates) (The Great 1906 San Francisco Earthquake 2018).

The two states to have suffered the most from earthquakes in the United States since 1950 have been Alaska and California. Table 1.2 shows tremors with Richter scales of more than 7.0 that have occurred in these two states.

Table 1.2 Earthquakes in Alaska and California with Intensities of More Than 7.5 (Richter scale) (Alaska) and More Than 6.5 (California) since 1950*

State	Date	Magnitude	Deaths	Damage**
Alaska	March 9, 1957	8.6		1
Alaska	July 10, 1958	7.8		1
Alaska	March 28, 1964	9.2	15	$284 million
Alaska	February 4, 1965	8.7		1
Alaska	March 30, 1965	7.6		
Alaska	July 30, 1972	7.6		1
Alaska	February 2, 1975	7.6		2
Alaska	May 7, 1986	8.0		2
Alaska	November 30, 1987	7.9		1
Alaska	March 6, 1988	7.8		1
Alaska	June 10, 1996	7.9		
Alaska	November 3, 2002	7.9		$56 million
Alaska	November 17, 2003	7.8		
Alaska	June 23, 2014	7.9		
California	July 21, 1952	7.7	12	$60 million
California	October 15, 1979	6.9		$30 million

State	Date	Magnitude	Deaths	Damage**
California	November 8, 1980	7.2	5	$2.75 million
California	October 18, 1989	6.9	62	$5.6 billion
California	April 25, 1992	7.1		$75 million
California(Yucca Valley)	June 28, 1992	7.6	3	$72 million
California(Big Bear)	June 28, 1992	6.7		2
California	January 7, 1994	6.7	60	$40 billion
California	September 1, 1994	7.0		1
California	October 16, 1999	7.2		
California	December 22, 2003	6.6	2	$300 million
California	June 15, 2005	7.2		

Source: "The Significant Earthquake Data Base." 2018. U.S. Geological Survey. https://www.ngdc.noaa.gov/nndc/struts/form?t=101650&s=1&d=1. Accessed on April 16, 2018.

*Empty cells = no data.

**1 = less than $1 million.

2 = about $1–$5 million.

3 = about $5–$24 million.

4 = more than about $24 million.

No data: none reported.

Tsunamis

A tsunami is a very large wave, or series of waves, caused by some type of disruption on the ocean floor. The most common types of disruptions are earthquakes or volcanic eruptions on the ocean floor or landslides along the coastline. Tsunamis may occur anywhere in the world, but about 80 percent of such events occur in the Pacific Ocean. They were once called *tidal waves* because of their similarity to very high tidal movements. That term has, however, now fallen into disuse.

Tsunamis differ from normal wind waves on the basis of two characteristics: wavelength (from crest to crest or trough to trough of the wave) and amplitude (height of the wave). The wavelength of a wind wave tends to be about 100 meters (300 feet), with an amplitude of about 2 meters (7 feet). By contrast, tsunami waves have wavelengths of up to 200 kilometers

(120 miles) and amplitudes of about 1 meter (3 feet). They travel at speeds in excess of 800 kilometers per hour (500 miles per hour).

As a tsunami wave approaches a coastline, it slows down, causing an increase in amplitude that may reach well over 100 kilometers. The highest tsunami wave ever recorded reached 524 meters (1,720 feet) in height. That event was triggered by a landslide along the shore of Lituya Bay, Alaska, on July 9, 1958. Most tsunamis have amplitudes much less than that of the Lituya event, generally amounting to about 50 meters in amplitude (Phillips 2011).

According to some experts, the worst tsunami in recorded history was caused by a 9.1 earthquake off the western coast of the island of Sumatra in Indonesia in December 2004. Energy released by the quake is said to have been equal to 23,000 nuclear bombs, enough to alter Earth's rotation as much as 2.3 centimeters (1 inch). Tsunami waves spread outward from the earthquake epicenter, reaching much of the southeastern coastline of the Indian Ocean. Wave amplitudes reached a maximum of about 10 meters (30 feet) in these areas, wiping away whole communities and natural areas. More than 225,000 deaths were attributed to the tsunami. Most heavily damaged was Aceh Province in northern Sumatra. Property damage from the event was estimated at $19.9 billion (Taylor 2014).

As to be expected, the parts of the United States most susceptible to tsunamis are states and territories bordering the Pacific Ocean, such as Alaska, Hawaii, American Samoa, Guam, and the Mariana Islands. Most heavily hit among these areas is the Hawaiian Islands, where more lives were lost due to natural disasters over the 20th century (221 people) than any other part of the United States. The largest of these events occurred on April 1, 1946, as the result of an earthquake off the Aleutian Islands that killed 5 people in Alaska and 159 in Hawaii. (The quake is sometimes referred to as the April Fools Earthquake because of the date on which it occurred and the perception the event was, somehow, a joke on the people of Hawaii.) One positive result from the tsunami was the creation of the Pacific Tsunami Warning Center, which began operations in 1949 (Manning 2009).

Volcanic Eruptions

As with other natural disasters, supernatural explanations for volcanic eruptions date back more than 5,000 years. One such myth arose in the Fiji Islands sometime around 2000 BCE. According to this story, volcanic eruptions on the islands were attributed to the work of a tribal chief, Nabukelevu. One early such eruption occurred when Nabukelevu became angry at the chief of a nearby island, Tanovo of the island Ono. In his effort to escape Nabukelevu's volcanic wrath, Tanovo dropped baskets of soil in the ocean, creating new islands in the chain (Nunn 2001).

Early Christian views on the origin of volcanoes can be found in accounts of the eruption of Mount Vesuvius in 79 CE. According to reports from the time, that event was ordered by God as retribution for the destruction of the temple of Jerusalem a few years earlier. Many other Jewish and Christian scholars also argued that volcanic eruptions occurred because of God's wrath and as a form of his punishment of humans for their evil deeds (Shanks 2018).

A volcanic eruption is an event in which magma (molten rock) and hot gases are expelled from deep under Earth's surface. The release of these materials may occur violently, with rocks the size of cars being thrown miles into the atmosphere, debris being spread over tens or hundreds of square miles, and poisonous gases flowing outward over that, and even greater, distance. A volcanic event typically results in the buildup of a cone-shaped structure that may have one of three major shapes—cinder, shield, or composite—depending on the mechanism by which the cone was formed. (Other volcano types have also been suggested. For illustrations of volcano types, see TomoNews US 2017.) A volcanic event often concludes with the collapse of some or all of the cone. The caldera (depressed region) that remains is often a visible indication of earlier volcanic activity in the region. Volcanoes may also occur in groups that are related to each other by a common source(s) of magma. Such arrangements are known as *volcanic group, volcanic complex,* or *volcanic sequence.*

The most modest (in terms of speed) of volcanic eruptions involves the slow, but steady, release of magma from an opening in the earth. Such events are often referred to as *effusive eruptions.* (For a video of a lava flow, see Lava Flows in Pahoa—Eruption Update 2014.) Some common forms of the solid rocks formed from such flows are aa, pahoehoe, and pillow lava. These materials differ in their appearance largely because of the way (such as speed) with which magma escapes from the earth. (For image of rock forms, see All Islands: Geology 2007.)

Volcanoes share some common features with earthquakes. But they also differ in some important ways. One such difference is their preservation throughout history. The evidence of earlier earthquakes is sometimes visible to the eye hundreds or even thousands of years after an event. In the case of volcanoes, that phenomenon may exist for millions of years. To the trained eye of a geologist, remnants of volcanoes that erupted millions of years ago are still visible. For example, the La Garita caldera in southwestern Colorado is still identifiable as a volcanic site; the eruption by which it was created has been dated to about 28 million years ago (Ort 1997; for a photo of the area, see Haraldsson 2010; an interesting timeline of volcanic action in Yellowstone National Park can be found at Geologic Event Cards 2018; a partial list of some of the oldest-known volcanoes can be found at Witze 2017).

Humans have been recording volcanic events for thousands of years. The earliest account of a volcanic eruption dates to a period between 29,000 and 35,000 years ago. This record consists of a group of drawings found in the Cave of Forgotten Dreams in southern France. The cave had been discovered in 1944, but the current interpretation of volcanic drawings was not completed until 2016. Supporting evidence of the age of these paintings comes from studies of extinct volcanoes in the area, whose activity has been dated to roughly the same period in history (Nomade et al. 2016).

Significant Volcanic Eruptions in History

As with earthquakes, volcanic eruptions have been studied for thousands of years and continue to be the source of research throughout the world. Scholars have now identified a number of the most dramatic eruptions in human history. By most accounts, the worst such event in history was the eruption of the Taupo Volcano in modern-day New Zealand in 180 CE. It has been said to be "the most violent eruption known in the world in the last 5000 years" (Taupo Volcano 2010). Very little information about this event is available from contemporary sources, so some researchers cite the "worst volcanic eruption" in modern history as the 1815 eruption of Mount Tambora in modern-day Indonesia.

Popular lore often cites the claim of "the worst volcanic disaster in human history" to the eruption of Mount Vesuvius in 79 CE. Located on the Bay of Naples, in Italy, the mountain had a long history of geological disruption. Modern research has found that the volcano had been erupting for at least 25,000 years prior to this event, which itself was preceded by a massive earthquake 17 years earlier in 62 CE. Much of what we know comes from the firsthand observations of the author and public official, Pliny the Younger (Gaius Plinius Caecilius Secundus or Gaius Caecilius Cilo).

One irony of the 79 eruption was that many citizens of Pompeii and Herculaneum, cities nearest to Vesuvius, were in the process of repairing and/or upgrading their homes and businesses because of the 62 event. These activities did not prevent the massive loss of life in the two cities, now estimated to have been more than 2,000. Modern archaeological research has uncovered hundreds of bodies, mostly in homes and shops, killed almost immediately by the eruption. According to Pliny's description of the event, a column of smoke and ash from the eruption may have reached a height as great as 30 kilometers (20 miles; 100,000 feet). Vesuvius remains active today, the only such volcano on the European continent. A future eruption would be far more destructive than that of 79 since the population that would be affected by such an event exceeds 3 million (Wallace-Hadrill 2011).

A second event of much wider global significance was the eruption of Mount Tambora, in modern-day Indonesia, in April 1815. The event had a Volcanic Explosivity Index (VEI) of 7. (The explosivity index is the measure of the relative intensity of a volcano's eruption.)

One description of the event is as follows:

Its noise reverberated loudly
Torrents of water mixed with ash descended
Children and mother screamed and cried
Believing the world had turned to ash.

The cause was said to be the wrath of God Almighty
At the deed of the King of Tambora
In murdering a worthy pilgrim, spilling his blood
Rashly and thoughtlessly. (Quoted in De Jong Boers 1995, 37)

The eruption began on April 5, 1815, with a mammoth explosion that could be heard as far away as the island of Sumatra, 2,600 kilometers (1,600 miles) from the volcanic site. Aftershocks, continued rumbling, and the release of ash occurred on sites as far away as West Java (1,100 kilometers; 700 miles away). These effects lasted for a period of up to three years, during which smoke and ash drifted around the globe. An estimated 71,000 or more people were thought to have been killed in the immediate eruption and related disasters that followed the original explosion. Darkening of the sky was so severe that the amount of sunlight striking Earth's surface declined by an appreciable effect. In fact, the extreme weather patterns and reduced temperature were sufficient to prevent the conduct of agriculture in much of the world. For this reason, the year following the eruption is sometimes known as the Year without a Summer (Klingaman and Klingaman 2014; Soon and Yaskell 2003).

Two other volcanoes are of interest primarily because of the enormous loss of human life involved in each. The first such event involved a volcanic explosion on the island of Krakatoa (also Krakatau) on August 27, 1883. The eruption was so strong that it was detected by seismographs around the world over a period of up to five days. The sound of the blast itself was heard as far away as Rodrigues Island, near Mauritius, 4,800 kilometers (3,000 miles) from the eruption. Ash from the event is said to have risen as high as 80 kilometers (50 miles) above Earth's surface. The death toll was officially listed at 36,417, although other estimates have placed that number at closer to 120,000. The island itself was essentially destroyed, with only the outermost sections surviving. The region has remained volcanically active ever since the eruption, and, in 1927, a new island began to emerge from the site of the previous island. The new island was called Anak Krakatoa, or Child of Krakatoa (Simkin and Fiske 1985; for an animation of the history of the island from the eruption to the present day, see Evolution of the Islands around Krakatoa from 1800 to 2005 2018).

The second event was an eruption from Mount Pelée on the French island of Martinique in the eastern Caribbean. Among other points, the eruption is of interest because it is the only volcanic eruption ever to occur on French soil, or on any of its territories. The first signs of an eruption were observed on April 23, 1902, but they were treated as unimportant because rumblings and the release of volcanic gases were relatively common on the mountain. Over the next two weeks, conditions on the mountain grew worse, and finally, on May 8, it erupted. Gases, ash, cinders, and rocky material rapidly covered the surrounding area, including the island's main city of St. Pierre, with a population of about 28,000. The entire city was almost destroyed in the event and has never been rebuilt in its original form. Death toll was placed at about 30,000, including everyone in St. Pierre, with the exception of three individuals who managed to survive because of the protected places in which they existed at the time of the eruption. Most deaths were attributed to the rapid flow of lava streaming from the volcano.

A massive rescue effort was initiated as soon as possible after the eruption. That effort was interrupted, however, by a second major eruption on May 20, killing an additional 2,000 people, most of them involved in the rescue effort. The event also resulted in the complete destruction of all remaining portions of St. Pierre. Additional, but less damaging, eruptions occurred in 1929 and ended in 1932. The volcano has been quiet ever since (Scarth 2006).

Volcanic Eruptions in the United States

Volcanic eruptions in the continental United States occur almost exclusively west of the Mississippi River, especially along the West Coast. They are even more common among the most western states of Alaska and Hawaii and in Pacific possessions such as American Samoa and the Northern Mariana Islands. Some of the events that occur in these locales provide very useful information about the nature of volcanic eruptions. The history of volcanoes in Hawaii is an example.

Some volcanic eruptions occur under water, on the seabed hundreds or thousands of feet below sea level. In a process similar to that which occurs on dry land, magma released from such events leads to the formation of volcanic cones. As an underwater cone grows larger and larger, it may ultimately break the water's surface and form a new landform, an island. Such is the background for the birth and evolution of the Hawaiian Islands.

The first islands to be born from volcanic islands were those in the western end of the archipelago, Ni'ihau and Kaua'i. Sometime about 5 million years ago, underwater volcanoes began to erupt, releasing magma that was to form these two islands. Over time, erosion wore away at both islands, so that very little visible evidence of the formation is still available (A Short Geologic History of Kauai, Hawaii, 2014).

As erosion was occurring on Ni'ihau and Kaua'i, a similar process was occurring eastward of these two islands. The process resulted in the formation of Oahu (build up and erosion), followed by such events on even more easterly islands of Moloka's, Maui, and Lana'i (Volcanoes Are "Everywhere" 2007). Today, only a small number of active volcanoes exist on the Hawaiian Islands. Four of those volcanoes can be found on the Big Island of Hawaii, one on the island of Maui, and one on the seafloor east of the Big Island.

In some ways, the most interesting of these volcanoes is Lōʻihi. It has not yet emerged from the ocean, with its highest point about 969 meters (3,180 feet) below sea level. It last erupted during July 16–August 9, 1996, and is expected to reach the surface of the water (if it continues to erupt at its current rate) in about 200,000 years (Lōʻihi 2017). Each of other five volcanoes has some unique characteristic:

- Haleakala is the only active volcano on the island of Maui. It has erupted at least 10 times in the past 1,000 years, most recently sometime between about 600 and 400 years ago.
- Hualalai is the third most active volcano on the island of Hawaii. It has erupted three times in the past 1,000 years and eight times in the past 1,500 years. Its most recent eruption occurred in 1801. The Kona International Airport is built on the lava flow produced in that eruption.
- Mauna Kea is the highest volcano on the island of Hawaii, with an elevation of 4,207 meters (13,883 feet). Its most recent eruption dates to about 6,000–4,500 years ago. It is the only Hawaiian volcano known to have been covered with snow and ice during the most recent ice age.
- Mauna Loa is the largest volcano on Earth. It has erupted 33 times since 1843, most recently in 1984. That event lasted 22 days and produced lava flows that came within about

7.2 kilometers (4.5 miles) of Hilo, the largest population center on the island.

- Kilauea is the youngest and most active volcano on the island of Hawaii. It has erupted almost continuously since 1983, most recently in 2008. About 90 percent of the volcano's surface is covered with lava flows less than 1,100 years in age (Active Volcanoes in Hawaii 2017).

One of the most interesting volcanic systems in the United States is the Yellowstone caldera. A caldera is a large, bowl-shaped depression created when the top of a volcanic cone collapses into the space left after magma is ejected during a violent volcanic eruption. The Yellowstone caldera covers an area of about 4,000 square kilometers (1,500 square miles) in the southeastern part of Wyoming. It is the remnant of a series of three volcanic eruptions that occurred over a time period ranging from 2.1 million to 640,000 years ago. The source of these eruptions was a supervolcano, a massive lake of magma that escaped to Earth's surface during a group of volcanic eruptions with a VEI of 8 or higher. Such eruptions involve the release of at least 1,000 cubic kilometers (240 cubic miles). Conditions that produced the ancient volcanic eruptions continue to exist today. The superheated magma below the caldera is responsible for the geysers and hot springs that are such a common sight in Yellowstone National Park today. For this reason, researchers suggest that new eruptions of the supervolcano may occur in the near or more distant future (Yellowstone Volcano 2018; for a comparison of the magnitude of supervolcanoes with other major volcanoes in history, see Questions about Supervolcanoes 2018; for the latest research development on the supervolcano, see Yirka 2018).

Extreme Weather

The term *extreme weather* (or *extreme storm*) is commonly applied to an atmospheric event characterized by rapidly moving winds capable of doing extensive damage to human lives and properties. The most common extreme storms are hurricanes, cyclones, typhoons, and tornadoes. (The term *cyclone* also has the more general meaning of being a storm system in which winds rotate around a center of low atmospheric pressure.) The first three of these events occur over the oceans. They have common physical characteristics but differ from each other in the regions over which they occur. Hurricanes occur in the North Atlantic Ocean, cyclones over the Indian Ocean, and typhoons over the Pacific Ocean. Tornadoes occur over dry land in almost every part of the world. Some other forms of extreme weather that may be very destructive are blizzards, downbursts, dust storms, excessive precipitation, hail, high winds, ice storms, thunderstorms, and waterspouts.

Weather legends were common among Native American tribes. One example is the story about Neyooxetusei (Whirlwind Woman). She was the first woman to exist and created Earth by spinning around and around in empty space until the planet was formed. She then continued to exist as the spirit responsible for storms and tornadoes. Although her works often created terrible damage, she is also credited with the formation of many helpful features on the land (Pybus 1979).

A deity for extreme weather in Africa was Oya, generally known as the Mother Goddess of Storms. In a poem in her honor, she is said to have claimed that

> I work in ways deep
> ever present
> always moving
> I work in ways dramatic
> with thunder and lightning
> sweeping and uprooting
> I work in ways subtle
> pushing and prodding
> wearing and tearing
> I swirl you and twirl you. (Silvestra 2012)

As with earthquakes and volcanic eruptions, extreme storms are capable of producing and have caused widespread damage to life and property throughout human history. Researchers have found evidence for the presence of severe storms dating back to at least 1330 BCE (see, e.g., Gischler et al. 2008; McCloskey and Keller 2009; Urquhart 2009). Records of such events in prehistoric and ancient times are, however, quite sparse and somewhat uncertain. Possibly the best single source of such events, ranging from 716 BCE to 1950, is Chatfield (2017). Table 1.3 lists some of the earliest extreme weather events in that resource. (Designations of events are somewhat uncertain prior to the mid-16th century, when modern terminology of storm types was generally adopted [Williams 2018].)

Table 1.3 Examples of Possible Extreme Weather Events from Early History

Date	Type	Location	Event
July 5, 716 BCE	Tornado*	Rome	Romulus, a founder of Rome, is swept away in a severe weather storm.
182 BCE	Tornado*	Rome	Severe windstorm destroys buildings in Rome.
156 BCE	Tornado	Rome	Temple of Jupiter destroyed; house roofs blown off.
60 BCE	Tornado	Rome	Roofs blown off house; trees uprooted.
540 CE	Tornado	China	Trees destroyed by "dragons."
587 CE	Tornado*	France	A village is "destroyed" in a windstorm.
August 2, 782	Tornado	Cluain Bronaig, Ireland	Much destruction from a "most mighty wind."
March 17, 804	Tornado*	Corco-Baiscim, Ireland	1,010 deaths from a severe storm.
August 22, 1281	Typhoon	Kyushu, Japan	An invading fleet of Mongols is destroyed in a severe windstorm.
October 1495	Hurricane	Santo Domingo	Sinking of three ships reported by Christopher Columbus.

Date	Type	Location	Event
July 1, 1502	Hurricane	Santo Domingo	A fleet under the command of Spanish conquistador Francisco de Bobadilla is destroyed.
1518–1519	Tornado	Near Milan	Leonardo da Vinci makes a sketch of an extreme storm thought to be a tornado. The sketch shows the vortex of the cloud.

Source: Chatfield (2017), The Ancient World, B.C.; Dark Ages. Sources for each of these events are also listed in this reference.

*Uncertain event.

Due to improved detection and measurement technology, as well as better worldwide systems of communications, information about severe storms is much more complete and accurate after the beginning of the 20th century. Some of the most severe and damaging in each storm category are as follows. (For the modern system of characterizing severe weather systems, see Burt 2007, 221.)

Tornadoes

One can measure the severity of a tornado (or other extreme weather event) in a variety of ways, such as strongest winds, greatest drop in atmospheric pressure, largest amount of loss in property value, greatest number of deaths, or longest-lived storm. The definition one chooses determines one's decision about the "worst" tornado that ever occurred.

According to the World Meteorological Association, the most devastating tornado in human history occurred on April 26, 1989. The storm swept through the Manikganj district of Bangladesh, completely destroying the towns of Saturia and Manikganj Sadar. It caused damage over an area of about 150 square kilometers (60 square miles), killing an estimated 1,300 people, injuring more than 12,000, and leaving about

80,000 people homeless. The storm was classified as a 3.5 event on the Fujita scale. That system is a way of indicating the severity of a tornado. It ranges in values from F0 (winds of less than 73 miles per hour) to F5 (winds of 261–318 miles per hour) (Fujita Tornado Damage Scale 2018; World: Highest Mortality due to a Tornado 2018).

As devastating as the Bangladesh tornado was, it was significantly exceeded by a storm that struck the United States in 1925, the so-called Tri-State Tornado. This event holds a number of records in tornado statistics. It struck near Ellington, Missouri, at 1:01 P.M. on March 18, 1925. The storm continued on its path across Missouri, Illinois, and Indiana, finally reaching its conclusion at 4:30 P.M. on the same day, near Petersburg, Indiana. By that time the tornado had traveled the greatest distance of any such storm in history (523 kilometers; 327 miles) over the longest recorded time (4 hours 29 minutes) with the greatest forward speed (120 kilometers per hour; 73 miles per hour) and an intensity of F5.0 on the Fujita scale, the highest possible reading. An estimated 695 people were killed, the highest number in U.S. history and the second deadliest in world history. Property damage was estimated at $16.5 million (in 1925 dollars; $235 million in 2018 dollars) (Tri-State Tornado Facts and Information 2018). For a summary of the deadliest and costliest tornadoes in U.S. history, see Tables 5.1 and 5.2.

Hurricanes

The region struck most commonly by hurricanes is the coastal United States. That region ranges from the coasts of Texas in the south and west to the northernmost part of the nation, the shores of New England. Coastal southeastern Canada may also be affected by hurricanes. According to the National Oceanic and Atmospheric Administration (NOAA), the average number of hurricanes (Categories 1–5) in the

North Atlantic from 1968 to 2016 is 6.2, and the average number of major hurricanes (Categories 3–5) is 2.4 (Landsea 2017).

The worst hurricane on record is the Galveston Hurricane of 1900, also known as the Great Storm of 1900. (Sources differ as to the "most intense," "deadliest," and "worst" hurricanes, with disagreement, in particular, about pre-1900 storms for which limited data are available.) The 1900 event is also the worst natural disaster ever to strike the United States in recorded history. The lack of modern storm technology and poor communication systems limit the amount of specific information about the hurricane. It is believed to have originated near the Cape Verde Islands off the western coast of Africa as a tropical storm. It then swept westward, across the Caribbean Sea and the Florida Keys, to the southern coast of Texas. It reached Galveston late in the day on September 8 as a Category 4 hurricane. (Hurricanes are classified by means of the Saffir-Simpson Hurricane Wind Scale, a system based on the wind speeds of the storm.) Categories range from 1 (119–153 kilometers per hour; 74/95 miles per hour) to 5 (greater than 252 kilometers per hour; 157 miles per hour). By nighttime on September 8, the storm had turned north, headed for the Great Plains states. It then turned eastward, passing over the Great Lakes, New England, and southeastern Canada. It lost strength and was last seen over the ocean on September 15, at which time it had become a Category 1 hurricane.

Damage caused by the storm resulted not only from the powerful winds it carried but also from the lack of any type of hurricane warning system that would have alerted people to the oncoming storm. By the time the hurricane had dissipated, it had killed somewhere between 6,000 and 12,000 people (estimates vary) and had injured between 10,000 and 12,000 people, and more than 30,000 people had been left homeless. Given that the population of Galveston at the time was about 38,000, one could say that the city was largely destroyed. Property damage was estimated to be about $30 million ($840 million in 2018 dollars). Because of decreasing wind strength, deaths, injuries, and property damage were much smaller as the storm swept across the nation. (For a contemporary report of the storm, see Green 1900; 2000.)

A second powerful hurricane of historical interest was the Atlantic-Gulf Hurricane of 1919, also known as the 1919 Florida Keys Hurricane or the 1919 Key West Hurricane. The storm originated in the northern Caribbean Sea, swept northward across the Florida Keys, and then turned westward to the coast of Texas. It lasted from September 2 through September 16, 1919. At maximum intensity, it was listed as a Category 4 storm. As many as 900 people died in the storm, more than half on ships on the Gulf of Mexico. Property damage was thought to be about $22 million ($617 in 2018 dollars) (1919 Florida Keys Hurricane 2015).

Recent hurricane seasons have seen some of the deadliest and most destructive of hurricanes to strike the United States. The year 2017 was especially devastating. Three of the five costliest hurricanes in U.S. history occurred in that year: Harvey (tied for first), Maria (third), and Irma (fifth). (Hurricanes were first given female names in 1953. The first such named hurricane was Alice. The use of male names began in 1979. For a list of names in use, see Tropical Cyclone Names 2018.)

As an example, Maria originated in the Cape Verde Islands before reaching the Caribbean on September 16, 2017. At this point, it was designated as a Category 5 hurricane on the Saffir–Simpson Hurricane Wind Scale. It reached land first on the island of Dominica, where it eventually resulted in at least 31 deaths and 34 persons missing, along with an estimated property damage of $1.31 billion. It moved on to

Puerto Rico, where it struck on September 20, now as a Category 4 hurricane. The storm completely devastated the island, resulting in at least 65 deaths, although the total number of deaths is generally thought to be much greater. Property damage to the island and the nearby U.S. Virgin Islands was estimated by NOAA to be $90 billion. Almost two years after the event, much of Puerto Rico is without reliable electrical, medical, food, and other supplies (Pasch, Penny, and Berg 2018). Tables 1.4 and 1.5 show the deadliest and costliest hurricanes in U.S. history.

Table 1.4   Deadliest Hurricanes in U.S. History

Location/Name	Date	Category	Deaths
Galveston, TX	1900	4	8,000–12,000
Florida	1928	4	2,500–3,000
Katrina (LA, MS, AL, FL, GA)	2005	3	1,500
Louisiana	1893	4	1,100–1,400
Sea Islands (SC/GA)	1893	3	1,000–2,000
Georgia/South Carolina	1881	2	700
Audrey (LA/TX)	1957	4	>416
Florida Keys	1935	5	408
Last Island, LA	1856	4	400
FL/MS/AL	1926	4	372
Grand Isle, LA	1909	3	350
Florida Keys, TX	1919	4	287
New Orleans	1915	4	275
Galveston, TX	1915	4	275
New England	1938	3	256

Source: Landsea (2013).

Table 1.5   Costliest Hurricanes in U.S. History

Hurricane	Year	Category	Damage (in millions of dollars)
Katrina (FL, LA, MS)	2005	3	125,000
Harvey (TX, LA)	2017	4	125,000
Maria (PR, US, VI)	2017	4	90,000
Sandy (Mid-Atlantic and Northeast United States)	2012	1	65,000
Irma (FL)	2017	4	50,000
Ike (TX, LA)	2008	2	30,000
Andrew (FL, LA)	1992	5	27,000
Ivan (AL, FL)	2004	3	20,500
Wilma (FL)	2005	3	19,000
Rita (LA, TX)	2005	3	18,500
Charley (FL)	2004	4	16,000
Irene (Mid-Atlantic and Northeast United States)	2011	1	13,500
Matthew (Southeast United States)	2016	1	10,000
Frances (FL)	2004	2	9,800
Allison (TX)	2001	TS	8,500

Source: "Costliest U.S. Tropical Cyclones Tables Updated." 2018. National Hurricane Center. https://www.nhc.noaa.gov/news/UpdatedCostliest.pdf. Accessed on April 25, 2018.

Note: TS, tropical storm.

Typhoons and Cyclones

Cyclones that occur in the Indian Ocean are among the most devastating windstorms of any on Earth. The first such storm to have been recorded, and generally thought to be the deadliest such storm, hit Calcutta (now Kolkata), India, in October 1737. The cyclone with the highest-recorded winds swept through Midnapore, India, in October 1942. Those winds registered about 225 kilometers per hour (140 miles per hour) (Hazards of Cyclones 2018).

By the definition used here, cyclones are not now, nor have they ever been, an issue for the United States. Something similar can be said for typhoons, storms that occur in the western Pacific Ocean. The only regions of the United States affected by typhoons are the westernmost territories of American Samoa, Guam, the Northern Mariana Islands, and the Hawaiian Islands. Some records for typhoons reaching American shores include the following:

- Typhoon Tip was the largest and most intense typhoon in historical times. It formed in the northwest Pacific Ocean on October 12, 1979, and eventually reached a diameter of 1,380 miles (2,220 kilometers) (Evans 2012).

- Typhoon John lasted 31 days, traveling a total distance of 13,180 kilometers (7,115 miles), both records for typhoons (20th Anniversary of Hurricane/Typhoon John 2014).

- Typhoon Iniki (also known as Hurricane Iniki) is the worst storm ever to strike the Hawaiian Islands. It made landfall on the island of Kaua'i on September 11, 1992, as a Category 4 storm with winds of up to 230 kilometers per hour (145 miles per hour). It killed six people, caused $1.8 billion in damages. More than 14,250 homes and buildings were either heavily damaged or completely destroyed (Hurricane Iniki: Quick Facts about Hawaii's Most Powerful Storm 2017).

- Typhoon Paka formed in the southwest of Hawaii on November 28, 1997. It then traveled in a mostly westward direction, where it caused devastation in Guam, the Marshall Islands, and the Northern Mariana Islands. It was classified as a super typhoon, one with winds of more than 185 kilometers per hour (205 miles per hour). (For the system used in classifying typhoons, see Classification of Tropical Cyclones 2009.) Because of advance notices of the storm's arrival, no deaths were recorded from the storm, although it did result in property damage amounting to about $80 million (Houston, Forbes, and Chiu 1998).

Floods

For many people around the world, the earliest mention of a catastrophic flood may be the story in the Bible about a time in which God becomes disillusioned about his creation of Earth and humans with which he populated it. He decides to send a flood that will cover Earth and destroy all living things on it, both humans and other animals. He selects one person, Noah, to build an ark with which to survive the flood. He is to include other members of his family and two of every species living on Earth at the time.

Flood stories of this kind are not unique to the biblical, Jewish, or Christian traditions. Indeed, they date back as far as the Neolithic or Bronze ages in many parts of the world. For example, one such story in China may date back to the Neolithic period, sometime between 10000 and 2000 BCE. (Recent research suggests that there may be evidence that such a flood may actually have occurred during that period; see Wu et al. 2016.)

One such historical study (of many of its type) that closely matches that of the biblical flood can be traced to the Sumerian culture in about 2000 BCE. According to this story, the gods Anu, Enlil, Ninurta, Ennugi, and Ea have decided to unleash a huge flood that will destroy human civilization. But the god Ea relents and tells a man by the name of Utnapishtim of the forthcoming flood. He instructs Utnapishtim to build a boat of reeds taken from his home as a way of surviving the flood. (For an excellent review of flood myths throughout human history, see Dundes 1988.)

The National Weather Service (NWS) provides the following detailed definition for the term *flood*:

An overflow of water onto normally dry land. The inundation of a normally dry area caused by rising water in an existing waterway, such as a river, stream, or drainage ditch. Ponding of water at or near the point where the rain fell. Flooding is a longer term event than flash flood-ing: it may last days or weeks.

NWS then goes on to define a *flash flood*:

A flood caused by heavy or excessive rainfall in a short period of time, generally less than 6 hours, characterized by raging torrents after heavy rains that rip through river beds, urban streets, or mountain canyons. (Flood and Flash Flood Definitions 2018)

Floods in Recorded History

A recent and comprehensive review of the history of flooding worldwide notes that an average of 181 floods strike around the planet each year. Just over 80 percent of these floods were reported after the 1990s, a fact that undoubtedly reflects im-proved systems of reporting rather than any actual increase in the number of floods. These floods resulted in an estimated 539,811 deaths, 362,122 injuries, homelessness among 4,580,522 individuals, and 2,898,579,881 people affected overall by flooding over recorded history. These data suggest that floods are "the leading cause of natural disaster fatalities worldwide" (Doocy et al. 2013).

A 2018 document issued by the Swiss Re Institute reported that 55 significant flooding events had occurred in 2017, re-sulting in 3,515 deaths. (Swiss Re is an organization providing information for the insurance industry on relevant and up-to-date research on risk management.) The worst of those events occurred on December 8, 2017, as a result of heavy monsoon rains in the Indian state of Bihar. The flooding with the greatest-reported financial loss, $400 million, occurred in Peru on January 15 (Natural Catastrophes and Man-Made Disasters in 2017: A Year of Record-Breaking Losses 2018). The worst flooding in the United States in 2017 occurred in February as the result of heavy rains over denuded landscape. Five deaths were reported in the flooding, which caused an estimated $1.5 billion in property damage (Billion-Dollar Weather and Climate Disasters: Table of Events 2018).

Flooding can be caused by a variety of events, including heavy rains, an overflowing river, strong winds along the coast, the breaking of a dam, loss of vegetation in an otherwise dry area, or unusually severe snow or ice melts. In many cases, flooding has accompanied the heavy rains that are associated with hurricanes, typhoons, or cyclones. For example, Hurricane Harvey, which struck Texas most heavily on August 25, 2017, brought with it between 40 and 61 inches of rain. Flooding also occurred on the Texas coast as the result of unusually high ocean storm surges caused by the hurricane's heavy winds. The city of Houston was the site of particularly severe flooding, which received 29 inches of rain over a 48-hour period. Death toll from the storm and flooding was set at 88, while nearly 200,000 homes were destroyed and 874,500 people were displaced. Total property damage resulting from the storm was estimated at $125 billion (Liautaud 2018).

Floods are so common throughout the world that it is virtually impossible to say what the "earliest" or "most devastating" of such events was. By some accounts, one event that would fit into the latter category was the St. Magdalene Flood of 1342, so named because it occurred on the feast day of St. Mary Magdalen (July 25). The flood was caused by passage of a Genoa low, a cyclonic storm, over southern Europe, especially modern-day Germany. The storm caused flooding in a number of rivers seriously damaging a number of cities, including Cologne, Mainz, Frankfurt am Main, Würzburg, Regensburg, Passau, and Vienna. Destruction extended as far as northern Italy and the Danube River. The total number of casualties is not known, although an estimate of at least 6,000 is often cited (Albert 2017; a very useful resource for historical and more recent floods is O'Connor and Costa 2004).

(Assessing the severity of a flood is a complex procedure because of a number of factors: availability and reliability of data for older events; areas covered by a flood; period of time over which a flood continues; known numbers of deaths and injuries; and estimated economic costs in contemporary and current times. Such factors make it difficult to decide floods that meet the criteria or "most devastating," "costliest," "most harmful," or the like.)

A flood that has been said to be the worst of its kind in human history struck the Yangtze River in 1931. Flooding has long been common along the river, with notable floods having occurred in 1900, 1911, 1915, 1931, 1935, 1950, 1954, 1959, 1991, and 1998. These events have resulted from a variety of causes, including the denuding of land for agriculture, rapid population growth along the river, and political malfeasance. In any case, the immediate cause of the flood was heavy rainfall over a region that had experienced a two-year drought in the late 1920s. The rainfall began in April of the year but continued to be a problem until August. By that time, more than half a million people had lost their homes to rising waters. Of even greater significance was the flooding of rice paddy in the region, destroying the crop and removing the primary food source for the region's population. In addition to those killed in the flood itself, many more lost their lives as a result of malnutrition and starvation and, most important, disease caused by pollution of the river (Courtney 2018).

Floods in the United States

Flooding patterns in the United States have historically been significantly different from those in the rest of the world. In terms of deaths and injuries, for example, no U.S. flood comes close to the toll in terms of lives lost than those that struck China in the 1930s. The Great Flood of 1931 is thought to have resulted in an estimated 3.7 million deaths, followed by the 1887 flooding of the Hunag He River (900,000 deaths), a 1642 flood (300,000 deaths), and a flood in North China in 1939 (200,000 deaths) (Hays 2013). By contrast, the deadliest flood in U.S. history was the Johnstown (Pennsylvania) flood of 1889, in which an estimated 2,209 lives were lost. The flood occurred when the South Fork Dam on the Little Conemaugh River 23 kilometers (14 miles) upstream of Johnstown collapsed, releasing 14.55 cubic meters (513.8 cubic feet; 20 million tons) of water on an unsuspecting population. Property damage amounted to about $17 million (about $463 million in 2017 dollars), making it the second-worst natural disaster (after the Galveston storm and flooding of Galveston in 1890) (McCullough 2005).

In terms of property damage only, a number of U.S. floods approximates that of the worst floods in the world. One reason for this fact is that many regions affected by floods in the United States (and other developed countries) tend to be highly developed, compared to those in Third World or developing nations, such as those in Southeast Asia. By some estimates, the costliest flood ever recorded occurred in Thailand in August 2011. Heavy monsoon rains caused flooding along the Mekong River, resulting in an estimated property damage of at least $40 billion, the highest ever recorded.

Estimates vary widely as to the economic costs of flooding in the United States and other parts of the world. For example, some observers suggest that the costliest flood in the United States may have been the Great Mississippi and Missouri rivers floods in the spring and summer of 1993. Damage estimates range from about $15 billion to just over $30.2 billion (see, e.g., Changnon 2005; The 10 Costliest Floods in American History 2011). The floods began in May 1993 and continued through August of that year. They eventually covered a distance of about 1,200 kilometers (745 miles) and 700 kilometers (435 miles) in width (78,000 square kilometers or 30,000 square miles) within the Missouri–Mississippi basin (The Great Flood of 1993 1994).

Forest Fires

As with other types of natural disasters, forest fires (also commonly known as *wildfires*) are usually responsible for a significant number of deaths, injuries, homeless persons, property damage, and environmental devastation. Unlike almost other natural disasters, however, forest fires often have some important environmental benefits. (The study of such benefits, from both forest fires and other types of natural disasters, is known as *disturbance ecology*.)

One such benefit arises from the fact that some plants and animals are actually dependent on fire for their survival and reproduction. Under normal circumstances, a plant produces seeds that become mature and then drop to the ground. In some cases, however, the plant may retain the seed even after it has matured. Release of the seed does not occur until some environmental event ("trigger") occurs to bring about the event. This behavior is called *serotiny*. The most common trigger for serotiny is heat, such as that produced by a forest fire. Thus, many species of conifer trees such as giant sequoias, lodgepole pines, and jack pines are unable to reproduce until their cones have been exposed to temperatures of more than 50°C (100°F) (Nix 2017; for a video of serotiny, see Why the Giant Sequoia Needs Fire to Grow 2017).

Fire can also be beneficial as a way of destroying disease-causing organisms. Some such organisms may be resistant to every mechanism developed by trees and other plants to act against disease; only heat from fires is available to achieve this result. Diseases of animals may also be brought under control by fires that destroy pathogens without fatally affecting plants themselves (Benefits of Fire 2018; Zimmer 2017). Yet another benefit provided by forest fires is cleaning up the forest floor of dead plant material and other debris, returning nutrients to the soil in the process. The action also opens up an area for the growth of bushes and other plants that require sunlight for their development but that may be blocked by dead and dying plant materials around them (Benefits of Fire 2018).

All of these benefits are not to ignore the very serious harm that can be caused by forest fires. The earliest reliable evidence of forest fires on Earth dates to the Devonian period, about 360 million years ago. Plants had already existed long before this date, but fire was not possible until environmental conditions were adequate for it to begin. For example, a concentration of oxygen in the atmosphere high enough to support burning was needed, a condition that seems to have arisen only during the Devonian period. Today, evidence for such fires exists in fossil charcoal remains. Charcoal is the most common product resulting from the combustion of plant material (Rimmer et al. 2015).

The most serious forest fires in recorded history, not surprisingly, have almost always occurred in open areas with vast reaches of forest land, such as Siberian Russia, Canada, Australia, and the American West. Such fires often consist not of a single blaze confined to a relatively limited area but a group and/or series of fires spread throughout a region. Such is the case with the largest forest fire in recorded history, a group of events that occurred in the Siberian taiga in 2003. The term *taiga* applies to a biome characterized by coniferous forests consisting mostly of pines, spruces, and larches. A taiga is also known as a *boreal* or *snow forest*. Almost a third of the world's forests are to be found in taiga biomes in Siberia and Canada.

The 2003 conflagration actually consisted of more than 27,000 individual outbreaks, covering more than 2.4 million hectares (6 million acres), resulting in an estimated 14.0 billion rubles ($230 million) (Forest Fires in the Russian Taiga 2004; estimates of damage differ depending on the source consulted). On a single day in June, satellite images captured 157 discreet fires covering an area of 110,000 square kilometers (42,500 square miles). Smoke from the Siberian blazes covered areas of southern Japan, 5,000 kilometers (3,000 miles) away (Featured Image 2012; Seen from Space 2003). Of the 15 largest forest fires ever recorded, 6 have occurred in Canada, 3 in Australia, 4 in the United States, and 1 in Bolivia (Largest Brush and Forest Fires in Recorded History 2018).

Table 1.6   Some Devastating U.S. Forest Fires

Date	Name	Location	Acres	Deaths/ Damage
October 1825	Miramichi and Maine Fires	New Brunswick and Maine	3,000,000	160 deaths
1845	Great Fire	Oregon	1,500,000	–
October 1871	Peshtigo	Wisconsin and Michigan	3,780,000	1,500 deaths
September 1881	Lower Michigan	Michigan	2,500,000	169 deaths; 3,000 structures destroyed
September 1902	Yacoult	Washington and Oregon	>1,000,000	38 deaths
August 1910	Great Idaho	Idaho and Montana	3,000,000	85 deaths
October 1918	Cloquet-Moose Lake	Minnesota	1,200,000	450 deaths; 38 communities destroyed
1988	Yellowstone	Montana and Idaho	1,585,000	–
2004	Taylor Complex	Alaska	1,305,592	–
March 2006	East Amarillo Complex	Texas	907,245	12 deaths; 80 structures destroyed

Source: Historically Significant Wildland Fires. 2018. National Interagency Fire Center. https://www.nifc.gov/fireInfo/fireInfo_stats_histSigFires.html. Accessed on May 16, 2018.

Records of forest fires in the United States tend to be somewhat incomplete, since the U.S. Forest Service did not keep formal records until the middle of the 20th century. Table 1.6 summarizes some of the information available about some of the best known and most disastrous of these events.

Other Types of Natural Disasters

Among the other types of natural disasters that occur are mass wasting, drought and famine, and limnic eruptions.

Mass Wasting

The term *mass wasting* refers to events in which very large volumes of sand, soil, rock, and other materials are displaced either on land or under water. Mass wasting occurs when the force of gravity on a body of land exceeds the cohesive forces that hold that land together and in position. The major types of mass wasting are creeps, falls, flows, landslides, and slumps. Each type is characterized by a type of land flow indicated by its name. Mass wasting events are also known by common names, such as rock avalanches, rockslides, slumps, debris flow, topples, and spreads. Mass wastings are common not only on Earth but also on extraterrestrial bodies such as Mars, Venus, and Io, one of Jupiter's moons (Bulmer 2017).

Mass wastings can occur on many types of land under a variety of environmental circumstances. One such condition may be the introduction of water to an area (e.g., rainfall) that may reduce the friction that holds materials in place. Such events can occur slowly, over a period of weeks, months, or years. Or they may take place very quickly, resulting in the massive shifting of materials over a short period of time. Mass wastings of this type tend to be the most serious since humans may have little or no time to prepare for a disaster. Most often, mass wastings travel with speeds of about 30–50 miles per hour, although the fastest such events have been clocked at 200 miles per hour (Opar 2015).

The most powerful mass wasting in U.S. history occurred in 1980, when 2.8 billion cubic meters (100 billion cubic feet) broke off Mount Saint Helens in Washington State. A total of 57 individuals lost their lives in the event, the vast majority of them resulting from the volcanic eruption responsible for the event, with scores more injuries (Impact and Aftermath 1997). By comparison, the deadliest landslide in U.S. history took place in March 2014 just outside the town of Oso, in Washington State. A total of 43 people were killed in the slide itself, with an estimated property damage of at least $50 million to the sparsely populated area (Keaton et al. 2014).

Drought and Famine

Drought and famine differ from other types of natural disasters in at least two critical ways. First, events such as earthquakes, volcanic eruptions, and extreme weather tend to occur suddenly with little advance notice over which humans have little or no control. Drought and famine, on the other hand, are more likely to develop over months or years. Records of rainfall in California over the period 2011–2017, for example, show only small areas of drought covering the extreme northeastern and southeastern portions of the state. These regions were classified by the U.S. Drought Monitor at the time as being "dry" and of little concern to government officials. By January 2012, areas of "moderate drought" began to appear, followed shortly thereafter by pockets of "severe drought." These conditions slowly spread over larger areas until, in mid-2013, the first patches of "extreme drought" showed up, followed in 2014 by growing areas of "exceptional drought." On January 17, 2014, Governor Jerry Brown formally declared a drought state of emergency, three years after these conditions first began to appear (Kyle and Lauder 2017).

Droughts also differ from other natural disasters in that they often reflect the influence of human activities; they are, that is, not entirely "natural." A number of observers have noted, for example, that the California drought of 2011–2017 was also caused by increasing use of limited water resources in the state for agricultural, residential, municipal, and industrial purposes. That is, the state's growing economy continues to place strains on limited supplies of water (Zamora, Lustgarten, and Kirchner 2015).

The term *drought* is not easily defined and may have different meanings to different individuals. The U.S. Geological Survey notes that

to a farmer, a drought is a period of moisture deficiency that affects the crops under cultivation—even two weeks without rainfall can stress many crops during certain periods of the growing cycle. To a meteorologist, a drought is a prolonged period when precipitation is less than normal. To a water manager, a drought is a deficiency in water supply that affects water availability and water quality. To a hydrologist, a drought is an extended period of decreased precipitation and streamflow. (Questions and Answers about Drought 2016)

Famine, then, is a social, economic, and community problem in which very large numbers of people are unable to obtain adequate food to remain healthy, a condition that may lead to large numbers of deaths. Major droughts worldwide from 1900 to the present day have been responsible for anywhere from 100,000 deaths (Ethiopia, 1973) to more than 3 million fatalities (China, 1928) (Number of Deaths Caused by Majors Droughts Worldwide from 1900 to 2016 2018).

Probably the most disastrous and best-known drought in U.S. history occurred during the 1930s. Commonly known as the Dust Bowl, this event covered the Great Plains sector of the United States, a region reaching from the Rocky Mountains in the west to the Mississippi basin in the east and from southern Canada in the north to the Rio Grande River in the south. Land area included in the Great Plains is about 1.3 million square kilometers (500,000 square miles). The region is semiarid, experiencing irregular rainfall adequate to maintain a rich flora dominated by prairie grasses that survive by sending their roots deep into the soil.

Native Indian tribes survived by maintaining a largely nomadic life, in which they followed the countless number of bison that inhabited the region. Over the eons, they had developed a lifestyle that provided a somewhat problematic, but generally successful way of life based on the available plant life and an endless supply of their primary food, the bison. Early American settlers were less successful in dealing with these natural resources, however, as they began to move into the Great Prairies in the late 19th century. Eager to take advantage of ("put to productive use") the vast land mass, encouraged by extensive land giveaways by the federal government, these newcomers abjured the Native American lifestyle and set out to create massive farmlands on their newly granted properties. The first step in this transformation involved the removal of native grasses and other plants, exposing the soil to the devastating effects of rare but intense rainstorms.

By about 1930, the product of this land-use philosophy had become apparent. The Great Plains were no longer the lush repository of adequate food supplies (when properly managed) but extensive areas of denuded land. As the natural ebb and flow of weather patterns continued to sweep over the prairies, loosened top soil was churned by heavy winds and swept way, in some cases, reaching as far east as the Atlantic Seaboard. This ecological disaster continued throughout the decade, varying to some extent in various regions and at various times.

By the end of the decade, vast portions of the plains had become uninhabitable. Once-optimistic settlers were forced to sell their now-useless properties at hopeless losses, or simply to leave the region entirely, heading west and looking for a "new life" in California and other western states. Eventually, an estimated 2.5 million people left the states of Colorado, Kansas, Nebraska, New Mexico, Oklahoma, and Texas, the largest mass migration in U.S. history. Thus ended one of the most dramatic examples of a joint natural and human-made disaster in modern history (Dust Bowl 2009; Timeline: The Dust Bowl 2018; the term *dust bowl* refers to both the events that occurred during the 1930s and the land on which the devastation occurred).

Limnic Eruptions

The decay of organic matter at the bottom of lakes and ponds results in the formation of carbon dioxide and methane that normally rise to the water's surface in the form of small bubbles. Under some circumstances, significant amounts of those

gases may dissolve in the pond or lake water, eventually resulting in a saturated solution of gas in water, one in which the
water holds all the gas it can at some given temperature. Such
an event may be followed by the release of all dissolved gases
at once, in much the same way as dissolved carbon dioxide
in soda drinks is released suddenly when the drink's cap is
removed. Such an event in the natural world is called a *limnic
eruption*. The term *limnic* refers to events relating to freshwater
events.

Limnic eruptions are rare events, with only two such cases
confirmed in human history. Both occurred in the nation of
Cameroon, one at Lake Monoun in 1984 and another, two
years later, at nearby Lake Nyos. Both eruptions resulted in
the release of huge amounts of carbon dioxide that spread
across the adjacent land and caused the asphyxiation of large
numbers of humans and other animals. The larger of the two
eruptions, at Lake Nyos, is thought to have killed about 1,746
humans and about 3,500 other animals. The Nyos explosion
is estimated to have produced a plume rising from the surface
of the lake more than 100 meters (300 feet) tall, with a total
volume of gases of about 1.2 cubic kilometers (300,000 cubic
miles) (Lake Nyos—The Deadly Limnic Explosion 2007; for
a video description of the event, see Exploding Lakes in the
World 2015).

Sinkholes

According to one definition, a *sinkhole* is a topographical feature that consists of a hole in the ground with no external
drainage (Sinkholes 2018). Any water that flows into the hole
stays there and/or drains into the subsurface zone. A somewhat simpler definition of a sinkhole is simply a hole in the
ground produced by the collapse of a surface layer of rock, soil,
or other material. Sinkholes are also known by a number of
other names, including cenote, doline, sink, swallet, and swallow hole.

Sinkholes range in size from a few meters to a few kilometers in diameter and 1 meter to more than 25 meters in depth. They occur in many parts of the world but are seen most commonly in certain regions where surface and/or subsurface conditions favor their creation. Sinkholes generally develop over long periods of time, usually many years. But their actual appearances on Earth's surface tend to occur very quickly often in a matter of minutes.

The largest sinkhole ever recorded is located in Qattara, Egypt, about 250 kilometers (150 miles) west of Cairo. It is about 80 kilometers (50 miles) long, 120 kilometers (70 miles) wide, and 133 meters (436 feet) deep (Jennings 2014). The largest sinkhole in the United States is the Golly Hole, in Shelby County, Alabama. It is 100 meters (325 feet) long, 90 meters (300 feet) wide, and 40 meters (120 feet) deep (Nation's Largest Sinkhole May Be near Montevallo 1973).

Sinkholes occur when changes occur in underground rocks, usually as the result of changes in water flow in the region. Imagine, for example, an area in which subsurface rock consists of a water-soluble material, such as limestone or salt. Over time, water seeping through that rock will dissolve some of the limestone or salt, producing open spaces (such as caves). At first, enough rock remains to support the roof of this space, the ground above the open space. Eventually, however, the space (cave) may become so large that can no longer do so; the roof of the cave collapses, and a sinkhole forms.

Sinkholes are an example of one type of natural disaster whose formation can be affected by human activity. Humans often decide to remove underground rock or water for surface use, as in the mining of minerals, irrigation of crops, or watering of cattle. When that happens, rocky particles underground tend to collapse into a smaller space and are no longer able to support the overlying ground, and a sinkhole may form. One of the best-known examples of this phenomenon can be found in Florida, which has a high number of sinkholes. Those sinkholes have been produced when phosphate rock underground has been removed, leaving open spaces from which sinkholes may ultimately form (Pittman 2017). In the American West, a somewhat similar phenomenon has occurred as farmers have removed underground water over the years for use in irrigation. In some places, the loss of this underground water has resulted in the formation of sinkholes (Land Subsidence in the American West 2016).

The Genesis of Natural Disasters

From the dawn of civilization to the mid-19th century, virtually nothing existed that could remotely be called the *science of seismology*. During this period, natural disasters such as earthquakes, volcanic eruptions, tsunamis, and severe storms were explained by reference to controlling gods and goddesses or other supernatural beings. Even the earliest suggestions that earthquakes might be the result of "natural causes" were commonly softened with the acknowledgment that such events probably had a "miraculous" cause also (Martyn 1756, Chapter 1, 535).

Earthquakes and Volcanic Eruptions

That situation began to change, however, in about 1850 with the increasing use of controlled observations, careful experimentation, accurate measurements, systems for testing and confirming hypotheses, and other elements of the modern scientific method. From that point on, scholars with backgrounds in chemistry, physics, engineering, geology, mathematics, and other fields rushed to the sites of major earthquakes, such as those in Lisbon in 1755. There, they applied their specialized knowledge and skills to produce detailed descriptions of such events never before available. For example, British astronomer, geologist, and pioneer of seismological research John Michell provided what we would today call the simplest and perhaps most obvious observation about earthquakes. Such events are, he said, "waves set up by the shifting masses of rock miles below the surface . . . , the motion of the earth in earthquakes is partly tremulous and partly propagated by waves which succeed each another" (Ben-Menahem 1995; original source: Michell 1760, 8). Michell's observation established the basic facts of earthquake events; they occurred (1) deep within the earth (2) by the movement of rocky materials in contact with each other (3) causing the release of underground waves that could be detected and studied on Earth's surface.

Modest steps forward such as these eventually led to the development of the modern science of *seismology*, a term that was first used by Robert Mallet, Irish geophysicist and engineer, sometimes referred to as the father of seismology. The most critical tool used in early research (as it remains today) was the seismograph, a device for detecting waves associated with an earthquake. The first device of its type was invented in 1841 by Scottish physicist James David Forbes and named by him as *seismometer*. The current name for such a device, *seismograph*, was suggested in 1855 by Italian physicist Luigi Palmieri. Early seismographs had limited value, in that they detected only those waves traveling across Earth's surface. A far more useful device, one that could detect subsurface waves traveling thousands of kilometers through Earth, was later developed by British geologist and mining engineer John Milne. The Milne seismograph possessed a crucial new component: it was able to detect earthquake waves hundreds or thousands of kilometers beneath Earth's surface. The device was first tested successfully by German astronomer Ernst von Rebeur-Paschwitz. In 1889, von Rebeur-Paschwitz detected at his Berlin laboratory waves produced during an earthquake in Japan, a distance of about 9,000 kilometers (5,400 miles) (Dewey and Byerly 1969).

Facts about Earthquakes

Throughout the second half of the 19th century, a vast database of information about earthquakes was created. Some of the most essential features of that database included the following facts:

- Arguably the best source of information about earthquakes was the pattern of waves resulting from such events. Some information about earthquakes can be obtained, of course, from the visual movement of rocky materials on Earth's surface. This information tells one almost nothing, however, about where the quake originated or how it came about. In addition, the study of wave properties had been a major field of research by physicists since at least the later 18th century. By the mid-1800s, researchers had learned a great deal about the movement of waves through a vacuum, air, water, molten materials, and other substances. When this information was applied to the study of earthquakes, research could determine the type of material through which a wave traveled, the direction in which it was moving, its point of origin, and other essential information (Ben-Menahem 1995, 1207).

- At least three major types of earthquakes exist: p, primary waves; s, secondary waves; and surface waves. The first two of these waves are also known as *body waves* because they travel beneath the ground. P waves travel through both solid and liquid materials, while s waves travel only through solids. Surface waves are the slowest of all wave types but responsible for the greatest amount of damage caused by an earthquake. The differences between p and s waves allow a seismologist to determine the type of material through which they have traveled and, hence, the composition (solid versus liquid) of materials beneath Earth's surface (What Is Seismology? 2006).

- An analysis of earthquake wave patterns allowed geologists to predict some basic facts about the composition of Earth's interior. Among the earliest of the models thus produced was one suggested by German physicist Emil Wiechert in 1896. Wiechert hypothesized that Earth consisted of two parts, a dense interior region known as the *core* surrounded by a less-dense, rocky shell made of silicate materials. The high density of the core suggested to Wiechert that it was probably made of molten iron (Schroeder 2018). Over the decades, more sophisticated models of Earth's structure were hypothesized. Today, the most widely accepted of those models posits an inner core of about 1,220 kilometers (760 miles) in diameter and a temperature of about 6,000°C (11,000°F), surrounded by an outer core of about 2,260 kilometers (1,400 miles) in thickness and a temperature of about 2,700–7,700°C (5,000–14,000°F). The core itself is then surrounded by the mantle, with a maximum thickness of about 3,000 kilometers (1,800 miles) and a temperature of 500–4,000°C (900–7,200°F), and an outermost layer, the crust, of no more than 65 kilometers (40 miles) in thickness, on which all life exists. A fifth section, the asthenosphere, is the outer layer of the mantle, about 100–725 kilometers (60–450 miles) in thickness (Oceanography 101 2016).

- The science of seismology began to blossom in the mid-19th century with the development of features that are characteristic of all mature sciences: colleges and universities where the subject is taught, professional societies of experts in the field, journals and other regulations publications where research results are reported, and regular collections of up-to-date information in the field. One of the first of these collections was produced in 1862 by Robert Mallet. That map showed that, while earthquakes can and do occur at almost any place on the planet, they tend to be collected within certain specific regions. In those regions, they are far more likely to take place than in others on Earth. (An interpretation of Mallet's original map can be found at http://images.slideplayer.com/19/5752371/slides/slide_7.jpg.) Over the next century and a half, more and more accurate maps of this type have been produced (see, e.g., http://wphase.unistra.fr/zacharie/myImages/sumatra2012.html).

- A feature of particular interest in even the earliest of earthquake maps is the concentration of such events in very specific parts of the planet. The likelihood of an earthquake or volcanic eruption occurring along the western coast of North and South America, for example, is far greater than it is on the eastern coast or between coasts of these continents. Probably the most famous of these patterns is called the Ring of Fire, a concentration of earthquakes and volcanic eruptions that lies around the outer edges of the Pacific Ocean. (For a typical map of the Ring of Fire, see Explore the Ring of Fire 2004.)

- Typically, the best observable indication of earthquake activity is faulting. A *fault* is a break in Earth's surface between two blocks of rock. Faulting occurs when one of those blocks moves in relation to the other block. Three kinds of faults are most common. A *thrust fault* is one in which one of the blocks moves upward and over the top of the second fault. A *normal fault* is one in which a block moves downward in comparison to the other block. And a *strike-slip fault* is one in which the two blocks slide past each other in a horizontal plane (Meredith 2016; includes video demonstration of faulting). A study of faults is important in seismology because it may give an observer an immediate, on-the-spot demonstration of changes in Earth's surface or, at least, a historic record of where and how those changes have occurred (Elliott 2012).

The Genesis of Earthquakes

The preceding database provides a great deal of valuable information about the nature of earthquakes. It fails, however, to answer perhaps the most basis question of all: How do earthquakes occur? The answer to that question evolved over a period of more than 500 years from research in a number of apparently unrelated fields, including cartography, geography, and oceanography, and meteorology.

The story begins in the 16th century with an observation by Barbantian cartographer and geographer Abraham Ortelius that was to be "rediscovered" many times later in history. In his 1587 text, *Thesaurus Geographicus*, Ortelius suggested that a map of the world suggests that Earth's continents were, at one time in history, joined together in a single "supercontinent." A subsequent series of earthquakes and floods had, he proposed, torn that supercontinent apart. He argued that this process would be evident to anyone who "brings forward a map of the world and considers carefully the coasts of the three continents" (Romm 1994).

A host of later scientists came to a similar conclusion. In 1889, for example, British polymath Alfred Russel Wallace noted that such a hypothesis had been "a very general belief" among geologists for some time. The general view was that "during the course of known geological time the continents and great oceans had again and again changed places with each other" (Wallace 1889, 342).

The big problem for all these theorists was the mechanism by which such massive changes might take place. Imagine moving a continent a few hundred or thousands of miles across the face of the planet. It's difficult to imagine how even the most powerful natural disasters could produce such an effect. One of the many explanations developed was Italian geologist (and violinist) Roberto Montovani's Expanding Earth Theory. According to this theory, Earth's size (volume) has increased slowly over time, causing continents to break apart and move away from each other. This theory failed when researchers found no evidence that such an expansion had ever take place (Scalera 2009).

Another proposed mechanism was that of American geologist Franklin Bursley Taylor. In 1908, Taylor argued that Earth's capture of the moon during the Cretaceous period had produced forces strong enough to cause continents to "creep" across the face of the planet. Attempts to confirm this hypothesis also failed (Black 1979).

The author of the modern theory of continental drift was German meteorologist and geologist Alfred Wegener. In 1912, Wegener presented a paper, "Die Entstehung der Kontinente und Ozeane" ("The Origin of Continents and Oceans"), on the topic to the German Geological Society. In that paper, he summarized previous research on the subject and described a process by which Earth's land mass originally consisted of a single supercontinent, which he called Pangea. Wegener is considered to be the father of continental drift theory because his paper provided the first comprehensive collection of existing data and theories about the topic. Like his predecessors, however, Wegener was unable to offer an adequate theory as to the forces responsible for continental drift. His suggestion that continental drift was caused by centrifugal forces pulling on the planet's land masses was soon proved to be inadequate for such an explanation. (A translation of Wegener's original paper is available at Wegener 2002.)

As a consequence, Wegener's theory was soon relegated to the dustbin of scientific thought. And there it remained for almost 50 years. Throughout this period, a handful of geologists struggled with the challenge of continental drift. Among the leaders of this movement was British geologist Arthur Holmes. As early as 1920, Holmes had hypothesized that the cycling of heat within the mantle provides a driving force on the overlying crust. This force is adequate, he said, to account for the slow, but inexorable, movement of continents across the face of Earth. (An explication of Holmes's theory can be found at Holmes 1931.)

Holmes's theory was accepted only very slowly. But research evidence continued to accumulate as to its validity. One of the most powerful discoveries was that of the Great Global Rift in 1947 by a group of oceanographers headed by American oceanographer Maurice Ewing. The rift was found to be a region in the middle of the Atlantic Ocean in which upwelling of new material from the mantle could be conclusively demonstrated, providing solid evidence for Holmes's theory of continental drift (Heezen 1960).

By the late 1960s, the phenomenon of plate tectonics had been convincingly demonstrated. Plate tectonics is a theory that says that Earth's crust consists of a few massive "plates" that migrate slowly over Earth's surface under the force of convection currents in the underlying mantle. (For a map of proposed tectonic plates, see http://worldbuildingschool.com/adding-tectonic-plates-to-your-world-map/.) From time to time, two plates come into contact with each other in one of three ways. The two plates may move toward each other as a convergent event. In such a case, one plate often slips underneath the other plate in a process known as subduction. The two plates can also move away from each other, in a divergent pattern. In such a case, a rift between the two plates, such as the Great Global Rift, may form. Finally, the two plates may slide in one direction or the other against each other in a transform movement. These three types of plate interactions are very roughly comparable to the thrust, normal, and strike-slip faulting patterns described earlier. (An excellent overview of these features of plate tectonics is available at Marshak and Herrstrom 2018.)

The plates that underlie the oceans are less dense than those that underlie the continents. Thus, ocean plate/continental plate interactions are most likely to occur and to result in earthquakes than are ocean/ocean or continental/continental quakes. This fact explains earthquake patterns such as the Ring of Fire that has been known for many centuries. The San Andreas Fault along the eastern shores of the Pacific Ocean, for example, is responsible for most of the major earthquakes observed along the western coasts of North and South America. (For an excellent illustrated overview of current tectonic theory [except for abundant advertisements], see Media for Plate Tectonics 2018.)

The role of plate tectonics in the genesis of volcanic activity is now simple to understand also. As molten rock (magma) from the mantle moves upward in zones of plate contact, it may escape through these zones, either as slow-moving lava or in the form of explosive eruptions. (For an excellent video presentation of the connection of plate tectonics, earthquakes, and volcanic eruptions, see Tectonics of the Planet Earth 2013.)

The Genesis of Severe Storms

Given their powerful destructive effects, it may be somewhat surprising to hear that the formation of tornadoes, hurricanes, typhoons, and cyclones depends on only a few simple physical principles, such as the heating and cooling of water and air, and the flow of air across Earth's surface.

Tornadoes

Tornadoes, hurricanes, and typhoons all form because of specialized atmospheric conditions: significant differences in air temperature and variations in wind speed. In the case of a tornado, the first of these conditions is met when a mass of warm air begins to flow, as, in the most common of all cases, from the Gulf of Mexico over the central United States. There it encounters a mass of cold air, such as one flowing from Canada into the same region. When these two air masses come into contact, warm air moves upward and over cold air, forming a thunderstorm. The largest and most powerful of such storms is called a *supercell*. A supercell is a type of thunderstorm in which the interior of the storm consists of a deep, rotating updraft, known as a *mesocyclone*.

The second condition required for tornado formation is *wind shear*, a condition in which the wind blows in the same direction at different heights above the ground but at different speeds. Under these conditions, faster-moving winds may begin to "roll over" slower-moving winds below them. Eventually, a cylindrical wind pattern develops in which air "rolls" over the ground. (See How Do Tornadoes Form? 2017 for an illustration of this process.)

When the rolling cylinder of air encounters an area of warm ground, one part of the now-heated cylinder begins to rise. This rising air converts the rolling horizontal cylinder into a vertical rotating air mass. The collision of that air mass with a super-cell provides the conditions needed for tornado formation. As winds rotate faster and faster, one end of the rotating vortex may come into contact with the ground, forming the cloud-to-earth funnel cloud characteristic of tornadoes (Howard 2015).

Hurricanes

Like tornadoes, hurricanes are engines for converting heat energy into kinetic energy (wind). The process is powered by a simple pair of matched physical changes: evaporation and condensation. When a liquid, such as water, changes into a gas, such as water vapor, energy is absorbed. In the reverse process—gas to liquid—energy is released. This set of reactions—water vapor to liquid water droplets, back to water vapor, and back to droplets—is the fundamental process by which hurricanes (as well as typhoons and cyclones) are formed.

Hurricanes that strike the United States originate in the southern Atlantic Ocean, where temperatures reach at least 30ºC (80ºF) in the top 50 meters (165 feet) of seawater. These warm waters provide one element of the engine that is to become a hurricane. The second element is the prevailing wind patterns in this region of the planet, from the west coast of Africa to the east coast of North America, that is, from east to west.

Energy conversion in this system begins when the combination of heat and moving air causes seawater to begin to evaporate. The water vapor formed by this process is less dense than the surrounding air and is pushed upward in the atmosphere. After reaching a certain height, water vapor begins to cool, turns back into liquid water, and initiates the formation of a large cumulonimbus cloud. The cycle of evaporation and condensation in the clouds continues, producing higher, larger clouds, the nucleus from which thunderstorms develop.

As the process of cloud formation develops, a second force enters the picture: the wind. If the cloud formation story were to take place on a completely stationary platform, the next steps in the storm development would be quite different. But, of course, Earth is not a stationary platform; it is rotating on its own axis. This motion forces winds to flow not in a straight line but in a curved path around some central point. That point eventually becomes the center, or *eye*, of the hurricane (KSL Chicago 2017).

Under appropriate conditions, thunderstorm clouds continue to grow larger, and winds within them move ever faster and faster. Depending on the size of a cloud and its wind speeds, the storm may ultimately be classified as a *topical disturbance* (winds less than 40 kilometers per hour; 25 miles per hour), *tropical depression* (winds between 40 kilometers per hour [25 miles per hour] and 61 kilometers per hour [38 miles per hour]), *tropical storm* (winds between 63 kilometers per hour [39 miles per hour] and 119 kilometers per hour [74 miles per hour]), and *tropical cyclone* (greater than 119 kilometers per hour [74 miles per hour]) (How Does a Hurricane Form? 2018; for a more technical discussion of hurricane formation, see Hurricanes: Science and Society 2015).

References

"Active Volcanoes in Hawaii." 2017. Hawaii Volcanic Observatory. https://volcanoes.usgs.gov/observatories/hvo/hvo_volcanoes.html. Accessed on April 20, 2018.

Albert. 2017. "The 1342 St. Mary Magdalene Flood." Volcano Café. http://www.volcanocafe.org/the-1342-st-mary-magdalene-flood/. Accessed on April 29, 2018.

"All Islands: Geology." 2007. Sandwich Islands. http://www.sandwichislands.com/Graphics/lava.jpg. Accessed on April 17, 2018.

Allahdadi, Joseph N., and Joseph N. Pelton, eds. 2015. *Handbook of Cosmic Hazards and Planetary Defense*. Cham, Switzerland: Springer International.

Ambraseys, Nicholas. 2009. *Earthquakes in the Mediterranean and Middle East: A Multidisciplinary Study of Seismicity up to 1900*. Cambridge, UK: Cambridge University Press.

Avalos, Hector. 1995. *Illness and Health Care in the Ancient Near East: The Role of the Temple in Greece, Mesopotamia, and Israel.* Harvard Semitic Monographs 54. Atlanta: Scholars Press, 22(1).

"Benefits of Fire." 2018. Cal Fire. http://www.fire.ca.gov/communications/downloads/fact_sheets/TheBenefitsofFire.pdf. Accessed on May 14, 2018.

Ben-Menahem, Ari. 1995. "A Concise History of Mainstream Seismology: Origins, Legacy, and Perspectives." *Bulletin of the Seismological Society of America.* 85(4): 1202–1225. Available online at https://engineering.purdue.edu/~ce597m/Handouts/ConciseHistory_BenMenahem.pdf. Accessed on May 25, 2018.

"Billion-Dollar Weather and Climate Disasters: Table of Events." 2018. National Centers for Environmental Information. https://www.ncdc.noaa.gov/billions/events/US/1980-2018. Accessed on April 28, 2018.

Black, George W. 1979. "Frank Bursley Taylor: A Forgotten Pioneer of Continental Drift." *Journal of Geological Education.* 279(2): 67–70.

Bulman, Julian. 2012. "10 Worst Earthquakes from the Past." Listverse. https://listverse.com/2012/11/02/10-historic-earthquakes-from-antiquity/. Accessed on April 14, 2018.

Bulmer, Marko H. K. 2017. "Landslides on Other Planets." In John J. Clague and Douglas Stead, eds. *Landslides: Types, Mechanisms and Modeling.* Cambridge, UK: Cambridge University Press, Chapter 32.

Burt, Christopher C. 2007. *Extreme Weather.* New York: W. W. Norton.

Chatfield, Christopher. 2017. "Landmarks of World History: A Chronology of Remarkable Natural Phenomena." The Gallery of Natural Phenomena. http://www.phenomena.org.uk/. Accessed on April 22, 2018.

Changnon, Stanley A. 2005. "The 1993 Flood's Aftermath: Risks, Root Causes, and Lessons for the Future." *Journal of Contemporary Water Research & Education.* 130: 70–74. Available online at https://onlinelibrary.wiley.com/doi/pdf/ 10.1111/j.1936-704X.2005.mp130001012.x. Accessed on May 10, 2018.

Chester, David K. 2018. "Natural Disasters and Christian Theology." https://www.faraday.st-edmunds.cam.ac.uk/ resources/FAR268%20Chester.pdf. Accessed on April 27, 2018.

"Classification of Tropical Cyclones." 2009. Hong Kong Observatory. http://www.hko.gov.hk/informtc/class.htm. Accessed on April 26, 2018.

Courtney, Chris. 2018. "Central China Flood, 1931." Disas ter History.org. http://www.disasterhistory.org/central-china-flood-1931. Accessed on April 29, 2018.

De Jong Boers, Bernice. 1995. "Mount Tambora in 1815: A Volcanic Eruption in Indonesia and Its Aftermath." *Indonesia.* 60: 37–60.

Dewey, James, and Perry Byerly. 1969. "The Early History of Seismometry (to 1900)." *Bulletin of the Seismological Society of America.* 59(1): 183–227. Available online at https:// earthquake.usgs.gov/learn/topics/eqsci-history/early-seismometry.php. Accessed on May 24, 2018.

Doocy, Shannon, et al. 2013. "The Human Impact of Floods: A Historical Review of Events 1980–2009 and Systematic Literature Review." *PLOS Currents Disasters.* doi:10.1371/ currents.dis.f4deb457904936b07c09daa98ee8171a. Available online at http://currents.plos.org/disasters/article/ the-human-impact-of-floods-a-historical-review-of-events-1980-2009-and-systematic-literature-review/. Accessed on April 28, 20168.

Dundes, Alan. 1988. *The Flood Myth.* Berkeley: University of California Press.

"Dust Bowl." 2009. History. https://www.history.com/topics/ dust-bowl. Accessed on May 21, 2018.

"1811–1812 New Madrid, Missouri Earthquakes." 2018. U.S. Geological Survey. https://earthquake.usgs.gov/ earthquakes/events/1811-1812newmadrid/. Accessed on April 16, 2018.

Elliott, Austin. 2012. "Landers@20." Blogosphere. https://blogs .agu.org/tremblingearth/2012/06/28/landers-20/. Accessed on May 26, 2018.

Evans, Meghan. 2012. "Earth's Strongest, Most Massive Storm Ever." https://www.accuweather.com/en/weather-news/ typhoon-tip-earths-strongest-storm/87362. Accessed on April 26, 2018.

"Evolution of the Islands around Krakatoa from 1800 to 2005." 2018. https://upload.wikimedia.org/wikipedia/ commons/5/5b/Krakatoa_evolution_map-en.gif. Accessed on April 18, 2018.

"Exploding Lakes in the World." 2015. Exploding Lakes. https://www.youtube.com/watch?v=gPvvg0ZjIP4. Accessed on May 22, 2018.

"Explore the Ring of Fire." 2004. Weather Watch. http:// teacher.scholastic.com/activities/wwatch/volcanoes/explore .htm. Accessed on June 1, 2018.

"Featured Image." 2012. National Aeronautical and Space Administration. https://www.nasa.gov/mission_pages/fires/main/ world/20120913-siberia.html. Accessed on May 16, 2018.

Finkbeiner, Ann. 2015. "The Great Quake and the Great Drowning." *Hakai Magazine*. https://www.hakaimagazine .com/features/great-quake-and-great-drowning/. Accessed on April 14, 2018.

"Flood and Flash Flood Definitions." 2018. National Weather Service. https://www.weather.gov/mrx/flood_and_flash. Accessed on April 28, 2018.

"Forest Fires in the Russian Taiga." 2004. Taiga Rescue Network Fact Sheet. http://old.forest.ru/eng/publications/ trn-forestfires/forestfire.pdf. Accessed on May 16, 2018.

"Fujita Tornado Damage Scale." 2018. The Online Tornado FAQ. http://www.spc.noaa.gov/faq/tornado/f-scale.html. Accessed on April 23, 2018.

"Geologic Event Cards." 2018. Expedition: Yellowstone! https://www.nps.gov/common/uploads/teachers/lessonplans/Geologic-Event-Cards.pdf. Accessed on April 17, 2018.

Gischler, Eberhard A., et al. 2008. "1500-Year Holocene Caribbean Climate Archive from the Blue Hole, Lighthouse Reef, Belize." *Journal of Coastal Research*. 24(6): 1495–1505.

Grady, Constance. 2017. "When the Dragon Ate the Sun: How Ancient Peoples Interpreted Solar Eclipses." Vox. https://www.vox.com/culture/2017/8/18/16078886/total-solar-eclipse-folklore. Accessed on April 12, 2018.

"The Great Flood of 1993." 1994. National Oceanic and Atmospheric Administration. https://www.weather.gov/media/publications/assessments/93_Flood.pdf. Accessed on May 11, 2018.

"The Great 1906 San Francisco Earthquake." 2018. U.S. Geological Survey. https://earthquake.usgs.gov/earthquakes/events/1906calif/18april/. Accessed on April 16, 2018.

Green, Nathan C. 1900; 2000. *Story of the 1900 Galveston Hurricane*. Gretna, LA: Pelican Publishing.

Haraldsson, Einar. 2010. "La Garita Caldera." Flickr. https://www.flickr.com/photos/rodor54/5183943931. Accessed on April 17, 2018.

Hays, Jeffreys. 2013. "Floods in China." Heavy Rains and Floods in China. http://factsanddetails.com/china/cat10/sub65/item395.html. Accessed on May 10, 2018.

"Hazards of Cyclones." 2018. Meteorological Centre, Ahmedabad. http://www.imdahm.gov.in/cycdisasters.htm#Cyclones_in_the_Indian_Seas. Accessed on April 26, 2018.

Heezen, Bruce C. 1960. "The Rift in the Ocean Floor." *Scientific American*. 203(4): 98–110.

Holmes, Arthur. 1931. *Nature*. 128: 559–605. Available online at http://www.mantleplumes.org/WebDocuments/ Holmes1931.pdf. Accessed on May 31, 2018.

Houston, Sam, Greg Forbes, and Arthur Chiu. 1998. "Super Typhoon Paka's (1997) Surface Winds over Guam." http://www.aoml.noaa.gov/hrd/project98/sh_proj1.html. Accessed on April 26, 2018.

"How Do Tornadoes Form?" 2017. eschooltoday. http:// eschooltoday.com/natural-disasters/tornadoes/how-do-tornadoes-form.html. Accessed on June 8, 2018.

"How Does a Hurricane Form?" 2018. SciJinks. NOAA. https:// scijinks.gov/hurricane/. Accessed on June 8, 2018.

Howard, Brian Clark. 2015. "How Tornadoes Form and Why They're So Unpredictable." National Geographic. https:// news.nationalgeographic.com/2015/05/150511-tornadoes-storms-midwest-weather-science/. Accessed on June 8, 2018.

"Hurricane Iniki: Quick Facts about Hawaii's Most Powerful Storm." 2017. Hawaii News Now. http://www.hawaiinew snow.com/story/36315106/hurricane-iniki-quick-facts-about-hawaiis-most-powerful-storm. Accessed on April 26, 2018.

"Hurricanes: Science and Society." 2015. Graduate School of Oceanography. University of Rhode Island. http://www .hurricanescience.org/science/science/primarycirculation/. Accessed on June 8, 2018.

"Impact and Aftermath." 1997. U.S. Geological Survey. https:// pubs.usgs.gov/gip/msh/impact.html. Accessed on May 19, 2018.

Jennings, Ken. 2014. *Condé Nast Traveler*. https://www.cntraveler .com/stories/2014-06-02/qattara-depression-maphead. Accessed on June 5, 2018.

Keaton, Jeffrey R., et al. 2014. "Turning Disaster into Knowledge." https://snohomishcountywa.gov/Document Center/View/18180/GEER_Oso_Landslide_Report_ July2014. Accessed on May 19, 2018.

Kim, Kyle, and Thomas Suh Lauder. 2017. "275 California Drought Maps Show Deep Drought and Recovery." *Los Angeles Times*. http://www.latimes.com/local/lanow/la-me-g-california-drought-map-htmlstory.html. Accessed on May 20, 2018.

Klingaman, William K., and Nicholas P. Klingaman. 2014. *The Year without Summer: 1816 and the Volcano That Darkened the World and Changed History*. New York: St. Martin's Griffin.

KSL Chicago. 2017. "Why Do Hurricanes Spin the Way They Do?" Kids Science Labs. https://kidssciencelabs.com/blog/2017/9/23/why-do-hurricanes-spin-the-way-they.do. Accessed on June 8, 2018.

"Lake Nyos—The Deadly Limnic Explosion." 2007. The World of Danescombe. https://productforums.google.com/forum/#!topic/gec-world-danescombe-moderated/YGla04E8B28. Accessed on May 22, 2018.

"Land Subsidence in the American West." 2016. USGS Groundwater Information. https://water.usgs.gov/ogw/pubs/fs00165/. Accessed on June 5, 2018.

Landsea, Chris. 2013. "What Have Been the Deadliest Hurricanes for the USA?" Hurricane Research Division. NOAA. http://www.aoml.noaa.gov/hrd/tcfaq/E12.html. Accessed on April 25, 2018.

Landsea, Chris. 2017. "How Many Tropical Cyclones Have There Been Each Year in the Atlantic Basin? What Years Were the Greatest and Fewest Seen?" Hurricane Research Division. NOAA. http://www.aoml.noaa.gov/hrd/tcfaq/E11.html. Accessed on April 24, 2018.

"Largest Brush and Forest Fires in Recorded History." 2018. World Atlas. https://www.worldatlas.com/articles/largest-brush-and-forest-fires-in-recorded-history.html. Accessed on May 16, 2018.

"Lava Flows in Pahoa—Eruption Update." 2014. YouTube. https://www.youtube.com/watch?v=ddzU-rkzKF0. Accessed on April 17, 2018.

Liautaud, Alexa. 2018. "Homeless after Harvey: A Crisis." Vice News. https://news.vice.com/en_ca/article/7xedqb/homeless-after-harvey-a-crisis-in-texas. Accessed on April 29, 2018.

"Lōʻihi." 2017. Volcano Hazards Program. U.S. Geological Survey. https://volcanoes.usgs.gov/volcanoes/loihi/. Accessed on April 20, 2018.

Ludwin, Ruth S., et al. 2005. "Dating the 1700 Cascadia Earthquake: Great Coastal Earthquakes in Native Stories." *Seismological Research Letters.* 76(2): 140–148.

Manning, Darrel. 2009. "Remembering the Hilo Tsunami of 1946." Damon Tucker: Hawaii News & Information. http://damontucker.com/2009/05/11/remembering-the-hilo-tsunami-of-1946/. Accessed on May 12, 2018.

Marshak, Stephen, and Eileen Herrstrom. 2018. "Planet Earth and You." University of Illinois. https://www.coursera.org/learn/planet-earth/lecture/7zhBk/2-b-1-discovering-plate-tectonics, et seq. Accessed on May 31, 2018.

Martyn, John. 1756. *The Philosophical Transactions.* London: Lockyer Davis and Charles Reymer.

McCloskey, T. A., and G. Keller. 2009. "5000 Year Sedimentary Record of Hurricane Strikes on the Central Coast of Belize." *Quaternary International.* 195(1–2): 53–68.

McCullough, David. 2005. *The Johnstown Flood.* New York: Simon & Schuster.

"Media for Plate Tectonics." Found in "Timeline of the Development of the Theory of Plate Tectonics." "View All Media." 2018. Britannica. https://www.britannica.com/science/plate-tectonics/Timeline-of-the-development-of-the-theory-of-plate-tectonics. Accessed on May 30, 2018.

Meredith, Liz. 2016. "Types of Faults." YouTube. https://www.youtube.com/watch?v=A_ZRtS3QGHw. Accessed on May 26, 2018.

Michell, John. 1760. "Conjectures Concerning the Cause, and Observations upon the Phænomena of Earthquakes." London: The Royal Society. Available online at https://ia800205.us.archive.org/17/items/Michell1760sc82C/Michell1760sc82C.pdf. Accessed on May 24, 2018.

"The Modified Mercalli Intensity Scale." 2018. U.S. Geological Survey. https://earthquake.usgs.gov/learn/topics/mercalli.php. Accessed on February 15, 2019.

"Nation's Largest Sinkhole May Be near Montevallo." 1973. *The Tuscaloosa News*. https://news.google.com/newspapers?id=cBIdAAAAIBAJ&sjid=MpwEAAAAIBAJ&pg=5787%2C5468505. Accessed on June 5, 2018.

"Natural Catastrophes and Man-Made Disasters in 2017: A Year of Record-Breaking Losses." 2018. sigma. Swiss Re Institute. http://media.swissre.com/documents/sigma1_2018_en.pdf. Accessed on April 28, 2018.

"1919 Florida Keys Hurricane." 2015. Hurricanes: Science and Society. University of Rhode Island. http://www.hurricanescience.org/history/storms/1910s/FloridaKeys/. Accessed on April 24, 2018.

Nix, Steve. 2017. "Serotiny and the Serotinous Cone." ThoughtCo. https://www.thoughtco.com/serotiny-and-the-serotinous-cone-1342894. Accessed on May 14, 2018.

Nomade, Sébastian, et al. 2016. "A 36,000-Year-Old Volcanic Eruption Depicted in the Chauvet-Pont d'Arc Cave (Arde'che, France)?" *PLOS ONE*. 11(1): e0146621.

"Number of Deaths Caused by Majors Droughts Worldwide from 1900 to 2016." 2018. Statista. https://www.statista.com/statistics/267695/number-of-deaths-worldwide-due-to-drought/. Accessed on May 20, 2018.

Nunn, Patrick D. 2001. "On the Convergence of Myth and Reality: Examples from the Pacific Islands." *The Geographical Journal*. 167(2): 125–138.

"Oceanography 101." 2016. Geology Café. http://geologycafe.com/oceans/chapter3.html. Accessed on May 25, 2018.

O'Connor, Jim E., and John E. Costa. 2004. "The World's Largest Floods, Past and Present: Their Causes and Magnitudes." U.S. Geological Survey. Circular 1254. https://pubs.usgs.gov/circ/2004/circ1254/pdf/circ1254.pdf. Accessed on April 29, 2018.

Opar, Alisa. 2015. "Slip-Sliding Away." National Resources Defense Council. https://www.nrdc.org/onearth/slip-sliding-away. Accessed on May 19, 2018.

Ort, Michael. 1997. "La Garita Caldera." Archive Today. http://archive.li/o8bzq. Accessed on April 17, 2018.

Pasch, Richard J., Andrew B. Penny, and Robbie Berg. 2018. "Hurricane Maria: (AL152017)." National Hurricane Center. https://www.nhc.noaa.gov/data/tcr/AL152017_Maria.pdf. Accessed on April 25, 2018.

Phillips, Campbell. 2011. "The 10 Most Destructive Tsunamis in History." *Australian Geographic*. http://www.australiangeographic.com.au/topics/science-environment/2011/03/the-10-most-destructive-tsunamis-in-history/. Accessed on May 11, 2018.

Pittman, Craig. 2017. "The Clock Is Ticking on Florida's Mountains of Hazardous Phosphate Waste." *Sarasota Magazine*. https://www.sarasotamagazine.com/articles/2017/4/26/florida-phosphate. Accessed on June 5, 2018.

"Poseidon (Earthshaker, Dark-Haired One, Neptune)." 2018. GreekGods.org. https://www.greek-gods.org/olympian-gods/poseidon.php. Accessed on April 27, 2018.

Pybus, Nani Suzette. 1979. "Whirlwind Woman: Native American Tornado Mythology and Global Parallels." http://citeseerx.ist.psu.edu/viewdoc/download?doi=10.1.1.633.56 13&rep=rep1&type=pdf. Accessed on April 27, 2018.

"Questions about Supervolcanoes." 2018. Yellowstone Volcanic Observatory. https://volcanoes.usgs.gov/volcanoes/yellowstone/yellowstone_sub_page_49.html. Accessed on April 21, 2018.

"Questions and Answers about Drought." 2016. U.S. Geological Survey. https://water.usgs.gov/edu/qadroughts.html. Accessed on May 20, 2018.

Rimmer, Susan M., et al. 2015. "The Rise of Fire: Fossil Charcoal in Late Devonian Marine Shales as an Indicator of Expanding Terrestrial Ecosystems, Fire, and Atmospheric Change." *American Journal of Science.* 315(8): 713–733. Available online at https://digitalcommons.wcupa.edu/cgi/viewcontent.cgi?article=1014&context=geol_facpub. Accessed on May 14, 2018.

Romm, James. 1994. "A New Forerunner for Continental Drift." *Nature.* 367(6462): 407–408.

Scalera, Giancarlo. 2009. "Roberto Mantovani (1854–1933) and His Ideas on the Expanding Earth, as Revealed by His Correspondence and Manuscripts." *Annals of Geophysics.* 52(6): 615–649. Available online at https://www.annalsof geophysics.eu/index.php/annals/article/view/4622/4689?acceptCookies=1. Accessed on May 30, 2018.

Scarth, Alwyn. 2006. *La Catastrophe: The Eruption of Mount Pelee, the Worst Volcanic Eruption of the Twentieth Century.* New York: Oxford University Press.

Schroeder, Wilfried. 2018. "Some Aspects in Emil Wiechert's Scientific Work." Working Group History of Geophysics and Cosmic Physics. http://verplant.org/history-geophysics/Wiechert.htm. Accessed on May 25, 2018.

"Seen from Space." 2003. Space Technology Directorate (Japan). http://www.eorc.jaxa.jp/en/earthview/2003/tp030801.html. Accessed on May 16, 2018.

"Shaanxi Earthquake 1556 (Worst Death Toll)." 2018. Armage ddon Online. https://armageddononline.org/shaanxi-earthquake-1556-worst-death-toll/. Accessed on February 15, 2019.

Shanks, Hershel. 2018. "The Destruction of Pompeii—God's Revenge?" Bible History Daily. https://www.biblicalarchaeology.org/daily/ancient-cultures/ancient-near-eastern-world/the-destruction-of-pompeii-gods-revenge/. Accessed on April 27, 2018.

Shonting, David, and Cathy Ezrailson. 2017. Chicxulub: The Impact and Tsunami: The Story of the Largest Known Asteroid to Hit the Earth. Cham: Springer International Publishing.

"A Short Geologic History of Kauai, Hawaii." 2014. Volcano Café. https://volcanocafe.wordpress.com/2014/10/20/a-short-geologic-history-of-kauai-hawaii/. Accessed on April 20, 2018.

Silvestra. 2012. "Oya—The Dark Goddess of Storms, Destruction and Change of the Yoruba People." https://goddessinspired.wordpress.com/2012/04/15/oya-the-dark-goddess-of-storms-destruction-and-change-of-the-yoruba-people/. Accessed on April 27, 2018.

Simkin, Tom, and Richard S. Fiske, eds. 1985. *Krakatau 1883: The Volcanic Eruption and Its Effects.* Washington, DC: Smithsonian Press.

"Sinkholes." 2018. The USGS Water Science School. https://water.usgs.gov/edu/sinkholes.html. Accessed on June 5, 2018.

Soon, Willie, and Steven H. Yaskell. 2003. "Year without a Summer." *Mercury.* 32(3): 13–14.

"Taupo Volcano." 2010. GNS Science. https://www.gns .cri.nz/Home/Learning/Science-Topics/Volcanoes/New-Zealand-Volcanoes/Taupo-Volcano. Accessed on April 17, 2018.

Taylor, Alan. 2014. "Ten Years since the 2004 Indian Ocean Tsunami." https://www.theatlantic.com/photo/2014/12/ ten-years-since-the-2004-indian-ocean-tsunami/100878/. Accessed on May 12, 2018.

"Tectonics of the Planet Earth." 2013. YouTube. https://www .youtube.com/watch?v=Kg_UBLFUpYQ. Accessed on June 1, 2018.

"The 10 Costliest Floods in American History." 2011. *Atlantic.* https://www.theatlantic.com/business/archive/2011/05/the-10-costliest-floods-in-american-history/239309/#slide1. Accessed on May 10, 2018.

"1755 The Great Lisbon Earthquake and Tsunami, Portugal." SMS Tsunami Warning. https://www.sms-tsunami-warning .com/pages/tsunami-portugal-1755#.XGdAL-hKg2w. Accessed on February 15, 2019.

"Timeline: The Dust Bowl." 2018. American Experience. PBS. https://www.pbs.org/wgbh/americanexperience/features/ dust-bowl-surviving-dust-bowl/. Accessed on May 21, 2018.

TomoNews US. 2017. "Volcano Types." YouTube. https:// www.youtube.com/watch?v=y2Yd-XzMcO4. Accessed on April 17, 2018.

"Tri-State Tornado Facts and Information." 2018. Tornado Facts and Information. http://www.tornadofacts.net/tri-state-tornado-facts.php#facts. Accessed on April 23, 2018.

"Tropical Cyclone Names." 2018. National Hurricane Center. https://www.nhc.noaa.gov/aboutnames.shtml#atl. Accessed on April 25, 2018.

"20th Anniversary of Hurricane/Typhoon John." 2014. Hurricane Research Division. Atlantic Oceanographic and Meteorological Laboratory. https://noaahrd.wordpress

.com/2014/08/11/20th-anniversary-of-hurricanetyphoon-john/. Accessed on April 26, 2018.

Urquhart, Gerald R. 2009. "Paleoecological Record of Hurricane Disturbance and Forest Regeneration in Nicaragua." *Quaternary International*. 195(1–2): 88–97.

"Volcanoes Are 'Everywhere.'" 2007. Astral News. http://www .astralnewz.com/volcanoes.html. Accessed on April 20, 2018.

Wallace, Alfred Russel. 1889. *Darwinism: An Exposition of the Theory of Natural Selection, with Some of Its Applications.* London: Macmillan.

Wallace-Hadrill, Andrew. 2011. "Pompeii: Portents of Disaster." BBC. http://www.bbc.co.uk/history/ancient/romans/pompeii_ portents_01.shtml. Accessed on April 18, 2018.

Wegener, A. 2002. "The Origins of Continents." *Geologische Rundschau*. 3: 276–292. Available online at http://www0 .unsl.edu.ar/~bibliogeo/index_archivos/wegener.pdf. Accessed on May 31, 2018.

"What Is Seismology?" 2006. Michigan Tech University. http:// www.geo.mtu.edu/UPSeis/waves.html. Accessed on May 25, 2018.

"Why the Giant Sequoia Needs Fire to Grow." 2017. Nature on PBS. https://www.youtube.com/watch?v=lmNZGr9Udx8. Accessed on May 14, 2018.

Williams, Ashley. 2018. "Experts Uncover the Origins of 10 Common Weather Terms." AccuWeather. https://www .accuweather.com/en/weather-news/experts-uncover-the-origins-of-10-common-weather-terms/70002110. Accessed on April 22, 2018.

Witze, Alexandra. 2017. "Earth's Lost History of Planet-Altering Eruptions Revealed." *Nature*. 543(7645): 295–296.

"World: Highest Mortality due to a Tornado." 2018. World Meteorological Organization's World Weather & Climate Extremes Archive. https://wmo.asu.edu/content/world-highest-mortality-tornado. Accessed on April 23, 2018.

Wu, Q., et al. 2016. "Outburst Flood at 1920 BCE Supports Historicity of China's Great Flood and the Xia Dynasty." *Science.* 353(6299): 579–582.

"Yellowstone Volcano." 2018. My Yellowstone. https://www .yellowstonepark.com/things-to-do/yellowstone-supervolcano. Accessed on April 21, 2018.

Yirka, Bob. 2018. "New Evidence for Plume beneath Yellowstone National Park." Phys.org. https://phys.org/news/ 2018-03-evidence-plume-beneath-yellowstone-national .html. Accessed on April 21, 2018.

Zamora, Amanda, Abrahm Lustgarten, and Lauren Kirchner. 2015. "California's Drought Is Part of a Much Bigger Water Crisis. Here's What You Need to Know." ProPublica. https://www.propublica.org/article/california-drought-colorado-river-water-crisis-explained. Accessed on May 20, 2018.

Zimmer, Carl. 2017. "Fire May Be the Only Remedy for a Plague Killing Deer and Elk." *New York Times.* https://www .nytimes.com/2017/06/26/science/chronic-wasting-disease-deer-elk-prions.html. Accessed on May 14, 2018.

Natural disasters are events that occur in the physical world without, in most cases, human involvement. Tectonic plates may shift, causing earthquakes, volcanic eruptions, and tsunamis. Underground caves may collapse, resulting in the formation of sinkholes. Sections of a mountain may break off, producing a mudslide or landslide. Winds blowing across a warm section of the ocean may induce strong storms that may become hurricanes.

The operative phrase in the preceding paragraph, however, is *in most cases*. The reason is that human activities may initiate, increase, or decrease the probability of a natural disaster occurring. The following sections describe such possibilities.

The Impact of Human Activities on Natural Disasters

The most common types of natural disasters in which human activities may be involved are earthquakes, tropical storms, landslides, forest fires, and sinkholes.

Earthquakes

A variety of human activities have resulted in the occurrence of seismic activity. Earthquakes produced in this manner are commonly called *induced earthquakes*.

A brush fire in Ventura, California. Though the fire consumed 25 acres, it was quickly controlled by more than 100 firefighters and water-dropping helicopters. (Georg Henrik Lehnerer/Dreamstime.com)

Problems

Among the most widely discussed of all human-caused earthquakes are those that have occurred in the state of Oklahoma over the second decade of the 21st century. Oklahoma lies within the central United States, where earthquakes are generally uncommon and mild. Geological evidence suggests that the last major earthquake activity in the region occurred during the Quaternary period about 3,400 years ago. Since that time and up to about 2010, the number of such events has been "extremely low" (Hough and Page 2015). That situation then began to change with the number of earthquakes in the state increasing from 41 in 2010 to 903 in 2015. (See Table 2.1. The number of such earthquakes has since dropped substantially. See Whitehead 2018.)

What caused this fairly dramatic change in the number of earthquakes observed in Oklahoma over the period of a few years? One answer originally given to that question was the increased use of hydraulic fracturing ("fracking") for the recovery of oil and natural gas reserves. Fracking is a process by which a liquid is injected at high pressure into underground rocks to

Table 2.1 Earthquake Activity in Oklahoma, 2010–2017

Year	Earthquakes
2010	41
2011	67
2012	35
2013	110
2014	579
2015	903
2016	623
2017	304

Source: "Earthquakes in Oklahoma: What We Know." 2017. Earthquakes in Oklahoma. http://earthquakes.ok.gov/what-we-know/. Accessed on June 26, 2018.

open existing fractures that may already occur in the rocks. The process releases oil and gas from underground reserves with much less cost and effort than is possible with traditional drilling procedures. At least partially for logical reasons, one might assume that breaking rock apart underground might increase the risk of an induced seismic event. Researchers, industrial executives, and politicians have been debating for over a decade as to whether this logical explanation actually applies to the production of induced earthquakes.

An early study by the U.S. National Research Council (NRC) concluded that fracking is *not* a major cause for such events. In its 2012 report, *Induced Seismicity Potential in Energy Technologies*, the NRC said that "the process of hydraulic fracturing a well as presently implemented for shale gas recovery does not pose a high risk for inducing felt seismic events" (Induced Seismicity Potential in Energy Technologies 2013, 1). On a number of occasions, the U.S. Geological Survey (USGS) has repeated this conclusion. In its web page on "Myths and Misconceptions" about induced earthquakes, the agency states clearly that "Fracking is NOT causing most of the induced earthquakes" (Myths and Misconceptions 2018).

This conclusion has not, however, achieved unanimous or even widespread support from researchers in the field. Some studies of areas other than Oklahoma claim to have found definitive evidence that fracking *does* cause induced earthquakes in these areas. A 2016 study of induced earthquakes in western Canada, for example, found that "hydraulic fracturing has been inferred to trigger the majority of injection-induced earthquakes in western Canada" (Bao and Eaton 2016).

All of these studies is not to suggest that fracking and earthquakes are completely unrelated. Indeed, as the USGS and many researchers have pointed out, it is often the liquid disposal process from fracking that is implicated in the production of earthquakes. An environmentally critical phase of fracking is disposal of liquids used in the process. Estimates vary, depending on specific characteristics of a fracking operation, but the

USGS reports that anywhere from 1.5 million to 16 million gallons of water are used in a single fracking operation (How Much Water Does the Typical Hydraulically Fractured Well Require? 2018). The question is, how can that contaminated water be disposed of in an environmentally sensitive way?

The most common solution to this problem is the injection of waste water and other liquids into deep wells. This procedure has a long history in the United States, dating back at least to the 1930s. During that early period, petroleum companies disposed of liquid wastes produced during drilling operations in deep wells (Clark, Bonura, and Van Voorhees 2005). Some of the best information about the relationship of deep well injection and earthquakes dates back to the 1960s at the Rocky Mountain Arsenal in Colorado. The facility was used by the U.S. military for the development of chemical weapons. Liquid wastes from the operation were injected into a specially drilled well 3,671 meters (12,045 feet) deep. A total of 4–6 million gallons of liquid were injected into the well from 1962 to 1965 (Evans 1966).

Early on, questions were raised about possible connections between the arsenal's deep well injection process and an increase in earthquakes in the Denver area. Researchers found that injection patterns quite closely matched the occurrence of earthquakes. Among the 710 earthquakes reported in the Denver area between 1962 and 1965, the majority occurred within a 5-mile radius of the injection site. One study of the phenomenon concluded that "the volume of fluid and pressure of fluid injection appear to be directly related to the frequency of earthquakes" (Evans 1966, 23).

A number of recent studies have shown a similar correlation between the volume of liquids injected into deep wells and the frequency of induced earthquakes. Such studies tend to conclude that a relatively small number of cases exist in which disposal is associated with earthquakes. Such occurrences may, nonetheless, create "an array of issues" and "has affected oil and gas wastewater disposal in some areas" (Folger and Tiemann

2016; also see Ellsworth 2013; Fernandez 2015; Hippauf 2015; Walsh and Zoback 2015).

Although injection wells as a source of induced earthquakes have received widespread attention in the past few decades, they are by no means the only—or even the most common— cause of such events. Among other human activities that may be correlated with earthquake activity are mining operations, the construction of reservoirs and other artificial lakes, groundwater extraction, geothermal facilities, construction of tall buildings or other heavy structures, excavation for tunnels, and nuclear explosions. According to The Human-Induced Earthquake Database (HiQuake), the most common cause of induced earthquakes historically and worldwide is activities associated with mining. Thirty-seven percent of the projects listed in the HiQuake database, which contains 766 events ranging from 1868 to 2016, are mine-related events. The next most common cause of induced earthquakes, according to HiQuake, is impoundment of water for reservoirs (22%), followed by conventional oil and gas operations (14%) and geothermal facilities (8%). Fracking and waste fluid disposal rank fifth and sixth in the database, accounting for just 6 percent and 5 percent, respectively, of all earthquake events (Foulger et al. 2018; the HiQuake database can be accessed at http://inducedearthquakes.org/).

The earliest record of mining-related earthquakes dates back to 1900 in the Kolar goldfields of India. Having been abandoned, the mines collapsed, setting off a series of earthquakes throughout the region. The specific type of earthquake produced by such an event is known as a *rock burst* (Guha 2000).

The first-recorded seismic event associated with the construction of water storage facilities occurred following the construction of the Oued Fodda Dam in Algeria in 1932. For about five months following completion of the dam, a group of earthquakes were detected in the area surrounding the new dam. Seismic activity soon ended, and residents of the area suffered no serious consequences of the quakes (Joint Panel on

Problems Concerning Seismology and Rock Mechanics; Division of Earth Sciences; National Academy of Sciences; National Academy of Engineering 1972, 15).

More serious seismic activity has been attributed to the construction of other dams throughout the world, including the Monteyard (France), Grandval (France), Hoover (United States), Kariba (Zambia/Zimbabwe), Kremasta (Greece), and Vaiont (Italy) dams. One of the most destructive of these events struck the Koyna Dam reservoir in Maharashtra, India, in 1967. The 6.3 magnitude earthquake and aftershocks resulting from construction of the new dam killed 180 people and injured another 1,500 individuals. The seismic event was felt in Mumbai (Bombay), about 230 kilometers (140 miles) from the dam (Gupta 2002).

Possibly the most disastrous of all reservoir-caused earthquakes is thought to have occurred in 2008 in Sichuan Province, China, the so-called Wenchuan earthquake. The event has been blamed for 461,751 deaths and injuries, about 45 million homes destroyed, and economic losses of an estimated $150 million. Although no completely conclusive evidence is available, the 8.0 magnitude earthquake has generally been attributed to construction of the massive Zipingpu Reservoir that lies on the Shuimo-Miaoziping fault line that also contains the epicenter of the earthquake. As of late 2018, the preponderance of expert opinion appears to support this explanation of the earthquake's origin (Xiao 2012; for a good general review of this topic, see Rothé 1969).

Geothermal facilities hold the promise for providing clean energy at a modest cost in certain specific parts of the world where geological features are suited to such operations. In recent years, however, some question has arisen as to the possible environmental impact of such facilities. The most discussed of these discussions has involved the occurrence of an earthquake in Pohang, South Korea, in 2017. During drilling for the geothermal plant, an earthquake—the second largest in the nation's modern history, with a magnitude of 5.5—struck the region around Pohang. The quake resulted in injuries to about 90 people and $52 million in damage to the new facility. Two studies provided significant evidence that drilling at the proposed geothermal site was responsible for seismic shocks immediately below the drilling site (Grigoli et al. 2018; Kim et al. 2018).

Solutions

The risk posed by induced earthquakes in Oklahoma and other states needs to be placed in perspective. The vast majority of such earthquakes are of relatively low magnitude, usually less than 3.0. And the more damaging earthquakes for which information is available have produced no deaths and only a handful of minor injuries (Fieldstadt 2016; Passut 2018; Weinhold 2012). The most serious problems caused by such quakes have been property damage. Although no overall estimate of such damage appears to be available, the economic cost of the most severe earthquakes may run into the tens of millions of dollars (Krehbiel 2015).

Such costs are, of course, substantial for individual property owners. But they pale in comparison to the profits made by fossil-fuel energy companies. According to one estimate, the oil and gas industry in Oklahoma "supports thousands of jobs, remits millions in state and local taxes, and generates billions of dollars of economic output" (Davis and Fisk 2017). Under those circumstances, government officials must weigh carefully the risks posed by induced earthquakes compared to the economic benefit of operations by which those events are created.

Given this need to balance risks and benefits of monitoring induced earthquakes, industry and governmental agencies have adopted a variety of programs for reducing the hazards posed by such events without seriously interfering with the efforts of the oil and gas industry. On the federal level, four agencies have important roles in the monitoring and/or regulation of waste disposal sites and induced earthquakes. Under the Safe Drinking Water Act of 1974, the U.S. Environmental Protection Agency (EPA) is required to prevent contamination of underground sources of drinking water. In accordance with that act, the EPA has developed a comprehensive program of inspection and regulation of disposal wells that applies to more than 700,000 such sites in the United States. The wells are classified into one of six categories, based on the type of material introduced into a well, as shown in Table 2.2. A company must present evidence to the EPA that its operations will meet all relevant safe drinking water standards in order to receive a permit for construction and operation of a well. The number of wells in each class varies widely from state to state. For example, as of 2013, there were 52,016 Class II wells in Texas, 29,505 in California, 16,658 in Kansas, and 10,629 in Oklahoma, compared to one such well in this class in Washington, and none in Arizona or North Carolina (Induced Seismicity Potential in Energy Technologies 2013, Table 4.2, 120).

For two other agencies, the Bureau of Land Management and the U.S. Forest Service, monitoring of disposal wells is limited to specific types of land, all federal lands in the United

Table 2.2   EPA Disposal Well Categories

Class	Wells
I	Hazardous and nonhazardous wastes into deep, isolated rock formations.
II	Fluids associated with oil and natural gas production.
III	Fluids used to dissolve and extract minerals.
IV	Hazardous or radioactive wastes into or above a geologic formation that contains an underground source of drinking water.
V	Nonhazardous fluids. Most Class V wells are used to dispose of wastes into or above underground sources of drinking water.
VI	Carbon dioxide (CO_2) into underground subsurface rock formations for long-term storage, or geologic sequestration.

Source: "Underground Injection Control Well Classes." 2016. Environmental Protection Agency. https://www.epa.gov/uic/underground-injection-control-well-classes. Accessed on June 30, 2018.

States in the former case and national forest lands in the latter. In both cases, the agencies are responsible for surface features of the well, such as surface facilities and surface impacts (Induced Seismicity Potential in Energy Technologies 2013, 127).

The fourth federal agency involved in the monitoring of disposal wells is the USGS. By its nature, USGS is intimately involved in a host of earthquake and disposal wells issues, such as recording and reporting earthquakes; the investigation of possible induced earthquakes; promoting knowledge, tools, and practices for earthquake risk reduction; and improving earthquake resilience. These activities are carried out within the department's Earthquake Hazards Program, which also houses the National Earthquake Information Center. One example of the services provided by the USGS is its seismic data processing and interpretation program. In this program, small, portable seismometers can be provided at a site where foreshocks or an actual induced earthquake may appear. The data collected from these seismometers can then be used for companies, regulators, and other agencies to learn more about the site of the earthquake, progression in major shocks and aftershocks, and other characteristic features of that specific event (Preventing Human-Caused Earthquakes 2016). Another important service provided by the USGS is the agency's annual Short-Term Induced Seismicity Model. Each year, the agency collects all data that may be relevant to the possible occurrence of natural and induced earthquakes throughout the United States. It then uses these data to develop a map showing the likelihood of an earthquake occurring during the current year in all parts of the nation (Short-Term Induced Seismicity Models 2018; for an example of the use of these data, see Simmers et al. 2017).

In addition to federal actions, many states have developed programs for preventing or reducing the damage caused by induced earthquakes. In most cases, these actions are based on new or more stringent requirements on industries to determine, monitor, and respond to the risk of such events as a

consequence of their operations. More specifically, these regulations often require that industries (1) conduct such testing
and research as may be needed to determine the potential risk
of earthquakes as a result of company activities; (2) provide this
information to state regulatory agencies as an element of the
permit application process; (3) monitor for earthquakes once
permits have been approved and operations have been started;
and (4) modify or discontinue operations if seismic action is
detected at a work site. (A summary of the specific actions
taken by the Oklahoma Corporation Commission to deal with
induced earthquakes is available at http://www.occeweb.com/
News/2017/02-24-17EARTHQUAKE%20ACTION%20
SUMMARY.pdf. Also see Earthquakes in Oklahoma: What
We Are Doing 2017.)

One of the common methods for dealing with induced
earthquakes is the so-called traffic light system (or protocol)
(TLS or TLP). This system is based most commonly on the
use of three indicator lights that correspond to the red, yellow,
and green lights typically used in traffic lights. It requires that
instruments be available at waste disposal sites where induced
earthquakes may be expected to occur. The readings on those
instruments determine the light color selected for that specific
operation. The selection of light colors and the definitions
provided for each color differ from agency to agency. In an
early version of the system used in the Basel Deep Heat Mining project in Switzerland, for example, four colors were used
to indicate possible earthquake risk: green: no seismic activity
detected; yellow: activity reported by some observers; amber:
activity reported by many observers; and red: activity felt by
most observers (Kao n.d.).

Each light color can then be used to determine the type of
activity by a company to reduce the risk of seismic activity at a
site. In the Basel system, for example, the following protocols
were used: green: no action required; yellow: company must
inform regulators and not increase rate of flow into a well;
amber: rate of flow into a well must be reduced; red: pumping

must stop and ancillary actions may be required. Such actions might include adding a concrete base to the bottom of the well and/or removing some or all of the liquid present in the well (Kao n.d.; for the original report on this system, see Häring et al. 2008).

A limited number of options are available to property owners whose assets may be threatened or affected by induced earthquake. One obvious step is to purchase earthquake insurance. Insurance for any type of earthquake (natural or induced) is typically not included in a standard homeowner insurance policy. But separate policies can be purchased for such events. This type of insurance is generally not widely purchased in the midwestern states, largely because the risk of earthquakes is so low in that region. Overall, only about 8 percent of homeowners in the Midwest carry earthquake insurance (Facts + Statistics: Earthquakes and Tsunamis 2018).

The increase in induced earthquakes since about 2010, however, has changed that situation significantly. In Oklahoma, for example, the rate of earthquake insurance policies written increased from 2 percent in 2006 to 15 percent in 2015 (a rate higher than even California). The total value of premiums during this period increased from $4.579 million to $18.858 million (Man-Made Earthquakes in Oklahoma—A Headache for Insurers 2017). In the long run, an increased reliance on earthquake insurance policies has turned out to be more beneficial to insurance companies than to property owners who have purchased the insurance. Between 2010 and 2016, insurers in Oklahoma paid out $5.1 million in claims to policyholders, while earning $211 million in policy premiums. During the same period, 1,800 claims were filed for earthquake damage, of which 292 received payments for the damage, a reimbursement rate of just over 16 percent (Earthquake Damage Claims 2017; Jones and Killman 2017; for the situation in other states, see Ryan 2016).

Another option available to individual property owners is legal action against companies that use deep well injection in their operations. Given the glacial pace at which legal cases work their way through the courts, it is still too early to say how effective this line of action will be in recompensing property owners for damage done by induced earthquakes. (For a recent summary of legal cases in this area, see Marek 2018; for an interesting discussion on induced earthquake liability issues and a proposed Model State Induced Seismicity Fund, see Konschnik 2017.)

In some cases, there is little or nothing that can be done to avoid the environmental risks (e.g., induced earthquakes) that may result from an industrial operation. In such cases, the benefits may so completely exceed the risks that the operation is allowed to go forward. A recent example of this situation was the construction of the Three Gorges Dam on the Yangtze River in Hubei Province, China. Completed in 2003, the dam was designed to control flooding in the area and to provide an inexpensive source of electrical power for surrounding communities. Experts acknowledge in advance that the impounding of nearly 40 cubic kilometers (10 cubic miles) of water posed a threat to underlying rock strata, with the accompanying risk of induced earthquakes. While recognizing that threat, however, the Chinese government decided that the benefits accruing from the dam were sufficient to overcome the possible risks of earthquakes. And so the dam was built. (Predictions of seismic activity turned out to be accurate. For a report on such events, see Miao et al. 2011.)

Among the most effective methods of controlling the damage caused by earthquakes are building codes. A building code is a set of rules that specify the standards for constructed objects, such as buildings and other commercial and residential structures. Most governmental bodies today have extensive and comprehensive regulations that developers must meet in order to get a permit for construction. The state of California, for example, has a detailed list of regulations required for construction of a building that will be reasonably resistant to seismic shocks. These requirements cover items such as the type of frame used for the building (concrete, steel, composite, or other); the types of beams, columns, and load-bearing walls; roof structures, balconies, and decks; reviewing stands, bleachers, yards, terraces, and similar structures; elevator systems; storage racks and wall-hung cabinets; snow loads and wind loads; and corridors, lobbies, and exit ways, all of which supplement many other regulations dealing, for example, with siting, plumbing, electrical, and other aspects of the building (Chapter 16 Structural Design 2018). California's building code is based on standards established by the American Society of Civil Engineers, as outlined in its publication *Minimum Design Loads and Associated Criteria for Buildings and Other Structures (7–16)* (American Society of Civil Engineers 2017; other agencies have developed similar seismic building codes; see, for example, NEHRP Recommended Seismic Provisions for New Buildings and Other Structures. 2009 Edition 2018; 2018 International Building Code 2018, Chapter 16).

Sinkholes

In some parts of the world, the likelihood of a sinkhole's formation can be significantly increased as a result of human activities. Some particularly interesting examples of such events can be found as a result of the phosphate industry's activities in the state of Florida. Ancient geological activity in some parts of the state resulted in the formation of deep-lying limestone rock overlain by clay, sand, and other types of rocks. Phosphate resources in these areas have led to the development of a substantial industry in which those resources are used for the production of fertilizers and other commercially valuable phosphate products. One by-product of the industry's operations is acidic waste, which may percolate into the subsurface area, dissolving limestone rock. The caves produced by this dissolution process are then unable to support overlying rocky layers, which collapse in the formation of giant sinkholes. One of the first and most thoroughly studied of these events was a sinkhole that formed on June 27, 1994, in a work area at the New Wales Plant of IMC-Agrico Company in Polk Country, Florida. The hole was 160 feet across and 200 feet deep, ending within the underlying limestone area. On discovery of the sinkhole, operations were immediately discontinued at the site (Fuleihan, Cameron, and Henry 1997). The resolution of the Polk County event involved redirecting waste products into a new storage area, lined to prevent harmful chemicals from soaking into the ground. The event also prompted state regulators to adopt a new, comprehensive plan for the treatment of phosphate wastes in the state (Rule Chapter: 62-673 2018).

Landslides

Problems

Of all types of natural disasters, landslides are among the events most likely to occur because of human activities. Landslides occur most commonly because of two major changes in an area: a change in the slope angle of the region or changes in the structure and/or composition of the area. The natural tendency of land to flow downward along a slope is at least partially dependent on its slope angle, the angle formed between a horizontal ground level and the level of the land's surface. The steeper the slope angle, the more likely it is that land will flow downward. (This effect is in large part, of course, because of the gravitational attraction of material that lies along the slope.)

Two major factors can affect the slope angle and, therefore, increase or decrease the likelihood of a landslide: material can be removed from the toe (bottom) of the slope, or material can be added to the crown (top) of the slope. For example, suppose that a road is being planned to run along the lower edge of a sloping area (a hill or a mountain). In order to construct that road, material will probably have to be cut away and removed from the slope. The slope angle will increase, gravitational attraction on the slope material will increase, and the probability of a landslide will increase. A similar effect may occur as a result of changes at the top of a slope. For example, a new irrigation system that significantly increases the amount (and, hence, the weight) of water placed on top of a slope may be installed. The additional weight may become greater than the slope itself can support, and sections of the slope crown may break off in a landslide. Some other activities that might produce the same result are the construction of new roads, parking areas, industrial plants, and residential developments or the accumulation of heavy wastes from mining or other operations at the top of the slope. (For an excellent overview of human causes of landslides, see Jaboyedoff et al. 2016. For a good review of the causes of landslides in general, see Highland, Lynn, and Bobrowsky 2008.)

Humans also contribute to the occurrence of landslides because of the changes they make on a hilly or mountainous area. In addition to changes made at the toe or crown of a slope for new construction or other operations, they may cut down trees and clear land for new housing developments or other purposes. Loss of plant material reduces the ability of land to retain water, increasing the instability of land on a slope. Installation of new water systems (irrigation systems, water and sewer lines, and artificial ponds, for example) may also increase the pressure on a hillside, increasing the likelihood of landslides. (For case studies on human-caused landslides in various countries around the world, see Jaboyedoff et al. 2016; Nadim et al. 2011.)

Solutions

Because of the significant damage that human-caused landslides can cause, methods for reducing risks of such events have become an important field of research. Today, a number of methods are available for reducing the landslide risks posed by human activities. Among these procedures are the following:

Excavation: The addition of material to or removal of material from an area can reduce the risk of landslides. For example, materials can be removed from the crown of a slope or added to the toe of a slope to stabilize the area from top to bottom. Some existing materials at the top of a slope can also be replaced by less dense materials, reducing the force on the slope overall. Changes can also be made in the surface of a slope to reduce gravitational forces. For example, benches can be cut into the face of a slope to reduce pressure on the land area.

Strengthening a slope: Physical changes can be made to a slope that makes it more resistant to loosening and sliding. One technique that is often used involves covering the face of a slope with a plastic or wire mesh that holds materials in place. It is also possible to install a buttress along the bottom of a slope by adding heavy rocks to the area, thus strengthening the toe of the slope when compared to its crown. Various types of dams can also be installed along the face of a slope to reduce the rate of water flow, providing more resistance to the loss of material from the slope.

Drainage control: Other forms of control over the rate of flow down a slope are also available. Ditches, drainage systems, trenches, retaining walls, and other systems are examples of such techniques. In some cases, these structures may be filled with water-absorbing material to reduce the rate of water flow on the surface. An example of a common type of drainage control system is the gabion wall, a box or cage filled with rocks, concrete, and/or sand and soil. A gabion wall absorbs flowing water and allows it to soak into the surface of a slope. Planting of new vegetation along a slope also increases the rate of water absorption on the slope, thus reducing the risk of landslide. In some areas, the development of natural ecological systems, with improved soils, native plants, and physical enclosures, has provided an aesthetically pleasing way of reducing landslide risk. (For more information on the many types of mediation now available for landslide-sensitive areas, see Highland and Bobrowsky 2008, Appendix C; Lacasse and Choi 2011; Popescu and Sasahara 2009.)

As with earthquakes, many communities now employ special building codes to prevent or ameliorate the effects of landslides. The state of Oregon, for example, has instituted a number of code requirements dealing with potential landslides, such as cut, fill, and sloping of the lot in relationship to the location of the foundation; building setback requirements from the top and bottom of slopes; and foundation design requirements to accommodate the type of soils, the soil-bearing pressure, and compaction and lateral loads from soil and ground water on sloped lots.

Forest Fires

Forest fires have long been a serious problem in the United States. At one point in history (1930), there were nearly 200,000 such fires annually, affecting more than 50 million acres of land. Those numbers have dropped dramatically. In 2017, there were only 71,499 such fires on just over 10 million acres of land (Total Wildland Fires and Acres [1926–2017] 2018). That improvement is somewhat deceiving, however, as forest fires in the modern day are more likely to destroy homes, farms, and other property and threaten larger numbers of individuals who live there than was the case in an earlier era.

Problems

Studies now confirm that human activities account for 84 percent of such fires, with lightning and other natural events responsible for the remaining 16 percent (Balch et al. 2017; other sources cite different numbers; for example, see Purposes and Techniques of Fire Management 2018). The human activities that account for these forest fires have been classified by the U.S. Forest Service into one of about a dozen categories, including the use of mechanical equipment, smoking, campfires, debris burning, railroad traffic, arson, children (playing with fire), fireworks, power lines, and other miscellaneous or undefined causes (Short 2014, 7). Note that all of these causes, except for arson, are unintentional causes of fires. That one intentional cause (arson) accounts for about 21 percent of all forest fires, second only to debris burning (29%), and greater than equipment use (11%), campfires (5%), and children's activities (5%) (Rice 2017).

An important element of the growing threat posed by forest fires is the recent tendency of builders to construct homes in areas known as the *wildland-urban interface* (WUI). The WUI is defined as the region in which houses come into contact with, or lie close to, undeveloped wildland vegetation. Recent research has showed that at least 60 percent of new homes built in the United States since 1990 have been constructed in WUI regions. According the U.S. Census Bureau data, an estimated 46 million homes, populated by 120 million people, now exist on 220 million acres of WUI (2014 Quadrennial Fire Review Final Report 2015, 28). This trend is troubling since WUI areas are typically at significantly greater risk for forest fires than are typical urban areas. Almost by definition, then, WUI homes are in constant danger from destruction by wildfires.

Solutions

The fundamental principle behind fire forest prevention programs is, and long has been, education. The more people know about the causes of forest fires, the more likely they are to act in ways to prevent such events from occurring. The vast majority of educational programs about forest fires fall into one of two categories: individual and community. One of the oldest and best-known educational programs in the first category is Smokey Bear, originally conceived in 1944 by a consortium of the U.S. Department of Agriculture's Forest Service, the National Association of State Foresters, the Ad Council, and the advertising agency Foote Cone & Belding (now FCB). The Smokey Bear program focuses on three general areas of forest fire prevention: campfire safety, backyard debris burning, and equipment use and maintenance. The first topic, for example, deals with practices such as the proper way to pick a campfire site, how to prepare the campfire pit, how to build a campfire, and how to maintain and extinguish a campfire (Prevention How-Tos 2018). Smokey Bear information is also available in similar formats from a number of other sources. See, for example, Fire Prevention 2018.

A second approach to forest fire prevention focuses on larger groups of individuals, such as communities that may be threatened by such events. Many of these programs emphasize the issues posed by building homes and other structures in WUI and ways of reducing fire risks in such areas. One such organization is Community Planning Assistance for Wildfire (CPAW), an organization created in 2015 to help both urban and rural communities deal with issues surrounding the construction of buildings in WUI. The services offered by CPAW include land-use planning, wildfire risk assessment, capacity building, and research in the field. As of late 2018, more than two dozen communities had become members of CPAW, including Ashland, Oregon; Austin, Texas; Boise, Idaho; Chelan (city and county), Washington; Lewis & Clark County, Montana; Pigeon Forge, Tennessee; San Diego, California; and Santa Fe, New Mexico (Community Planning Assistance for Wildfire [CPAW] 2018).

Another such program is Firewise, cosponsored by the U.S. Forest Service, U.S. Department of Agriculture, U.S. Department of the Interior, and National Association of State Foresters. Firewise provides materials and individual expert assistance to aid individual homeowners and community groups with suggestions for reducing the risk of forest fires in a specific area. Federal, state, and/or local grants may also be available to individuals and communities to carry out recommendations from Firewise advisers (Firewise USA 2018; for other community fire protection organizations, see Prevention and Education 2018; Your Role in Fire-Adapted Communities 2012).

As with other natural disasters, building codes have been developed to prevent or reduce the likelihood of a forest fire. Arguably, the best single resource for such codes is the National Fire Protection Association, which has nine codes dealing with various aspects of forest fires. Those codes include standards for Fire Protection Infrastructure for Land Development in Wildland, Rural, and Suburban Areas; Water Supplies for Suburban and Rural Fire Fighting; Reducing Structure Ignition Hazards from Wildland Fire; Wildland Fire Management; Use of Class A Foams in Manual Structural Fire Fighting; Wildland Fire Fighter Professional Qualifications; and Wildland Fire Apparatus (Wildfire Codes and Standards 2018).

Floods

One area in which human activities can, and often do, have very significant impacts on natural disasters is flooding. Of course, flooding *is* a natural disaster that occurs in most cases because of heavy rains or melting snow. But humans can worsen or even create such events by poor planning of developed areas.

Problems

The flow of water through rivers and streams, across the surface, or along other natural pathways is controlled to a major degree by the rock and soil conditions over and through which water moves. Trees, bushes, grasses, and other plant material growing in these areas all have extensive and complex root systems that tend to bond soil together and prevent it from being washed away. When this natural system of control is disrupted by human activities, soil is eroded and water that would normally be retained in the ground is carried away in a flood.

Some of the most common activities that produce such conditions are development of natural lands for housing, commercial sites, industrial buildings, roads and parking lots, and mass transit systems. Natural sinks (points of collection) for water are removed by such activities and replaced by materials such as concrete, stone, and asphalt. These materials are impervious to water, which flow more rapidly over the surfaces than they do over natural soil conditions. When even normal amounts of rain fall on such surfaces, flooding may occur where such events were essentially unknown previous to development. (For discussions of the nature of this problem in two specific geographical areas, see Flinker 2010 [Rhode Island] and Bogost 2017 [Houston, Texas].)

Flooding as a result of human activities results in a problem of not only *quantity of water* but also *quality of water*. The flow of floodwater over impervious surfaces has a tendency to dissolve and suspend a wide variety of harmful pollutants, such as natural sediments—sand and clay, pesticides and herbicides, other types of synthetic organic materials, heavy metals, oil and grease products, bacteria and viruses, and compounds of nitrogen and phosphorus. All of these materials have significant effects on human health, explaining the need to close public facilities such as beaches and lakes, other types of recreational areas, urban waterways, fishing sites, and shellfish bed closures (Strassler, Pritts, and Strellec 1999).

Solutions

Once again, the keys to flood prevention are education and regulation. A number of public service announcements, brochures, videos, school programs, and websites have been developed to educate the general public. School children have often been the main target of such educational program. For example, a Facebook page called "Flood Risk Education" has been developed "to promote the teaching of flood risk and floodplain management in schools." The web page contains a list of events of interest to individuals working in the field of flood education, photographs and videos of programs in the field, and a link to local flood models currently in existence (Flood Risk Education 2018). Another good source of educational information and programs about flood risk is the National Weather Service (NWS). The NWS website contains helpful information on flood safety before, during, and following a flood; state flood information sources; flood hazards; forecasts and observations; and other topics. It also lists public service announcements, brochures, pamphlets, and videos on flood education available from the agency (Flood Safety Outreach and Education 2018).

One focus of flood education is the need for property owners to have insurance against such disasters. Ordinary homeowners insurance typically does not cover losses resulting from water damage caused by flooding; a special flood insurance policy is needed to cover such damages. Given that 41 million Americans (12% of the population) live in a flood zone, one might expect such policies to be popular in many parts of the nation. This does not appear to be the case, and, in fact, the number of such policies written has decreased every year from a high of 5,700,235 in 2009 to 4,081,470 in 2016 (the last year for which data are available) (Total Policies in Force by Calendar Year 2018). The effects of this trend can sometimes be striking. In the area around Houston, Texas, for example, 9 percent of residents had dropped flood insurance in the five-year period preceding the devastation caused by Hurricane Harvey in 2017. For many people, the explanation for abandoning flood insurance was, as one resident put it, "that's just another bill I can't afford," except the damages caused by Harvey were far beyond almost anyone's flood insurance premiums (Condon et al. 2017; also see Ryan 2017).

A key element in the flood insurance program in the United States is the National Flood Insurance Program, created by the U.S. Congress in 1968. The aim of that program was to provide a way for citizens to buy affordable flood insurance guaranteed by the U.S. government. The program has long been popular in the country, with an estimated 5 million policies providing $1.28 trillion in coverage, as of February 2018 (Horn and Brown 2018). How long that program will survive in its current form is uncertain, however. President Donald Trump announced in early 2018 that he was recommending that FEMA cut back on the program in order to save money (Warmbrodt 2018).

An increasingly common method for reducing the risk of flooding is the adoption of local and state ordinances that prescribe the conditions for building within and otherwise altering a floodplain. In 2013, FEMA published a model for such ordinances that has since been adopted in one form or another by a number of governmental bodies. Illustrative of the types of requirements included in the FEMA document are the following:

- All proposed subdivisions must have one or more lots set aside for open space.
- Such new subdivisions must have sewer, gas, electrical, water, and other utilities constructed in such a way as to eliminate or reduce possible flood damage.
- New subdivisions must also have at least one road that connects to an area outside the floodplain.
- All facilities that are hazardous, toxic, or a threat to water quality, such as chemicals, explosives, gasoline, propane, buoyant materials, animal wastes, fertilizers, flammable liquids, pollutants, or other materials, are prohibited from a flood hazard area.
- Critical facilities, such as schools, nursing homes, hospitals, police, fire and emergency operations installations, water and wastewater treatment plants, electric power stations, and installations that produce, use, or store hazardous

materials or hazardous waste, must have the lowest floor at some predetermined height above a typical flood level.

• Human alterations of natural sand dunes are prohibited in certain specified areas. (For the complete model code, see Model Ordinance for Floodplain Management under the National Flood Insurance Program and the Endangered Species Act 2012.)

Drought

Drought is a normal event in many parts of the world. Yet the meaning of a *drought* can differ widely from place to place. The wettest city in the United States, for example, is New Orleans, with an annual rainfall of 62.7 inches. By comparison, average rainfall in Las Vegas, Nevada, is 4.2 inches per year (Osborn 2018). A year in which only 4 inches of rain fall in New Orleans, then, makes essentially no difference to the drought status of the city; it would be a "no drought" condition. A decrease in rainfall of 4 inches in Las Vegas would mean no rain at all in the year: a severe drought for the region.

Problems

The region of the United States with the lowest annual rainfall is the Mountain Region, consisting of the states of Arizona, Colorado, Idaho, Montana, Nevada, New Mexico, Utah, and Wyoming (Average Annual Precipitation by State 2018). Rainfall differs considerably from year to year in this region and the state of California, where such records have been studied intensively. In California, severe droughts have occurred in the three-year periods 1918–1920, 1922–1924, 1929–1931, 2007–2009, and 2012–2014 (California's Most Significant Droughts: Comparing Historical and Recent Conditions 2015, Table 3.1, 41). Between these drought periods, precipitation remained at normal, or even elevated levels.

But these data reflect only changes that take place only because of *natural* variations in precipitation, patterns over which humans have essentially no control. But human activities since the beginning of the 20th century have dramatically affected these drought patterns. One major reason for these changes has been population growth. Between 1900 and 2017, population in the state grew from 1,485,053 to 39,356,653, an increase of more than 2,500 percent. The largest part of that increase occurred in the period from 1950 to the present day (Rosenberg 2018).

Therefore, what does population growth have to do with drought in California? Well, essentially everything. With a population of only a few million, the state was able to meet all water needs from natural sources: rain and water runoff from adjacent mountain ranges. But as population grew, new demands for water began to arise. Water was needed to irrigate the blossoming agricultural industry and to meet the needs of rapidly growing urban areas, as well as to protect so-called environmental water, water needed to maintain river flow, sustain habitat in lakes and rivers, protect wetlands, and preserve the state's existing water resources. In response to this problem, the state began to develop a large and complex system for collecting water from as many natural sources as possible for delivery to urban areas and the agricultural industry, both of which were located in classically arid regions.

California's modern water production system consists of two major elements: collecting, storing, and delivering water from existing rivers and snow melts; and removing water from underground sources. Probably the most important step in the first of these avenues was the Colorado River Compact of 1922. The agreement was hammered out among seven states bordering the Colorado River after an arduous and contentious series of meetings held in 1921 and 1922. The contract awarded certain fixed amounts of water to each state, ranging from 0.05 million acre-feet per year for Arizona to 4.40 million acre-feet annually for California. The seven states, federal government, and Indian tribes asking for water rights were not all completely satisfied with the conditions of the compact, and a series of agreements were later negotiated, and at least one major court battle (collectively called "The Law of the River") raged for at least the next half century (The Law of the River 2008; Water in the West and California's Drought 2015).

For many years, The Law of the River agreements provided California with adequate amounts of the water it needed for urban, agricultural, and environmental purposes. But increasing demands also prompted greater use of a second resource: groundwater. Groundwater is water stored underground in the soil within pores and crevices of rock. It occurs naturally when rain and snow travel through rivers and lakes, eventually sinking into the ground. The region in which groundwater is stored is called the *aquifer*, and the top of the aquifer, from which groundwater can be retrieved, is the *groundwater table*. Groundwater can be collected for (primarily) irrigation and (secondarily) urban use by sinking wells into the aquifer. The critical factor in using groundwater for human needs is that the rate of retrieval should always be less than the rate of recharge (the rate at which water flows into the aquifer). If that balance is not maintained, an aquifer may be depleted, eventually to the point that it can no longer be used as a source of water.

The largest aquifer in California underlies that Central Valley, the nation's most important single agricultural region, for a distance of about 400 miles. The aquifer is filled with water that seeped into the earth at least 10,000 years ago. The USGS estimates that the state has withdrawn about 125 million acre-feet (41 trillion gallons) from this aquifer during the period 1920–2013. The water is being removed at a rate much greater than it is being replaced. One consequence of this pattern, of course, is that aquifers are being drained, with less and less water available for human use. A second result is that, as water is removed from the ground, the earth's surface sinks into the empty spaces produced. According to one estimate, some parts of the Central Valley had sunk 30 feet by the 1970s from the beginning of historic records, and an additional drop of the same amount is predicted by 2030 (Halverson 2015).

Solutions

An important part of the drought problems faced by many areas, including California, is the complaint that governmental agencies have not planned adequately for droughts that everyone knows will be coming at some time in the future. A number of organizations have developed a series of recommendations for dealing with this issue. As an example, the Pacific Institute, in partnership with the California-Nevada Section of the American Water Works Association, University of California Berkeley Water Center, and University of California Davis Extension's Collaboration Center, held a series of meetings in 2015 around the theme of Where We Agree. The report produced by this effort made a number of suggestions for reducing the human effects on droughts in California:

- Expand indoor and outdoor water conservation and efficiency efforts that target residential, commercial, industrial, and institutional users.
- Increase water reuse at a variety of scales, from a more decentralized building-scale system to a more centralized municipal scale, by adopting a suite of policies to make it more affordable and convenient.
- Adopt stormwater policies, guidelines, and incentives to facilitate stormwater capture and use.
- Improve resilience for future droughts by enhancing planning and data collection and reducing constraints on short-term water transfers during droughts, provided they are protective of ecosystems and communities.
- Improve the reliability and adequacy of funding for water infrastructure.

- Integrate water management activities to foster innovative solutions that result in projects that provide multiple services and benefits.
- And invest in groundwater storage and develop an integrated strategy for maximizing the potential of these projects. (Quoted in full from Cooley et al. 2016; for the full report, see http://pacinst.org/wp-content/uploads/2016/03/Where_We_Agree_Building_Consensus_on_Solutions_to_CAs_Urban_Water_Challenges.pdf)

Much of the effort to reduce drought involves direct recommendations to individuals and companies. For example, the advocacy group Environment California suggests ways of reducing one's personal use of water indoors by checking for leaks in the home water system; choosing to wash dishes by hand rather than in a dishwasher; installing so-called low-flow showerheads; reducing the length of time one showers; limiting the use of a washing machine to full loads only; turning off the water when it is not actually in use, such as brushing one's teeth or washing one's hair; plugging the sink when shaving; buying water-saving devices, such as low-flow toilets and energy-efficient washing machines; and installing aerators on kitchen faucets to reduce water flow. Some recommendations for outdoor water systems include limiting watering of lawns and gardens to early morning or late evening; using a broom rather than a hose to clean outdoor concrete spaces, such as sidewalks and driveways; switching to xeriscaping (plants that grow well in arid conditions) instead of water-dependent plants; collecting rainfall for irrigation; limiting the amount of water used for car washing; mulching garden areas to reduce evaporation of ground water; aerating the soil so that it absorbs more water; and raising the height of the lawnmower (Solving the Drought 2018). Many of the suggestions for water conservation for schools, hospitals, businesses, and other commercial entities include the same recommendations as those listed earlier. They also may include ideas for incorporating water conservation into the routine activities of the company, such as informing employees about the problems of and solutions to water overuse, conducting water use audits, and setting company goals for water conservation (see, e.g., Business Water Conservation Tips 2018).

The U.S. Congress has historically been rather timid about adopting legislation designed to reduce the risk of drought resulting from human activities. Most legislation passed before the mid-2010s dealt with relief for farmers and other individuals damaged because of drought conditions (Folger, Cody, and Carter 2013). That situation changed somewhat beginning in about 2015, with the occurrence of severe drought conditions in California and other western states. A number of bills have been introduced in the House and Senate since that time, taking a somewhat different approach to drought conditions, requiring that the federal and state governments take more actions that reduce the risk of drought rather than trying to ameliorate its effects. One approach in these bills has been to require, by whatever means possible, to increase the amount of water available to drought-prone areas. That goal seems admirable, although it is not always clear as to where that water will come from and/or how it will be delivered to needy areas.

Another approach involves weakening the Endangered Species Act of 1973. Currently, large amounts of water are set aside and protected from human use to ensure that various endangered species will have the water resources they need to survive. Some federal legislation attempts to solve that problem by simply exempting some regions from enforcing the act, thus increasing the amount of water available for human activities. A third approach requires the federal government to increase construction of dams and reservoirs, often in areas that are currently protected by legislation such as the Wild and Scenic Rivers Act of 1968.

Finally, some federal legislation has attacked the drought problem simply by allowing federal actions to override existing state and local legislation. The implied assumption here is that the federal government often knows better and/or is better able to provide water conservation methods than are individual state entities (Weiser 2016). In fact, the great majority of legislation for drought relief at the federal level has not been very successful. A number of bills have either failed the House into which they were introduced or passed one House but failed in the other. (As an example, see H.R.23—Gaining Responsibility on Water Act of 2017; H.R.2898—Western Water and American Food Security Act of 2015; S.2533—California Long-Term Provisions for Water Supply and Short-Term Provisions for Emergency Drought Relief Act.)

Both the quality and quantity of drought legislation have been greater in some individual states than it has been at the national level. Not surprisingly, such has been the case where drought has been a long-standing problem, and a state has struggled to adopt legislation to deal with the prevention and control of, and recovery from, disastrous droughts. In the state of California, such efforts go back to the earliest days of the state's existence. Over time, new laws were continually introduced to update, correct for, or otherwise improve drought policies. The state's modern-day policies were first established in 1967 with the creation of the state Water Resources Control Board. The agency was charged with balancing all competitive uses of water available within the state. The agency continues its mission today, although the problems it faces are so extensive and complex that it usually does not function very effectively (California State Water Resources Control Board 2018; Weiser 2015a).

The most recent spate of drought legislation in California was inspired by one of the longest and most severe droughts in the state's history, starting as early as 2007 and extending into 2017. The event has been called "the state's worst ever, based on more than 100 years of record-keeping" (Weiser 2015b). One example of the most recent legislation adopted has been the Sustainable Groundwater Management Act (SGMA), a group of three bills signed into law by Governor Jerry Brown in 2014.

The law sets out a new groundwater policy consisting of the following elements:

- Requires that regions with groundwater resources at greatest risk to halt overdraft recovery of such resources and establish a system for balanced pumping and recharge.
- Sets time limits for local and regional agencies to reach these goals: 2040 for the most seriously compromised water basins, and 2042 for other threatened basins.
- Authorizes the formation of local Groundwater Sustainability Agencies (GSAs) to adopt Groundwater Sustainability Plans (GSPs) that outlines plans for managing basins sustainably.
- Allows the state to create and operate temporary GSAs in areas that do not create such agencies until such areas are able to create their own agency. (The 2014 Sustainable Groundwater Management Act: A Handbook to Understanding and Implementing the Law 2015; the law itself can be found at https://water.ca.gov/-/media/DWR-Website/Web-Pages/Programs/Groundwater-Management/Sustainable-Groundwater-Management/Files/2014-Sustainable-Groundwater-Management-Legislation-with-2015-amends-1-15-2016.pdf?la=en&hash=ADB3455047A2863D029146E9A820AC7DE16B5CB1)

In 2018, the state of California went one step further on drought prevention, adopting two bills that require both urban and agricultural suppliers of water in the state set specific standards for the sustainable use of water. Those standards must be approved by the State Water Resources Control Board. They require that standards provide limits of 55 gallons per day for personal use by 2025, 52.5 gallons per day by 2030, and 50 gallons per day by 2030. The bill also provides incentives for water suppliers to recycle water (Governor Brown Signs Legislation Establishing Statewide Water Efficiency Goals 2018 [provides link to the final version of the bills]).

Finally, drought is enough of a problem at some times and in some parts of the world and the United States that imaginative and creative ideas are now beginning to appear. The website Inhabitat has reviewed a number of these "out-of-the-box" suggestions. (Inhabitat is a "green design and lifestyle site that provides coverage of environmental news and the latest in sustainable design.") Among those technologies are the following:

- Desalination of ocean waters.
- Fog catching nets to collect atmospheric water.
- Cloud seeding to produce artificial rainfall.
- "Harvesting" of water vapor that exists in the air, but that is not expected and does not actually fall to the ground as precipitation.
- Wastewater recycling.
- Large pipelines that carry water from even more distant locations than those now in existence. (Cameron 2015)

Extreme Weather and Climate Change

Of all types of natural disasters, extreme weather might seem to be the less susceptible to human influence. Consider the power of a hurricane or tornado: What is it that human beings might do to increase, decrease, or otherwise modify some such occurrence? Well, the answer is that, as unlikely as it may seem, human actions appear to be—and probably already actually are—able to affect the genesis, movement, intensity, length, and other features of severe storms. Those human activities are the result of climate change, modifications in global and regional climate patterns, especially over the past century or so.

Climate Change

The topic of climate change (also known as *global warming*) has been studied intensively over at least the past 50 years (and, in some ways, much longer than that). Today climatologists (scientists who study climate) have reached a number of conclusions about current climate problems and trends into the near and more distant future. They base these conclusions on two types of research. First, very detailed records about all kinds of climate-related events are available, some dating back hundreds of years. Researchers review these data to see if they can describe the events from which these data arose. They then can say what they believe those events were like in the past.

Second, researchers try to predict future trends by constructing mathematical models. These models are based on trends from the past with their best guesses as to what is likely to occur in the future. These models have been available for quite a while now, and they get more accurate the more they are used. Therefore, predictions about future climate trends produced in 2018 (often by more than one model) keep getting better and better as time passes (Climate Models 2018).

Both types of predications, past and future, have various degrees of certainty about this knowledge, ranging from virtual certainty to doubtful. The definitions of these terms are based on the probability of each one's happening or having happened: virtually certain 99–100 percent probability, very likely 90–100 percent, likely 66–100 percent, about as likely as not 33–66 percent, unlikely 0–33 percent, very unlikely 0–10 percent, exceptionally unlikely 0–1 percent (Pachauri et al. 2014, 2). Some examples of those conclusions are as follows:

It is *virtually* certain that the planet's annual average temperature is increasing. That is, global warming is now taking place. Information from a variety of sources on different Earth systems confirms this trend. For example, temperature measurements by four major agencies (NASA Goddard Institute for Space Studies, Met Office Hadley Center/Climatic Research Unit, NOAA National Climatic Data Center, and Japanese Meteorological Agency) show strikingly similar trends, with temperatures rising from a low point in 1900 to a centuries-old peak in 2010 (Graphic: Earth's Temperature Record 2018). The hottest year in recorded history was 2016, followed by 2015, 2017, 2014, and 2010 (Ten Hottest Years Globally 2018). The hottest decade in recorded history is the 2010s, followed by the 2000s, 1980s, and 1990s (Dahlman 2017; data on which these graphs are based can be found at GISS Surface Temperature Analysis [GISTEMP] 2018, see "Global-Mean Monthly, Seasonal, and Annual Means").

It is *very likely* that human activities have contributed to the frequency and intensity of global temperature changes observed since the mid-20th century, to loss of Arctic sea ice since the 1970s, to increase heat content in the upper atmosphere, and to the rise in global sea levels since the 1970s.

It is *very likely* that human activities will result in more frequent and longer-lasting heat waves and that extreme precipitation events will become more intense and more frequent in many regions.

It is *very likely* that human activities will continue to contribute to the rise of sea levels, an increase in the salinity and acidity of the oceans, and the loss of sea ice in the future.

It is *likely* that the period 1983–2012 was the warmest 30-year period in the Northern Hemisphere for at least the past 1,400 years and that human activities have more than doubled the likelihood of heat waves in some parts of Earth and contributed to the number and intensity of storm surges.

It is *likely* that the mass of glaciers and sea ice has been shrinking since at least 1991, with the greatest loss of ice between 2002 and 2011. Similar effects are likely to occur for permafrost regions and early spring snow falls.

It is *likely* that the frequency of droughts in currently arid regions will increase by the end of the 21st century, for which one consequence will be that "the interaction of increased temperature; increased sediment, nutrient and pollutant loadings from heavy rainfall; increased concentrations of pollutants during droughts; and disruption of treatment facilities during floods will reduce raw water quality and pose risks to drinking water quality" (Pachauri et al. 2014, 69).

It is *about as likely as not* that currently agreed-upon systems for reducing global warming will prevent annual average global temperatures from increasing by less than 2°C.

It is *unlikely* that global sea levels will rise by more than a meter by the end of the 21st century. (All examples are selected from Pachauri et al. 2014. No examples of *very unlikely* and *exceptionally unlikely* in the report.)

Therefore, what do these findings and predictions have to say about the effects of human activities on natural disasters in the future?

Extreme Weather

Predicting future weather patterns, let alone future climate patterns, is a complex problem. So many factors are involved in the evolution of a storm that it is usually difficult to determine how much each of many factors may contribute to the development and intensity of a storm. A large amount of research has been conducted on the potential effects of climate change on hurricanes, tornadoes, and other types of severe storms, such as winter snowstorms. The evidence adduced from that research is somewhat contradictory, but in general, it appears that the number and intensity of winter snowstorms have been increasing in most parts of the United States since at least 1980 and are likely to increase even more in the coming decades (Climate Change Impacts in the United States 2014). The reason for these changes appears to be a greater availability of the energy needed to produce such storms, primarily increases in atmospheric temperatures and wind shear factors (Trapp et al. 2007; also see Seeley and Romps 2015). Some research has begun to show an interesting side effect to this future. It appears that the seemingly "minor" difference between a temperature increase of 1.5°C and 2.0°C can have major effects on the number and intensity of severe storms. This line of research suggests that the target for climate control suggested by many observers (2.0°C) may actually be too high (Barcikowska 2018; based on Barcikowska et al. 2018).

The effect of climate change on hurricanes has also been studied in some detail. Given some inconsistencies in research results, there seems to be common agreement that there may be fewer hurricanes in the future, but those that do develop are likely to travel more slowly and be more severe than those in the past (Kossin 2018). The simplistic reason for this trend is that ocean water is the source of energy needed in the development of a hurricane. The warmer the seawater, the greater the amount of water evaporation, the more heat energy there is released from the evaporation, and the more intense the hurricane that develops. Abundant evidence dating back to the 1850s indicates that seawater has been warming at an accelerating pace from that period to the present day. The decadal temperature decreased from about 0.2°C in 1850–1860 to its lowest point in the period, −0.6°C in 1910–1920, before increasing to +0.4°C in 2018 (Extended Reconstructed Sea Surface Temperature [ERSST] v4 2018). According to one expert in the field, the magnitude of future hurricanes is likely to reflect the general rule that each degree (Fahrenheit) in ocean warming produces a 10-mile-per-hour increase in wind speeds in a hurricane. Since the oceans have already warmed (in 2018) by nearly 1.6°F over the 20th-century average, this new information may be of particular importance in predicting the characteristics of future hurricanes (Global Climate Report— May 2018 2018).

One of the interesting consequences of future hurricane behavior may be the need for a new intensity category. Currently, hurricanes are rated on a 1–5 basis on the Saffir–Simpson Hurricane Wind Scale, with the upper limit on that scale (Category 5) being "157 mph or more." But the recorded speed for two 2017 hurricanes, Irma and Maria, already reached the upper level of the Category, about 180 miles per hour. This trend suggests to at least a few observers that a new Category 6, or even

Category 7, might need to be added to the scale to describe the worst future hurricanes (Fleshler 2018).

Based on the results of hurricane research, one might expect climatologists to have some ideas about the possible effects of climate change on the formation and intensity of tornadoes. In fact, such is not the case. Given that our understanding of tornadoes is already quite limited, it perhaps should not be surprising that very little is known about the way global warming might affect the genesis of tornadoes. In commenting on his recent study of tornado patterns over the past half century, Columbia University's Michael Tippett said that "the fact that we don't see the presently understood meteorological signature of global warming in changing outbreak statistics [about tornadoes] leaves two possibilities: Either the recent increases are not due to a warming climate, or a warming climate has implications for tornado activity that we don't understand. This is an unexpected finding" (Evarts 2016; for the study cited, see Tippett, Lepore, and Cohen 2016). (Interestingly enough, the only tornado feature that so far has been associated with climate change is new pathways across the United States for such events. See Agee et al. 2016.)

Other Natural Disasters

Most experts in the field of climate change now believe that global warming is likely to have an impact on many types of natural disasters other than severe storms. For example, the changes in hurricane characteristics are likely to result also in changes in floods usually associated with such events. As those storms begin to move more slowly and carry larger amounts of water, the flooding they produce is likely to increase in severity. According to one recent study, the flooding associated with Hurricane Harvey in 2017 was about 38 percent greater than would be expected in a nonwarming planet (Risser and Wehner 2017). A second report on the event estimated an increase of about 15 percent in flooding as a result of climate change (van Oldenborgh et al. 2017). Based on studies such as these, whatever the specific value, increased flooding as a result of climate change appears to be very likely.

Another way that global warming affects flooding patterns is through storm surges. A *storm surge* is defined as an abnormal rise in sea level as the result of a storm. As sea levels rise, storm surges may carry ocean waters so high that they begin to flood coastal communities. Some research suggests that changes of this type are already taking place (Rahmstorf 2017).

Increased flooding is to be expected as a result of climate change and also because of increased temperatures of the atmosphere and water. As temperatures rise, the rate of evaporation from the oceans, lakes, and other bodies of water also rises. At the same time, a warmer atmosphere is able to hold a larger quantity of water vapor. Specifically, an increase in air temperature of 1°F increases the air's ability to hold water vapor by about 4 percent. A larger concentration of water in the air, then, results in increased frequency and amounts of precipitation. Depending on the land on which the precipitation falls, it may not be absorbed as fast as it reaches Earth, causing flooding in the area (Abraham 2017).

Interestingly enough, the changes in the water cycle just described can also result in an increase in the likelihood of droughts. As the atmosphere warms, water in the soil is likely to evaporate more rapidly, just as seawater does. Soil dries out, becomes hard, and is less able to absorb rain that does fall on it. Also warmer temperatures increase the rate of evapotranspiration, the loss of water from plant material. Warmer air temperatures also tend to promote evaporation from lakes, ponds, rivers, streams, and other inland bodies of water. Finally, a warmer atmosphere is likely to reduce the size of snowpacks, which, in many parts of the world, is a major source of water for agricultural and urban use. At least some experts in the field of drought have decided that recent research has "clearly demonstrated that climate change has played a role in recent droughts" (Cook 2018; for a report on the anthropogenic connection with drought, see Diffenbaugh, Swain, and Touma 2015).

Another area in which climate change appears to be influencing natural disasters is forest fires. The principle involved is that global warming causes increased loss of moisture from the ground (as with droughts), increasing the aridity of an area as well as hardening soil. Precipitation that does occur in such areas is more likely to run off the surface of the land, rather than sinking into the ground. As a result, trees, bushes, grasses, and other forms of plant life tend to dry out and become more susceptible to fire. One recent study attempted to sort out natural factors leading to increased aridity in an area, compared to anthropogenic effects. That study found that about 55 percent of the aridity in western U.S. forests between 1979 and 2015 could be accounted for by climate change (Abatzoglou and Williams 2016). Another way in which climate change affects the risk of forest fires is the timing of the arrival of spring. Abundant evidence is now available that spring is arriving earlier and earlier each decade, probably as a result of climate change. But this trend means that snow melts earlier, the ground dries out too soon, and plant life becomes more arid and more susceptible to fire (Early Spring's Domino Effect 2010; Westerling 2016).

Possibly one of the most interesting developments of the study of anthropogenic effects on natural disasters is the recent discovery that researchers are now apparently able to connect specific, individual events with climate change. One review of the trend notes that it is now routinely possible to investigate "the influence of climate change on events ranging from the Russian heat wave of 2010 to the California drought, evaluating the extent to which global warming has made them more severe or more likely to occur" (Harvey 2018; for a detailed report on this phenomenon, see Committee on Extreme Weather Events and Climate Change Attribution. Board on Atmospheric Sciences and Climate. Division on Earth and Life Studies 2016).

Preparation and Recovery

Natural disasters all carry with them an inherent problem: in many cases, humans have little or advance notice of such events. They may not be able to escape from a threatened area or protect property in that area. This fact means that two features are always of importance in thinking about natural disasters. First, what kinds of warning systems can be developed to let people know that a disaster is likely or imminent? Second, what types of recovery programs should be in place to help survivors following a disaster?

Warning Systems

Probably the most common type of warning system is the TLS, described earlier for induced earthquakes. This type of system usually involves three steps: (1) be aware that an event may take place, (2) get ready to move out of your area to avoid the event, and (3) move. One form of this warning system is called "ready, set, go," in which one first makes whatever preparations possible in case of a disaster (ready), becomes aware that a disaster may be imminent and makes plan for evacuation (set), and then leaves the threatened area (go) (Ready, Set, Go! 2018).

Many warning systems use descriptive terms to indicate the relative threat of a disaster. Among the most common of these terms are *advisory*, *watch*, and *warning*. One example of such a system is the landslide warning system, established in 1986 by a working group of the USGS. The terminology used in that system is as follows:

- *Advisory*: A general statement about the potential of landslide activity in a given region. It may include general statements about rainfall conditions and list precautions to be taken in the event of heavy rainfall.
- *Watch*: Landslide activity will be possible but is not imminent. Residents in the area should check preparedness and stay informed about developing weather patterns.

- *Warning*: Landslide activity is occurring and extreme caution should be taken (When Does the U.S. Geological Survey Issue a Landslide Advisory, and under What Conditions? 2018; for a somewhat dated, but very good, overview of early warning systems, see Grasso 2001).

Recovery

For much of U.S. history, recovery from natural disasters was regarded as a problem for local communities. Affected businesses, transportation and communication systems, and individuals and their families were thought to be the responsibility of just those groups: people and groups relied on aid and assistance from others in the local community. That situation began to change in 1906 when the San Francisco earthquake produced widespread damage far exceeding than ever recorded on the continent. The U.S. Congress appropriated $2.5 million for flood, blankets, tents, and other relief needs (Lesson 3: When Disaster Strikes, What Can Government Do? 2018). Over the next century, Congress continued to expand and diversify the services that the federal government would provide to devastated areas, often supplementing state and local efforts and sometimes providing services above and beyond those efforts (Baca 2008; History of Federal Disaster Policy 2015; Mener 2007).

The intricacies of modern-day disaster relief programs at the state, local, and federal levels go far beyond the space limitations of this book. Suffice to say that the majority of relief policies include a number of common elements, many of which are within the range of common sense. The most recent edition of the U.S. Department of Homeland Security's "National Disaster Recovery Framework," for example, sets out eight "guiding principles" that should underlie a disaster recovery program. They are as follows:

- Pre-disaster recovery planning: Agencies at all levels should have developed recovery program *prior* to the occurrence of any such event so that communities can go into action if and when a disaster strikes.

- Individual and family empowerment: Recovery efforts should focus on the need for individuals and families to begin rebuilding their lives as soon as possible after a disaster strikes. These efforts should be designed so as not to discriminate against individuals of any race, color, ethnicity, national origin, religion, sex, sexual orientation, gender identity, age, or disability.

- Leadership and local primacy: Recovery program depends on the coordinated efforts of agencies at all levels of government.

- Engaged partnerships and inclusiveness: Recovery programs must recognize the contributions that can be made by individuals from any area of local government.

- Unity of effort: The success of a recovery program depends to a large extent on the ability of a relief effort to efficiently coordinate the skills and activities of all parts of the community.

- Timeliness and flexibility: Recovery services must be available as soon as possible after a disaster, and provisions must be possible for changing circumstances that may follow such an event.

- Resilience and sustainability: As part of the pre-disaster planning, efforts should be made to identify specific vulnerabilities and resources relevant to various types of disaster.

- Psychological and emotional recovery: Planners must take into account and plan for psychological and emotional issues that arise as the result of a natural disaster, issues that may be at least as important as basic issues such as food, water, and health care (National Disaster Recovery Framework, Second Edition 2016; see also Pre-Disaster Recovery Planning Guide for State Governments 2016).

Given the plethora of research on and recommendations about natural disaster recovery programs, it may seem a bit strange that considerable criticism has been raised about governmental efforts to deal with such issues in real life. This criticism is aimed at state, local, and federal agencies, as well as nonprofit, private organizations, such as the Red Cross. (As an example of these critiques, see Atkin 2017; Barrand 2018; Mayer 2012.)

Over the past decade, each new catastrophic disaster appears to have been followed by specific complaints about the handling of recovery efforts for that event. Most recently, these denunciations have been brought against efforts by rescue agencies, most commonly, FEMA, for their inadequate efforts to provide relief in the aftermath of Hurricane Maria in September 2017. Nearly a year later (2019), criticism is still being lodged about FEMA's failures in dealing with problems in Puerto Rico following that event (see, e.g., Vinik 2018). One of the most interesting features of this issue is that the agency itself eventually released a report pointing out its own failures in meeting the island's needs after the hurricane. Some of the points raised in the FEMA report were the following:

- The agency vastly underestimated the population impacted, cellular service interrupted, power outages, hospitals impacted, and area of the island requiring search and rescue.
- FEMA mis-estimated the costs (in terms of personnel and expense) of the 2017 hurricane season, leaving it with inadequate resources to deal with Hurricane Maria.
- FEMA did not have enough trained personnel on the ground to deal with Maria-caused problems.
- The agency shipped the vast majority of stocked supplies to the U.S. Virgin Islands, leaving the amount available for Puerto Rico dramatically short.
- Supplies from FEMA as well as contract agencies were inadequately tracked so that workers were unsure as to what supplies were available or where they had been sent.

- Communication systems were seriously inadequate because of a lack of cell phones, destruction of cell towers, and collapse of the electric grid. (All points taken from 2017 Hurricane Season FEMA After-Action Report 2018, vi–ix. The report also contains a number of recommendations for improving responses to future disasters. For a good summary of the report, see Robles 2018)

Conclusion

Almost every type of natural disaster can be, and often is, affected by human activities. For each type of disaster, those effects produce new problems, for which solutions must be found. Sometimes those solutions can be highly effective although, in the majority of cases, the power of natural disasters greatly overcomes the efforts of humans. Governmental agencies and private organizations have been developing prevention and recovery efforts for natural disasters for many years, although the efficiency of those efforts has sometimes been called into question.

References

Abatzoglou, John T., and A. Park Williams. 2016. "Impact of Anthropogenic Climate Change on Wildfire across Western US Forests." *Proceedings of the National Academy of Sciences of the United States of America.* 113(42): 11770–11775. Available online at http://www.pnas.org/content/pnas/113/42/11770.full.pdf. Accessed on July 18, 2018.

Abraham, John. 2017. "Global Warming Is Increasing Rainfall Rates." *Guardian.* https://www.theguardian.com/environment/climate-consensus-97-per-cent/2017/mar/22/global-warming-is-increasing-rainfall-rates. Accessed on July 18, 2018.

Agee, Ernest, et al. 2016. "Spatial Redistribution of U.S. Tornado Activity between 1954 and 2013." *Journal of*

Applied Meteorology and Climatology. 55(8): 1681–1697. Available online at https://journals.ametsoc.org/doi/ pdf/10.1175/JAMC-D-15-0342.1. Accessed on July 17, 2018.

American Society of Civil Engineers. 2017. *Minimum Design Loads and Associated Criteria for Buildings and Other Structures.* Reston, VA: American Society of Civil Engineers.

Atkin, Emily. 2017. "America's Natural Disaster Response Is Its Own Disaster." *New Republic.* https://newrepublic.com/ article/145019/americas-natural-disaster-response-disaster. Accessed on July 20, 2018.

"Average Annual Precipitation by State." 2018. Current Reports. https://www.currentresults.com/Weather/US/ average-annual-state-precipitation.php. Accessed on July 13, 2018.

Baca, Anna Maria. 2008. "History of Disaster Legislation." Federal Emergency Management Agency. https://www .fema.gov/pdf/dae/200809.pdf. Accessed on July 20, 2018.

Balch, Jennifer K., et al. 2017. "Human-Started Wildfires Expand the Fire Niche across the United States." *Proceedings of the National Academy of Sciences of the United States of America.* 114(11): 2946–2951. Available online at http:// www.pnas.org/content/pnas/114/11/2946.full.pdf. Accessed on July 6, 2018.

Bao, Xuewei, and David W. Eaton. 2016. "Fault Activation by Hydraulic Fracturing in Western Canada." *Science.* 354(6318): 1406–1409.

Barcikowska, Monika. 2018. "Climate Change and Severe Storms in Europe—New Science Shows We Need a Lower Temperature Target." Environmental Defense Fund. http:// blogs.edf.org/climate411/2018/06/19/climate%20change% 20and%20severe%20storms%20in%20europe%20new%

20science%20shows%20we%20need%20a%20lower%20 temperature%20target/. Accessed on February 17, 2019.

Barcikowska, Monika J., et al 2018. "Euro-Atlantic Winter Storminess and Precipitation Extremes under 1.5°C vs. 2°C Warming Scenarios." *Earth Systems Dynamics*. 9: 679–699. https://doi.org/10.5194/esd-9-679-2018. Available online at https://www.earth-syst-dynam.net/9/679/2018/esd-9-679-2018.pdf. Accessed on July 17, 2018.

Barrand, Jamie. 2018. "FEMA: Criticism." High Beam Research. https://www.highbeam.com/topics/fema-criticism-t10091. Accessed on July 20, 2018.

Bogost, Ian. 2017. "Houston's Flood Is a Design Problem." *Atlantic*. https://www.theatlantic.com/technology/ archive/2017/08/why-cities-flood/538251/. Accessed on July 10, 2018.

"Business Water Conservation Tips." 2018. Tualatin Valley Water District. https://www.tvwd.org/media/22789/ business_tips.pdf. Accessed on July 14, 2018.

"California State Water Resources Control Board." 2018. https://www.waterboards.ca.gov/. Accessed on July 14, 2018.

"California's Most Significant Droughts: Comparing Historical and Recent Conditions." 2015. California Department of Water Resources. https://water.ca.gov/LegacyFiles/water conditions/docs/California_Signficant_Droughts_2015_ small.pdf. Accessed on July 13, 2018.

Cameron, Charley. 2015. "10 Solutions to Tackle the California Drought." Inhabitat. https://inhabitat.com/ possible-solutions-to-tackle-the-california-drought/. Accessed on July 15, 2018.

"Chapter 16 Structural Design." 2018. California Building Code 2016. https://up.codes/viewer/california/ca-building-code-2016-v2/chapter/16/structural-design#16. Accessed on February 17, 2019.

Clark, J. E., D. K. Bonura, and R. F. Van Voorhees. 2005. "An Overview of Injection Well History in the United States of America." *Developments in Water Science.* 52: 3–12. Available online at https://www.env.nm.gov/wqcc/Matters/ 14-15R/Item32/007B_RobertFVanVoorhees-Overview Publication06-15-15.pdf. Accessed on June 27, 2018.

"Climate Change Impacts in the United States." 2014. U.S. Global Change Research Program. https://www.nrc.gov/ docs/ML1412/ML14129A233.pdf. Accessed on July 17, 2018.

"Climate Models." 2018. NOAA. Climate.gov. https://www .climate.gov/maps-data/primer/climate-models. Accessed on July 17, 2018.

Committee on Extreme Weather Events and Climate Change Attribution. Board on Atmospheric Sciences and Climate. Division on Earth and Life Studies. 2016. *Attribution of Extreme Weather Events in the Context of Climate Change.* Washington, DC: The National Academies Press. Available online at https://www.nap.edu/read/21852/chapter/1. Accessed on July 18, 2018.

"Community Planning Assistance for Wildfire (CPAW)." 2018. https://planningforwildfire.org/. Accessed on July 7, 2018.

Condon, Bernard, et al. 2017. "Flood Insurance Policies in Houston Plunged before Harvey." *Chicago Tribune.* http:// www.chicagotribune.com/news/nationworld/ct-houston-harvey-flood-insurance-20170830-story.html. Accessed on July 11, 2018.

Cook, Benjamin. 2018. "Guest Post: Climate Change Is Already Making Droughts Worse." Carbon Brief. https:// www.carbonbrief.org/guest-post-climate-change-is-already-making-droughts-worse. Accessed on July 18, 2018.

Cooley, Heather, et al. 2016. "Where We Agree: Building Consensus on Solutions to California's Urban Water

Challenges." Pacific Institute. http://pacinst.org/publication/where-we-agree-building-consensus-on-solutions-to-californias-urban-water-challenges/. Accessed on July 13, 2018.

Dahlman, LuAnn. 2017. "Climate Change: Global Temperature." Climate.gov. https://www.climate.gov/news-features/understanding-climate/climate-change-global-temperature. Accessed on July 16, 2018.

Davis, Charles, and Jonathan M. Fisk. 2017. "Mitigating Risks from Fracking Related Earthquakes: Assessing State Regulatory Decisions." *Society & Natural Resources.* 30(8): 1009–1025. doi:10.1080/08941920.2016.1273415. https://www.libarts.colostate.edu/polisci/wp-content/uploads/sites/35/2017/02/Chuck-Davis_fracking-and-earthquakes-2017.pdf. Accessed on June 29, 2018.

Diffenbaugh, Noah S., Daniel L. Swain, and Danielle Touma. 2015. "Anthropogenic Warming Has Increased Drought Risk in California." *Proceedings of the National Academy of Sciences.* 112(13): 3931–3936. Available online at http://www.pnas.org/content/pnas/early/2015/02/23/1422385112.full.pdf. Accessed on July 18, 2018.

"Early Spring's Domino Effect." 2010. Union of Concerned Scientists. https://www.ucsusa.org/global_warming/science_and_impacts/impacts/springs-domino-effect.html#.W0-wbNJKg2w. Accessed on July 18, 2018.

"Earthquake Damage Claims." 2017. *Tulsa World.* https://www.tulsaworld.com/damage-claims/html_f5831a45-b2d0-58ca-a010-3c4f005c756e.html. Accessed on July 3, 2018.

"Earthquakes in Oklahoma: What We Are Doing." 2017. Earthquakes in Oklahoma. https://earthquakes.ok.gov/what-we-are-doing/. Accessed on July 1, 2018.

Ellsworth, William L. 2013. "Injection-Induced Earthquakes." *Science.* 341(6142): 142–149. doi:10.1126/science.1225942.

Evans, David M. 1966. "The Denver Area Earthquakes and the Rocky Mountain Arsenal Disposal Well." *The Mountain Geologist.* 3(1): 23–36.

Evarts, Holly. 2016. "Increasing Tornado Outbreaks: Is Climate Change Responsible?" State of the Planet. Columbia University. http://blogs.ei.columbia .edu/2016/12/01/increasing-tornado-outbreaks-is-climate-change-responsible/. Accessed on July 17, 2018.

"Extended Reconstructed Sea Surface Temperature (ERSST) v4." 2018. National Centers for Environmental Education. https://www.ncdc.noaa.gov/data-access/marineocean-data/ extended-reconstructed-sea-surface-temperature-ersst-v4. Accessed on July 17, 2018.

"Facts + Statistics: Earthquakes and Tsunamis." 2018. Insurance Information Institute. https://www.iii.org/fact-statistic/ facts-statistics-earthquakes-and-tsunamis. Accessed on July 1, 2018.

Fernandez, James B. 2015. *Deep-Well Injections and Induced Seismicity: Understanding the Relationship.* New York: Nova Publishers.

Fieldstadt, Elisha. 2016. "State of Emergency Declared in Oklahoma after Magnitude 5.6 Earthquake." NBC News. https://www.nbcnews.com/news/us-news/state-emergency-declared-oklahoma-after-magnitude-5-6-earthquake-n642 676. Accessed on June 29, 2018.

"Fire Prevention." 2018. Bureau of Land Management. https:// www.blm.gov/programs/public-safety-and-fire/fire-and-avi ation/get-involved/fire-prevention. Accessed on July 9, 2018.

"Firewise USA." 2018. National Fire Protection Association. https://www.nfpa.org/Public-Education/By-topic/Wildfire/ Firewise-USA/Firewise-USA-Resources. Accessed on July 9, 2018.

Fleshler, David. 2018. "The World Has Never Seen a Category 6 Hurricane. But the Day May Be Coming."

Los Angeles Times. http://www.latimes.com/nation/la-na-hurricane-strenth-20180707-story.html. Accessed on July 17, 2018.

Flinker, Peter. 2010. "The Need to Reduce Impervious Cover to Prevent Flooding and Protect Water Quality." Rhode Island Department of Environmental Management. http://www.dem.ri.gov/programs/bpoladm/suswshed/pdfs/imperv.pdf. Accessed on July 10, 2018.

"Flood Risk Education." 2018. Facebook. https://www.facebook.com/floodriskeducation/. Accessed on July 11, 2018.

"Flood Safety Outreach and Education." 2018. National Weather Service. https://www.weather.gov/safety/flood-education. Accessed on July 11, 2018.

Folger, Peter, Betsy A. Cody, and Nicole T. Carter. 2013. "Drought in the United States: Causes and Issues for Congress." Congressional Research Service. https://fas.org/sgp/crs/misc/RL34580.pdf. Accessed on July 14, 2018.

Folger, Peter, and Mary Tiemann. 2016. "Human-Induced Earthquakes from Deep-Well Injection: A Brief Overview." Congressional Research Service. https://fas.org/sgp/crs/misc/R43836.pdf. Accessed on June 27, 2018.

Foulger, Gillian R., et al. 2018. "Global Review of Human-Induced Earthquakes." *Earth-Science Reviews.* 178: 438–514.

Fuleihan, Nadim E., John E. Cameron, and James E. Henry. 1997. "The Hole Story: How a Sinkhole in a Phosphogypsum Pile Was Explored and Remediated." http://www.ardaman.com/FileRepository/Resources/6559f986-7427-47df-906b-3370fd94b973.pdf. Accessed on July 3, 2018.

"GISS Surface Temperature Analysis (GISTEMP)." 2018. NASA. https://data.giss.nasa.gov/gistemp/. Accessed on July 16, 2018.

"Global Climate Report—May 2018." 2018. National Centers for Environmental Information. https://www.ncdc .noaa.gov/sotc/global/201805. Accessed on July 17, 2018.

"Governor Brown Signs Legislation Establishing Statewide Water Efficiency Goals." 2018. Planting Seeds. https:// plantingseedsblog.cdfa.ca.gov/wordpress/?p=15470. Accessed on February 17, 2019.

"Graphic: Earth's Temperature Record." 2018. NASA: Global Climate Change. https://climate.nasa.gov/climate_resources/ 9/graphic-earths-temperature-record/. Accessed on July 16, 2018.

Grasso, Veronica F. 2001. "Early Warning Systems: State-of-Art Analysis and Future Directions." United Nations Environment Programme. https://na.unep.net/geas/docs/ Early_Warning_System_Report.pdf. Accessed on July 19, 2018.

Grigoli, F., et al. 2018. "The November 2017 Mw 5.5 Pohang Earthquake: A Possible Case of Induced Seismicity in South Korea." *Science*. 360(6392): 1003–1006. doi:10.1126/science.aat2010.

Guha, S. K. 2000. "Mining Induced Seismicity." In S. K. Guha, ed. *Induced Earthquakes*. Boston: Kluwer Academic Publishers, 159–215.

Gupta, Harsh K. 2002. "A Review of Recent Studies of Triggered Earthquakes by Artificial Water Reservoirs with Special Emphasis on Earthquakes in Koyna, India." *Earth-Science Reviews*. 58(2002): 279–310.

"H.R.23—Gaining Responsibility on Water Act of 2017. 115th Congress (2017–2018)." Congress.Gov. https:// www.congress.gov/bill/115th-congress/house-bill/23/all-actions?overview=closed#tabs. Accessed on July 14, 2018.

"H.R.2898—Western Water and American Food Security Act of 2015." 114th Congress (2015–2016). Congress.Gov.

https://www.congress.gov/bill/114th-congress/house-bill/2898/text. Accessed on February 17, 2019.

Halverson, Nathan. 2015. "9 Sobering Facts about California's Groundwater Problem." Reveal. https://www.revealnews.org/article/9-sobering-facts-about-californias-groundwater-problem/. Accessed on July 13, 2018.

Häring, Markus O., et al. 2008. "Characterisation of the Basel 1 Enhanced Geothermal System." *Geothermics*. 37(5): 469–495.

Harvey, Chelsea. 2018. "Scientists Can Now Blame Individual Natural Disasters on Climate Change." *Scientific American*. https://www.scientificamerican.com/article/scientists-can-now-blame-individual-natural-disasters-on-climate-change/. Accessed on July 18, 2018.

Highland, Lynn M., and Peter Bobrowsky. 2008. *The Landslide Handbook—A Guide to Understanding Landslides*. Reston, VA: U.S. Geological Survey. Circular 1325. Available online at https://pubs.usgs.gov/circ/1325/pdf/C1325_508.pdf. Accessed on July 5, 2018.

Hippauf, Dory. 2015. "QUAKElahoma." frackorporation. https://frackorporation.wordpress.com/2016/01/17/quakelahoma/. Accessed on June 27, 2018.

"History of Federal Disaster Policy." 2015. Office of Policy Development and Research (PD&R). U.S. Department of Housing and Urban Development. https://www.huduser.gov/portal/periodicals/em/winter15/highlight1_sidebar.html. Accessed on July 20, 2018.

Horn, Diane P., and Jared T. Brown. 2018. "Introduction to the National Flood Insurance Program (NFIP)." Congressional Research Service. https://fas.org/sgp/crs/homesec/R44593.pdf. Accessed on July 11, 2018.

Hough, Susan E., and Morgan Page. 2015. "A Century of Induced Earthquakes in Oklahoma?" *Bulletin of the Seismological Society of America*. 105(6): 2863–2870.

Available online at https://pasadena.wr.usgs.gov/office/hough/BSSA_Hough_Page_2015.pdf. Accessed on June 26, 2018.

"How Much Water Does the Typical Hydraulically Fractured Well Require?" 2018. USGS. https://www.usgs.gov/faqs/how-much-water-does-typical-hydraulically-fractured-well-require. Accessed on June 27, 2018.

"Induced Seismicity Potential in Energy Technologies." 2013. National Research Council. https://www.nap.edu/catalog/13355/induced-seismicity-potential-in-energy-technologies. Accessed on June 27, 2018.

Jaboyedoff, Michael, et al. 2016. Human-Induced Landslides: Toward the Analysis of Anthropogenic Changes of the Slope Environment. In Aversa Stefano et al, eds. *Landslides and Engineering Slopes—Experiences, Theory and Practices.* Boca Raton, FL: CRC Press, 217–232.

Joint Panel on Problems Concerning Seismology and Rock Mechanics; Division of Earth Sciences; National Academy of Sciences; National Academy of Engineering. 1972. "Earthquakes Related to Reservoir Filling." Washington, DC: The National Academies Press. Available online at https://www.nap.edu/download/20612. Accessed on June 28, 2018.

Jones, Corey, and Curtis Killman. 2017. "Earthquake Insurance: 3 in 20 Claims Approved in Oklahoma since 2010." *Tulsa World.* https://www.tulsaworld.com/earthquakes/earthquake-insurance-in-claims-approved-in-oklahoma-since/article_de588725-1475-592c-9025-bdcfbf9b8bcd.html. Accessed on July 3, 2018.

Kao, Honn. n.d. "A Review of Traffic Light Protocol for Induced Seismicity and Its Effectiveness in Canada." Natural Resources Canada. http://www.orogo.gov.nt.ca/sites/orogo/files/resources/induced_seismicity_workshop_-_review_of_traffic_light_protocol.pdf. Accessed on July 1, 2018.

Kim, Kwant-Hee, et al. 2018. "Assessing Whether the 2017 Mw 5.4 Pohang Earthquake in South Korea Was an Induced Event." *Science.* 360(6392): 1007–1009. doi:10.1126/science.aat6081.

Konschnik, Kate. 2017. "Regulating Stability: State Compensation Funds for Induced Seismicity." *Georgetown Environmental Law Review.* 29(2): 227–300.

Kossin, James P. 2018. "A Global Slowdown of Tropical-Cyclone Translation Speed." *Nature.* 558: 104–107.

Krehbiel, Randy. 2015. "Oklahoma Supreme Court Clears Way for Earthquake Lawsuits against Energy Companies." *Tulsa World.* http://www.tulsaworld.com/news/capitol_report/oklahoma-supreme-court-clears-way-for-earthquake-lawsuits-against-energy/article_546e6b34-4bfb-5298-a245-502c632a00dd.html. Accessed on June 29, 2018.

Lacasse, Suzanne, and Young Jae Choi. 2011. "Work Package 5.1—Toolbox for Landslide Hazard and Risk Mitigation Measures." SafeLand. https://cordis.europa.eu/result/rcn/54948_en.html. Accessed on July 5, 2018.

"The Law of the River." 2008. Bureau of Reclamation. Lower Colorado Region. https://www.usbr.gov/lc/region/g1000/lawofrvr.html. Accessed on July 13, 2018.

"Lesson 3: When Disaster Strikes, What Can Government Do?" 2018. Foundation for Teaching Economics. https://www.fte.org/teachers/teacher-resources/lesson-plans/disasterslessons/lesson-3-when-disaster-strikes-what-can-government-do/. Accessed on July 20, 2018.

"Man-Made Earthquakes in Oklahoma—A Headache for Insurers." 2017. Insurance Information Institute. https://www.iii.org/insuranceindustryblog/tag/induced-earthquakes/. Accessed on July 1, 2018.

Marek, Ben. 2018. "The Latest on Ladra: Updates on Induced Seismicity Tort Litigation." http://tjogel.org/

latest-ladra-updates-induced-seismicity-tort-litigation/. Accessed on July 3, 2018.

Mayer, Matt. 2012. "Congress Should Act on FEMA's Refusal to Reform." The Heritage Foundation. https://www.heritage .org/homeland-security/report/congress-should-act-femas-refusal-reform. Accessed on July 20, 2018.

Mener, Andrew S. 2007. "Disaster Response in the United States of America: An Analysis of the Bureaucratic and Political History of a Failing System." College Undergraduate Research. University of Pennsylvania. https://repository .upenn.edu/cgi/viewcontent.cgi?article=1068&context=curej. Accessed on July 20, 2018.

Miao, Dai, et al. 2011. "A Study on the Relationship between Water Levels and Seismic Activity in the Three Gorges Reservoir." *Renmin Changjiang: Journal of the Changjiang Water Resources Commission.* 41(17): 1–9. Available online at http://probeinternational.org/library/wp-content/ uploads/2011/06/3-Gorges-Report-26-5.pdf. Accessed on July 3, 2018.

"Model Ordinance for Floodplain Management under the National Flood Insurance Program and the Endangered Species Act." 2012. Federal Emergency Management Agency, Region 10. https://www.fema.gov/media-library-data/1383597893424-4747f702310a2bbc7e04ea83d66f 73f5/NFIP_ESA_Model_Ordinance.pdf. Accessed on July 12, 2018.

"Myths and Misconceptions." 2018. Induced Earthquakes. USGS. https://earthquake.usgs.gov/research/induced/ myths.php. Accessed on June 27, 2018.

Nadim, Farrokh, et al. 2011. "Deliverable 1.6: Analysis of Landslides Triggered by Anthropogenic Factors in Europe." SafeLand European Project Living with Landslide Risk in Europe: Assessment, Effects of Global Changes, and Risk Management Strategies. https://cordis.europa.eu/result/ rcn/54948_en.html. Accessed on July 5, 2018.

"National Disaster Recovery Framework, Second Edition." 2016. Department of Homeland Security. https://www .fema.gov/media-library-data/1466014998123-4bec85509 30f774269e0c5968b120ba2/National_Disaster_Recovery_ Framework2nd.pdf. Accessed on July 20, 2018.

"NEHRP Recommended Seismic Provisions for New Buildings and Other Structures. 2009 Edition." 2018. Federal Emergency Management Agency. https://www .fema.gov/media-library/assets/documents/18152. Accessed on July 7, 2018.

Osborn, Liz. 2018. "United States' Rainiest Cities." Current Results. https://www.currentresults.com/Weather-Extremes/ US/wettest-cities.php. Accessed on July 13, 2018. "Driest Cities in the United States." Current Results. https://www .currentresults.com/Weather-Extremes/US/driest-city.php. Accessed on July 13, 2018.

Pachauri, Rajendra K., et al. 2014. "Climate Change 2014 Synthesis Report." Intergovernmental Panel on Climate Change. http://ar5-syr.ipcc.ch/ipcc/ipcc/resources/pdf/ IPCC_SynthesisReport.pdf. Accessed on July 16, 2018.

Passut, Charlie. 2018. "Oklahoma Judge Approves Quake Lawsuit Class Action; More Wastewater Wells Shut." Shale Daily. http://www.naturalgasintel.com/articles/114484- oklahoma-judge-approves-quake-lawsuit-class-action-more- wastewater-wells-shut. Accessed on June 29, 2018.

Popescu, Mihail E., and Katsuo Sasahara. 2009. "Engineering Measures for Landslide Disaster Mitigation." In Kyoji Sassa and Paolo Canuti, eds. *Landslides—Disaster Risk Reduction*. Berlin: Springer, 609–631.

"Pre-Disaster Recovery Planning Guide for State Governments." 2016. Federal Emergency Management Agency. https://www.fema.gov/media-library-data/ 1485202780009-db5c48b2774665e357100cc69a14da68/ Pre-DisasterRecoveryPlanningGuideforStateGovernments- 1.pdf. Accessed on July 20, 2018.

"Preventing Human-Caused Earthquakes." 2016. U.S. Geological Survey. https://www.usgs.gov/news/preventing-human-caused-earthquakes. Accessed on June 30, 2018.

"Prevention and Education." 2018. U.S. Forest Service. https://www.fs.fed.us/fire/prev_ed/index.html. Accessed on July 9, 2018.

"Prevention How-Tos." 2018. Smokey Bear. https://smokey bear.com/en/prevention-how-tos. Accessed on July 9, 2018.

"Purposes and Techniques of Fire Management." 2018. *Encyclopedia Britannica.* https://www.britannica.com/science/forestry/Purposes-and-techniques-of-forest-management#ref393393. Accessed on July 6, 2018.

Rahmstorf, Stefan. 2017. "Rising Hazard of Storm-Surge Flooding." *Proceedings of the National Academy of Sciences.* 114(45): 11806–11808. Available online at http://www.pnas.org/content/pnas/early/2017/10/23/1715895114.full.pdf. Accessed on July 18, 2018.

"Ready, Set, Go!" 2018. City of Ashland. http://www.ash land.or.us/Page.asp?NavID=13512. Accessed on July 19, 2018.

Rice, Doyle. 2017. "Study: People Start 84% of U.S. Wildfires." *USA Today.* https://www.usatoday.com/story/weather/2017/02/27/wildfires-human-lightning-caused/98480888/. Accessed on July 6, 2018.

Risser, Mark D., and Michael F. Wehner. 2017. "Attributable Human-Induced Changes in the Likelihood and Magnitude of the Observed Extreme Precipitation during Hurricane Harvey." *Geophysical Research Letters.* 44(24): 12457–12464. Available online at https://agupubs.online library.wiley.com/doi/full/10.1002/2017GL075888. Accessed on July 18, 2018.

Robles, Francis. 2018. "FEMA Was Sorely Unprepared for Puerto Rico Hurricane, Report Says." *New York Times.*

https://www.nytimes.com/2018/07/12/us/fema-puerto-rico-maria.html. Accessed on July 20, 2018.

Rosenberg, Matt. 2018. "California Population." ThoughtCo. https://www.thoughtco.com/california-population-overview-1435260. Accessed on July 13, 2018.

Rothé, J. P. 1969. "Earthquakes and Reservoir Loadings." http://www.iitk.ac.in/nicee/wcee/article/4_vol1_A1-28.pdf. Accessed on June 28, 2018.

"Rule Chapter: 62-673." 2018. Florida Administrative Code & Florida Administrative Register. https://www.flrules.org/gateway/ChapterHome.asp?Chapter=62-673. Accessed on July 3, 2018.

Ryan, Kelsey. 2016. "Wichita Agents Fielding More Questions on Earthquake Insurance." *Wichita Eagle*. https://www.kansas.com/news/local/article53628805.html. Accessed on July 3, 2018.

Ryan, Kelsey. 2017. "If You Haven't Bought Flood Insurance, You're Not Alone." *Kansas City Star*. https://www.kansascity.com/news/politics-government/article170765492.html. Accessed on July 11, 2018.

"S.2533—California Long-Term Provisions for Water Supply and Short-Term Provisions for Emergency Drought Relief Act." 114th Congress (2015–2016). Congress.Gov. https://www.congress.gov/bill/114th-congress/senate-bill/2533/all-actions?q=%7B%22search%22%3A%5B%222533%22%5D%7D&overview=closed#tabs. Accessed on July 14, 2018.

Seeley, Jacob T., and David M. Romps. 2015. "The Effect of Global Warming on Severe Thunderstorms in the United States." *Journal of Climate*. 28(6): 2443–2458. Available online at https://journals.ametsoc.org/doi/pdf/10.1175/JCLI-D-14-00382.1. Accessed on July 17, 2018.

Short, K. C. 2014. "A Spatial Database of Wildfires in the United States, 1992–2011." *Earth System Science Data*. 6:127. doi:10.5194/essd-6-1-2014. Available online at

https://www.fs.fed.us/rm/pubs_other/rmrs_2014_short_
k001.pdf. Accessed on July 6, 2018.

"Short-Term Induced Seismicity Models." 2018. U.S.
Geological Survey. https://earthquake.usgs.gov/hazards/
induced/index.php#2018. Accessed on June 30, 2018.

Simmers, Rick, et al. 2017. "Potential Injection-Induced
Seismicity Associated with Oil & Gas Development,"
2nd ed. StatesFirst. http://www.gwpc.org/sites/default/files/
event-sessions/Nickolaus%20-%20seismicity.pdf. Accessed
on June 30, 2018.

"Solving the Drought." 2018. Environment California.
https://environmentcalifornia.org/page/cae/solving-drought.
Accessed on July 14, 2018.

Strassler, Eric, Jesse Pritts, and Kristen Strellec. 1999.
Environmental Protection Agency. Chapter 4. https://www
3.epa.gov/npdes/pubs/usw_b.pdf. Accessed on July 10,
2018.

"Ten Hottest Years Globally." 2018. Climate Central. http://
www.climatecentral.org/gallery/graphics/the-10-hottest-
global-years-on-record. Accessed on July 16, 2018.

Tippett, Michael K., Chiara Lepore, and Joel E. Cohen.
2016. "More Tornadoes in the Most Extreme U.S. Tornado
Outbreaks." *Science*. 354(6318): 1419–1423. doi:10.1126/
science.aah7393. Available online at http://lab.rockefeller
.edu/cohenje/assets/file/416TippettLeporeCohenExtreme
TornadoOutbreaks_SuppMatScience2016.pdf. Accessed on
July 17, 2018.

"Total Policies in Force by Calendar Year." 2018. Federal
Emergency Management Agency. https://www.fema.gov/
total-policies-force-calendar-year. Accessed on July 11, 2018.

"Total Wildland Fires and Acres (1926–2017)." 2018.
National Interagency Fire Center. https://www.nifc.gov/
fireInfo/fireInfo_stats_totalFires.html. Accessed on July 6,
2018.

Trapp, Robert J., et al. 2007. "Changes in Severe Thunderstorm Environment Frequency during the 21st Century Caused by Anthropogenically Enhanced Global Radiative Forcing." *PNAS*. 104(50): 19719–19723. Available online at http://www.pnas.org/content/104/50/19719#sec-2. Accessed on July 17, 2018.

"2018 International Building Code." 2018. International Code Council. https://codes.iccsafe.org/public/document/IBC2018/effective-use-of-the-international-building-code. Accessed on July 7, 2018.

"2014 Quadrennial Fire Review Final Report." 2015. Developed by Booz Allen Hamilton on Behalf Of: USDA Forest Service Fire & Aviation Management and Department of the Interior Office of Wildland Fire. https://www.forestsandrangelands.gov/QFR/documents/2014QFRFinalReport.pdf. Accessed on July 7, 2018.

"The 2014 Sustainable Groundwater Management Act: A Handbook to Understanding and Implementing the Law." 2015. Water Education Foundation. https://www.watereducation.org/sites/main/files/file-attachments/groundwatermgthandbook_oct2015.pdf. Accessed on July 15, 2018.

"2017 Hurricane Season FEMA After-Action Report." 2018. Federal Emergency Management Agency. https://www.fema.gov/media-library-data/1531743865541-d16794d43d3082544435e1471da07880/2017FEMAHurricaneAAR.pdf. Accessed on July 20, 2018.

van Oldenborgh, Geert Jan, et al. 2017. "Attribution of Extreme Rainfall from Hurricane Harvey." *Environmental Research Letters*. 12(12): 124009. Available online at http://iopscience.iop.org/article/10.1088/1748-9326/aa9ef2/pdf. Accessed on July 18, 2018.

Vinik, Danny. 2018. "FEMA's Plan Underestimated Puerto Rican Hurricane." Politico. https://www.politico.com/

story/2018/04/15/puerto-rico-hurricane-fema-disaster-523033. Accessed on July 20, 2018.

Walsh, F. Rall, III, and Mark D. Zoback. 2015. "Oklahoma's Recent Earthquakes and Saltwater Disposal." *Science Advances.* 1(5). doi:10.1126/sciadv.1500195.

Warmbrodt, Zachary. 2018. "As Congress Stalls, Trump Quietly Overhauls Flood Program." Politico. https://www .politico.com/story/2018/03/29/as-congress-stalls-trump-quietly-overhauls-flood-program-491384. Accessed on July 11, 2018.

"Water in the West and California's Drought." 2015. Colorado Springs Utilities. https://www.csu.org/Blog/archive/2015/ 04/07/water-in-the-west-and-californias-drought.aspx. Accessed on February 17, 2019.

Weinhold, Bob. 2012. "Energy Development Linked with Earthquakes." *Environmental Health Perspectives.* 120(10): A388. Available online at https://www.ncbi.nlm.nih.gov/pmc/ articles/PMC3491933/. Accessed on February 17, 2019.

Weiser, Matt. 2015a. "Water Files—Law & Politics: Drought-Focused Regulations Prove Hard to Enforce." *Sacramento Bee.* https://www.sacbee.com/news/state/california/water-and-drought/article32446875.html. Accessed on July 14, 2018.

Weiser, Matt. 2015b. "Water Files—Supply: Moving Water Only Works When There's Enough to Go Around." *Sacramento Bee.* https://www.sacbee.com/news/state/ california/water-and-drought/article32435193.html. Accessed on July 14, 2018.

Weiser, Matt. 2016. "Four Things to Note in Federal Drought Legislation." Water Deeply. https://www.newsdeeply.com/ water/articles/2016/03/18/four-things-to-note-in-federal-drought-legislation. Accessed on July 14, 2018.

Westerling, Anthony LeRoy. 2016. "Increasing Western US Forest Wildfire Activity: Sensitivity to Changes in the

Timing of Spring." *Philosophical Transactions of the Royal Society B. Biological Sciences.* 371(696): doi:10.1098/ rstb.2015.0178. Available online at https://www.ncbi.nlm .nih.gov/pmc/articles/PMC4874415/. Accessed on July 18, 2018.

"When Does the U.S. Geological Survey Issue a Landslide Advisory, and under What Conditions?" 2018. U.S. Geological Survey. https://www.usgs.gov/faqs/when-does-us-geological-survey-issue-a-landslide-advisory-and-under-what-conditions. Accessed on February 17, 2019.

Whitehead, Seth. 2018. "USGS Report: Oklahoma Earthquakes Have Decreased 'Rapidly' since 2015." Energy in Depth. https://www.energyindepth.org/oklahoma-earth quake-declines-continue-first-quarter-2018/. Accessed on June 27, 2018.

"Wildfire Codes and Standards." 2018. National Fire Protection Association. https://www.nfpa.org/Public-Education/By-topic/Wildfire/Codes-and-standards. Accessed on July 9, 2018.

Xiao, Fan. 2012. "Did the Zipingpu Dam Trigger China's 2008 Earthquake?" A Probe International Study. https:// pdfs.semanticscholar.org/b472/5921021258eb1655d6caa9 a859f90584b078.pdf. Accessed on June 28, 2018.

"Your Role in Fire-Adapted Communities." 2012. U.S. Fire Administration. https://www.usfa.fema.gov/downloads/ pdf/publications/fire_adapted_communities.pdf. Accessed on July 9, 2018.

3 Perspectives

Natural disasters are a topic of considerable interest to a wide range of people for a variety of reasons. For example, one may have lived through such an event; has special interest in a topic; is studying or researching some aspect of natural disasters; or is curious about earthquakes, sinkholes, landslides, tsunamis, or some other type of natural disaster. The essays in this chapter illustrate the range of personal experiences that may fall into this category.

Who Is Pele: A Native Hawaiian Perspective
Wendy Awai-Dakroub

When asking the question "Who is Pele?" one cannot give an accurate description because the question is complex. The best way to describe who Pele really is is to keep the explanation very basic and simple. Pele is the magma. Magma is meant for us to build life. Without that we have no land to stand on.

This question is complex because to many people who experienced eruptions in the 1970s and 1980s and recently in Puna (especially the residents of Leilani Estates), there is ongoing inner conflict when referring to Pele. Some welcomed her eruption as a powerful embodiment of creation: The beginning and ending of all things. Others wept in sorrow over her destruction. There is also the cultural appropriation of Pele caused by the influx of mainland spiritual groups selling "Pele experiences." Then there

---

Trash and debris piled up outside a Houston, Texas, business following Hurricane Harvey, which devastated the area in late August 2017. (Eric Overton/Dreamstime.com)

are the tour operators selling "lava tours" to visitors of the island hoping to catch a glimpse of Pele, all for profit. Finally, you have the media, who each have their own version of Pele, depending on the story they are telling. All these concepts combined add to the layer of sensitivity of the topic and to the community that has lost its homes and places to live.

Therefore, the easiest way to explain the complexity of the question "Who is Pele?" is to break it into three layers, the first of which is Pele in mythology. This answer is based on a myth that is a sacred narrative and is usually placed in primordial time, or a time before time really existed. It is usually taken as true by the people who hold that myth as part of their religion. The religion of the ancient Hawaiians was polytheistic, in which the forces of nature, such as war, fire, life, and water, were personified as deities. Ancient Hawaiians looked to the volcano goddess Pele for protection. Pele is known to be unpredictable, so Hawaiians have traditionally left gifts and offerings to keep her happy. That tradition continues till this day, and many Native Hawaiians still consider Pele as a supernatural being.

The second view of Pele comes from folklore. Folklore is a tale that takes place in some alternate or undefined time ("once upon a time" being just one example). It can involve human beings, animals, or any creature. In Hawaiian folklore, Pele is often portrayed as a wanderer, and sightings of the goddess have been reported throughout the island chain for hundreds of years. In these sightings or visions, she appears as either a very tall, beautiful young woman or an unattractive and frail elderly woman usually accompanied by a white dog. Those well versed in the legend say that Pele takes this form of an elderly beggar woman to test people—asking them if they have food or drink to share. Those who are generous and share with her are rewarded, while anyone who is greedy or unkind is punished with destruction of their homes or other valuables.

The third view of Pele is based on a Hawaiian chant known as *oli*. The oli falls into two broad categories: *mele oli* and *mele hula*. Mele hula are chants accompanied by dance and usуль

or musical instruments and are usually performed by a group. Ancient Hawaiians had no written language until the 1800s, so most information was passed through the use of song, dance, chants, and poems. Native Hawaiians used this method of recording information for the purpose of passing it on from one generation to the next, which is the reason that Native Hawaiians, until the present day, are always very mindful of their actions whenever presented with an oli.

Each of these layers serves its own purpose, which is to understand who Pele is. However, because of our human emotions and our need to understand and define things, who Pele is to you depends on which level of understanding you choose to acknowledge or accept. This is why the question is so complex.

It is important to note that Native Hawaiian people have great respect for Pele, which is why she is often referred to as "Madame Pele" or "The Pele." How they look at their relationship with Pele has a lot to do with nature, how it forms, and what it gives them. The adjective *The* in *The Pele* refers to that which is "Godly" because, as people we cannot ever be the energy, Pele is the magma. And this is the reason that a person can only create his or her own story based on his or her own belief system.

Native Hawaiians understand this and therefore rely on knowing their *mo'olelo* (story) through oli, which has been passed down from their ancestors. By listening to these stories, they have a simple, basic understanding of who Pele is. Pele is the magma. Pele is the lava. Pele is the rock. Pele is the sulfur. Pele is the smoke. She is the creator of the Hawaiian Islands.

Wendy Awai-Dakroub is a Native Hawaiian freelance writer and photographer based in Honolulu, Hawaii. She lives with her two children and husband on Oahu.

Unnatural Disasters
Trudy E. Bell

Powerful weather events may wreak destruction and claim human lives no matter how careful people may be. But through action or inaction, human beings also can unintentionally intensify—or even create—tragedy from natural weather events.

The most obvious short-term way individuals unnecessarily expose themselves to high risks is by not getting out of the way when warned. Some people refuse to follow official evacuation orders in advance of an oncoming hurricane. Instead, they try to drive through flooded streets, not realizing that water 2 feet deep has enough mass in a moving current to sweep away an SUV. Others threatened by a raging forest fire may decide to "ride it out" with a garden hose on the roof to try to protect their homes from falling embers. Mercifully, a few get lucky. But others succumb when belatedly trying to get to emergency shelters or medical assistance and may even put would-be rescuers in danger.

There are also less obvious, longer-term human decisions that affect risk. One factor is where individuals choose to (or can afford to) live. People looking to buy or build homes may not appreciate the actual magnitude of potential risks of certain locations or may not be able to afford a safer location. While the risk posed during any one year may seem low, it can be significant over the life of a typical 30-year home mortgage. Human settlement that ignores the inexorable realities and risks of nature courts tragedy.

Examples abound. Any structures built on a river's floodplain are at risk, even if the last big flood was more than a century ago. A luxurious house built atop cliffs overlooking the Pacific Ocean commands a spectacular view, but over the decades, natural erosion can weaken the cliff until a mudslide triggered by heavy rains could take down the home. Individuals living within or near the peace and beauty of a western U.S. forest may face the risk of wildfire during prolonged drought. And apart from threats posed by occasional hurricanes along the Atlantic Seaboard, increasing stretches of beachfront property are at risk from rising sea levels due to climate change—some neighborhoods now even suffering "sunny day flooding" from normal high tides.

A societal factor that increases risk is poor maintenance of dams, levees, and floodwalls. Major infrastructure of concrete and earth typically has a nominal 50-year lifetime—but only if it is regularly maintained against weathering, rodents, tree roots, or other forms of deterioration. The nation is dotted with more than 90,000 dams of all sizes (plus additional uncounted levees and floodwalls). Dams are rated by hazard potential: high-hazard potential dams are ones whose failure would likely kill people. Over 15,000 high-hazard potential dams exist nationwide.

Half of those high-hazard potential dams—erected during the infrastructure-building heyday of the 1960s and 1970s—are now older than half a century. More than a third are now in poor, unsatisfactory, or unknown condition, primarily because of underfunding from their owners (federal, state, municipal, and private). Yet some states actually exempt dams from safety requirements. The Federal Emergency Management Agency (FEMA), in its biennial report on the National Dam Safety Program for 2014–2015, warned "many Americans are living below structurally deficient, high hazard potential dams" and that "Americans are unaware of the risk" (FEMA 2016, 81).

Another societal way humans outright magnify a natural weather disaster into a full-fledged human tragedy is when multiple authorities do not enforce well-advised public policies. Examples include letting flood maps get out of date; downgrading the hazard potential of dams to circumvent required inspections; granting waivers to allow permits to build homes in flood-prone areas; or allowing coal ash or other toxic waste products to be piled along riverbanks without requiring any protective ground liner or top cover to prevent poisons from leaching into drinking water supplies during a flood. Why would anyone relax such commonsense safety guards? All too often, interested parties seek to reduce short-term costs or government spending, but commonly they do so by increasing future risk to countless human lives.

In short, many natural disasters could be significantly less calamitous if humans fully recognized the ferocity of nature and truly reduced risk to life and property.

Some steps can be taken at the federal level. One major need is funding efforts to revise flood maps along coastlines to reflect realistic calculations of the true future extent of flooding as a result of sea level rise and greater storm surge due to climate change. Another need is to remove perverse incentives in flood insurance regulations that reward rebuilding in the same flood-prone area instead of encouraging and enabling moving to safer ground.

Useful steps can also be taken locally through city hall. If ocean, river, or storm flooding poses a local risk, for example, one potential action is requiring the use of permeable pavements for streets and parking lots (instead of traditional impermeable asphalt) to reduce stormwater runoff and local flooding. Another useful step would be enacting and enforcing local zoning laws against building for human occupancy in flood-prone areas: instead, turn floodplains into public riverfront parks—which during floods allow the river room to swell with less risk to human lives.

Today, some large- and medium-sized U.S. cities—including New York City, Seattle, and Tulsa—are quietly evaluating risks and making preparations against important threats posed locally by different manifestations of extreme weather resulting from climate change. With an even longer-term global view, other urban centers are networking worldwide to explore and implement ways to slow the pace of climate change itself over forthcoming decades.

Reference

"The National Dam Safety Program: Biennial Report to the United States Congress, Fiscal Years 2014-2015 (P-1067, August 3)." 2016. Federal Emergency Management Administration. https://www.fema.gov/media-library-data/1470749866373-5de9234b8a02a3577c2646ffdf6eb087/FEMAP1067.pdf. Accessed on September 23, 2018.

Trudy E. Bell, MA, is a former editor for Scientific American *and* IEEE Spectrum *magazines and former senior writer for the University of California High-Performance AstroComputing Center. She has written, coauthored, or edited a dozen books; written several hundred articles on science and technology for national magazines; and edited two dozen reports for the Union of Concerned Scientists.*

Understanding the Communication Gaps between Disaster Prediction and Public Response
Sean Ernst

Oklahoma is no stranger to tornadoes. The state averages over 50 of the storms per year (NWS Norman 2018) and has suffered some of the worst tornadoes on record in the United States, such as the infamous May 3, 1999, F5 tornado in the city of Moore. It is tempting to assume that the residents of Central Oklahoma are some of the most tornado-savvy people on the planet, cool and collected during even the angriest of the state's spring storms. However, May 2013 took all of Oklahoman's expectations of tornado seasons and turned them on their heads. On May 19, supercells in Central Oklahoma produced several long-track tornadoes, including an EF4 that impacted Norman and Shawnee (NWS Norman 2013a). The day after, an EF5 tornado with winds estimated at over 200 miles per hour struck Moore, Oklahoma, sadly resulting in 24 fatalities (NWS Norman 2013b). Both events received extensive news coverage, with local TV stations' paid storm chasers and helicopter footage covering the tornadoes from beginning to end. National media was quick to descend on the scene, writing headlines about the impacts of the storms for days afterward (CBS News 2013).

Barely over a week later, on May 31, meteorologists in the region had noticed a pattern disturbingly similar to the tornado outbreaks on May 19 and 20 taking shape around the Oklahoma City metro. However, in addition to the threat of tornadoes, a significant flash flooding threat was anticipated for the area, mentioned in weather briefings conducted by the

National Weather Service (NWS) that morning. Media focus was more on the tornado threat, and when a massive, 2-mile-wide tornado developed during rush hour west of the metro, local media went into overdrive. Members of the public interviewed after the event reported receiving messaging to evacuate the city and "drive south." As a result, a huge number of residents, driven by fear, ignored years of practice sheltering in place and jumped in their cars, creating a traffic jam that encompassed much of the city.

Though the El Reno tornado claimed eight lives, all of which occurred in vehicles, the flash flooding that resulted from the slow-moving storm swept away 12 people sheltering from the tornado in drainage ditches. Most of these fatalities came from a single Guatemalan family, whose primary language was Spanish. Even without the language barrier faced by Spanish-speaking members of the community, members of the English-speaking population reported being surprised and unprepared for the flash flooding that occurred with the storm, and 23 high-water rescues were completed that day (NWS Norman 2013c).

The tornadoes and flash flooding in Oklahoma on May 31, 2013, are a tragic example of the critical importance of effective meteorological messaging and the deficiencies that exist in the current system. Individuals who had been in relative safety, sheltering in places away from the floodwaters, abandoned it due to ineffective or misguided communication and widespread fear. This is not the only time that communication missteps during natural disasters have resulted in tragedy, as multi-hazard crises like the El Reno event also commonly occur in landfalling hurricanes. In these situations, communicators ranging from emergency managers to broadcast meteorologists have reported being overwhelmed by the volume of warning information put out by the NWS (Demuth et al. 2012, 1138). Communication failures for vulnerable populations are not limited to meteorological disasters in the United States, as similar failures of the tsunami evacuation system in Indonesia have been reported, with individuals trying to drive away from the coast instead of going to predetermined shelters, or warnings not even reaching some populations (Witze 2014).

Groups such as the National Academy of Sciences have recognized the need for further improvement of the study of communication of weather information. In 2018, the academy published a consensus study report explaining that, even with the impressive advancements in forecast accuracy in recent decades, social and behavioral science research has not been leveraged at the level it needs to be to provide the greatest return on investment for these technical improvements (National Research Council 2018). For tornadoes specifically, work has begun at the National Severe Storms Laboratory in Norman, Oklahoma, just south of the Moore tornado's damage path, to use social science knowledge to change the way we communicate tornado risks (Karstens et al. 2018). Utilizing the social and behavioral sciences in understanding individuals' comprehension of warning information, not just for tornadoes but for all disasters, will prove critical in reducing the human impacts of major disasters in the modern era.

References

CBS News. 2013. "In Depth: Oklahoma Tornado Disaster." CBS Interactive Inc. https://www.cbsnews.com/feature/oklahoma-tornado-disaster/3/. Accessed on July 5, 2018.

Demuth, Julie L., et al. 2012. "Creation and Communications of Hurricane Risk Information." *Bulletin of the American Meteorological Society*. 93: 1133–1145.

Karstens, Chris D., et al. 2018. "Development of a Human-Machine Mix for Forecasting Severe Convective Events." *Weather and Forecasting*. 33: 715–737.

National Research Council. 2018. *Integrating Social and Behavioral Sciences within the Weather Enterprise*. Washington, D.C.: The National Academies Press. https://doi.org/10.17226/24865. Accessed on July 5, 2018.

NWS Norman. 2013a. "The Tornado Outbreak of May 19, 2013." National Weather Service. https://www.weather .gov/oun/events-20130519. Accessed on July 5, 2018.

NWS Norman. 2013b. "The Tornado Outbreak of May 20, 2013." National Weather Service. https://www.weather .gov/oun/events-20130520. Accessed on July 5, 2018.

NWS Norman. 2013c. "The Tornado Outbreak of May 31, 2013." National Weather Service. https://www.weather .gov/oun/events-20130531. Accessed on July 5, 2018.

NWS Norman. 2018. "Monthly/Annual Statistics for Tornadoes in Oklahoma (1950–Present)." National Weather Service. https://www.weather.gov/oun/ tornadodata-ok-monthlyannual. Accessed on July 5, 2018.

Witze, Alexandra. 2014. "Tsunami Alerts Fail to Bridge the 'Last Mile.' " *Nature*. 560(7530): 151–152. Available online at https://www.nature.com/news/tsunami-alerts-fail-to-bridge-the-last-mile-1.16516. Accessed July 5, 2018.

Sean Ernst holds a bachelor of science degree in meteorology, with minors in mathematics and psychology, from the University of Oklahoma. In 2018 he became a master's student at the University of Oklahoma's School of Meteorology, with a research interest in improving the communication of weather information. Sean has been interested in the weather from a young age, nicknamed "the weatherman" by his kindergarten teachers, and had his heart set on the University of Oklahoma for many years. He plans to work toward his PhD in meteorology before pursuing a research career in meteorology and communication.

Red Tide: The Insidious Killer
ChrisAnn Silver Esformes

One thing I've learned as a reporter on a barrier island on the Gulf Coast of Florida—and as a lifelong Floridian—is not all natural disasters rage as loudly as a hurricane. Sometimes tragedy creeps in silently with the wind and tide, leaving a trail of death, stench, and economic rubble in its meandering path.

On Anna Maria Island, a small barrier island on the south end of Tampa Bay, the week leading up to Hurricane Irma's U.S. landfall September 10, 2017, over the Florida Keys, was charged with adrenaline and buffered by exhaustion. When media outlets announced this could be the strongest hurricane ever to hit the United States, people were understandably scared.

A slight turn to the east as the storm approached Tampa Bay saved the area from potentially catastrophic damage. Since the hurricane pushed east of the island, storm surge was minimal.

The eye of the storm passed about 30 miles east of Anna Maria Island as a Category 3 early on Monday, September 11. After the cleanup crews made their first pass, the bridges reopened that day. The relief was palpable. Everyone I interviewed said a variation on the same theme: they thought they'd be returning to a wasteland.

The paper I write for went to press that night and was circulated the next day.

Irma brought some destruction to our area. Many were without power for close to two weeks, homes were damaged, and trees were knocked down.

But it happened fast and the remedy was clear: apply for Federal Emergency Management Agency funds and rebuild stronger structures.

However, when a natural disaster silently infiltrates an area, such as the red tide that devastated the Gulf Coast of Florida starting in late 2017 and peaking in July 2018, it works like a slowly mounting panic attack.

Red tide continues to linger in low levels on both coasts of Florida when this essay was written in October 2018.

Florida is no stranger to *Karenia brevis*, the neurotoxic algae that follows the wind and tide and causes or exacerbates respiratory illness in mammals, kills fish and shorebirds—not to mention the economy—and turns the water a reddish-brown murky shade.

Red tide has been reported in Florida since the 1700s, with the worst recent instance prior to the 2018 bloom lasting from 2004 to 2006, and peaking in 2005, according to the National Oceanic and Atmospheric Administration.

At its peak in August 2018, the red tide bloom along the Gulf Coast was 150 miles long and 10 miles wide, according to Mote Marine Laboratory in Sarasota. As part of its work, Mote rescues stranded marine life, researches the effects of red tide, and looks for ways to combat it.

Just after sunrise on August 22, 2018, my editor called to tell me that a dead dolphin had washed ashore on Anna Maria Island. It was the first reported dead dolphin in Manatee County since the red tide reached high levels in August.

As of October 17, 2018, 20 more dolphins had perished, likely due to red tide, along with 67 manatees and more than 200 sea turtles, according to the Florida Fish and Wildlife Conservation Commission.

When I arrived at the beach to meet Mote representatives retrieving the dolphin for research, I was shocked. I had been on that same beach the day before, and aside from dark water and a slight respiratory irritation, one would never have known red tide was there. On this day, however, the closest comparison I could make was that the beach looked like a scene from a marine-life war zone.

The beach was littered with dead fish, eels, and crabs. The decaying sea-life was so thick that walking on top of it was practically unavoidable. The stench was strong, burning my eyes and nostrils even with a mask, and for several yards out, the water was filled with dead fish floating in a sea of what looked like black coffee.

All because the wind had changed.

When Mote representatives arrived, they spotted something else bobbing on the surface of the water about 10 yards out: it was a dead sub-adult Kemp's ridley sea turtle, one of the rarest species in the world.

I took photos of the dead animals, and they ran in the paper that week.

This was hard work, not just physically but emotionally. Taking those pictures felt brutal. I had to remind myself it was for a good cause. But what was the cause?

As a journalist, I often must weigh the value of a difficult topic. I do not create the picture; I just capture the moment in history. However, I knew such photos would hurt an already-suffering tourism industry. And what good would coverage do for something created by nature?

But the answer is not so simple.

As of October 2018, Mote and other organizations are receiving federal and state funding to research the causes and possible cures for the toxic algae, and some believe pollution flowing from Lake Okeechobee and other water bodies, to the Gulf, as well as fertilizer runoff, is to blame.

The passage of hurricanes and other large storms through the gulf and cooler winter waters has been predicted to keep red tide at bay while researchers attempt to find a solution.

The goal is that my coverage of the red tide crisis has opened peoples' eyes to the fact planetary disasters do not necessarily happen quickly but are the result of a slow and insidious process.

While the federal and state governments continue to fund areas devastated by hurricanes, hopefully, funding for red tide research does not wane.

ChrisAnn Silver Esformes is a news reporter for a weekly newspaper, The Islander, *on Anna Maria Island, Florida. She received her MA in mass communication from the University of Florida. She is a native Floridian.*

The Great Galveston Hurricane of 1900
Madeline Clark Frank

In 1900, a Category 4 hurricane hit Galveston, Texas, in what is to this day the deadliest natural disaster in U.S. history. Over the course of a single day, 10,000 people were killed and the city was leveled. Galveston was transformed from a prominent port city to little more than rubble. Today, even the deadliest hurricanes to make landfall in the United States rarely result in more than 100 deaths. Advances in science and technology over the last century have allowed us to forecast storms to warn people when a hurricane is coming. Management agencies, such as FEMA, have also been established to provide resources for rescue and evacuation.

In 1900, the meteorologist assigned to the Galveston office of the U.S. Weather Bureau, the predecessor of today's National Weather Service, was Isaac M. Cline. He lived on the Texas Gulf coast with his wife, Cora, their three daughters, and his brother. His records and observations of the storm survived the devastation and are preserved in the Weather Bureau Archives.

Cline had minimal information available to him. His crude instruments could measure quantities such as temperature, air pressure, rainfall, and wind speed and direction. Other than those simple measurements, his only means of obtaining information was through telegraphs from other bureau offices. On September 4, Cline received a report of a tropical disturbance moving northward over Cuba, and on September 5, a telegraph from Key West, Florida, indicated that the disturbance was traveling northwest. While he did observe "rough seas with heavy southeast swells," on September 7, he had no indication that the storm reported over Cuba and Florida had abandoned its northward trajectory. The storm had turned into the Gulf of Mexico and was heading straight toward Galveston.

The storm's two days in the gulf was disastrous for two reasons. First, the warm ocean water served as a sort of battery for the storm, causing it to strengthen from the tropical disturbance reported over the telegraph to a full-fledged hurricane with winds blowing 130 miles an hour. Second, while the storm was over the ocean, no weather station could observe it. A ship in that area could have seen the storm, but since radio technology was still in its infancy at the time, the ship would have had no means to communicate its observations. This meant that Isaac Cline had no warning that the storm was bearing down on his city.

The hurricane struck Galveston in full force on Saturday, September 8, catching the city almost entirely unaware. At

11:45 A.M., Mr. Cline deployed his only means of communicating the danger to the public: a warning flag at the Weather Bureau office. By that point, even if the entire city could have seen the flag, there was no time to organize an evacuation.

Once the storm destroyed his instruments and tore down the warning flag, Cline left the bureau office. Wading through rapidly rising floodwater, Cline made his way to his family. Their home was well constructed, and about 50 people had taken shelter there. But before he could reach them, the storm surge ripped apart a railway trestle bridge and threw it "against the side of the house like a huge battering ram; the house creaked and was carried over in the surging waters and torn to pieces." Isaac rushed to save his family. He and his brother managed to rescue his three daughters, but tragically his wife, Cora Cline, was counted among the thousands who died that day.

The Great Galveston Hurricane was a terrible tragedy. But Category 4 hurricanes are not uncommon. Many have made landfall in the United States in the years since Galveston, and while they are no less dangerous now than they were then, we no longer count the dead by the thousands.

Take 2017's Hurricane Harvey. It was a Category 4 hurricane that made landfall on Texas's Gulf coast, remarkably similar to the Galveston storm. Harvey began its life in the middle of the Atlantic Ocean, far from any weather observation stations. But today, scientists from around the world use satellites from agencies like the National Oceanic and Atmospheric Administration, the National Aeronautics and Space Administration (NASA), the European Space Agency, and the Defense Meteorological Satellite Program to monitor and forecast weather over remote regions like the ocean. Even weather observations made by ships can be incorporated into forecasts, thanks to wireless communication.

Harvey made landfall in the early hours of August 26, 2017. Over the next several days, it flooded 300,000 buildings and 500,000 vehicles. FEMA reported 30,000 people rescued from the floodwaters and another 40,000 housed in emergency flooding shelters. Imagine what a difference a few days warning, trained emergency responders, and designated evacuation shelters could have made to the victims of the Galveston Hurricane. While Harvey tragically claimed the lives of 68 people, thousands were saved due to advanced warning of the storm.

Hurricanes and severe weather are a part of our world. We can't stop them, but we can understand them. While the Great Galveston Hurricane and Hurricane Harvey were remarkably similar storms, the death toll of the Galveston Hurricane was more than 100 times Harvey's. We were better equipped to track and predict Harvey, which allowed for timely emergency management, saving thousands of lives. The meteorological and technological advances of the past century may not be able to prevent hurricanes, but they can prepare us for them.

Madeline Clark Frank lives in Norman, Oklahoma, with her husband, Liam, and dog, Toby. She is a graduate student at the University of Oklahoma where she studies Arctic weather and sea ice.

After the Disaster: What Are the Next Steps?
Eloise Merrifield

On October 9, 2017, shortly after midnight, a wildfire started within the city limits of my hometown of Santa Rosa, California. By the time I woke up to the e-mail from my parents five hours later telling me that they and my sister were safe, 75 percent of the neighborhood I grew up in had already burned down. My parents were only passing along secondhand information, as they were on vacation in another part of the state and couldn't tell me whether our house was still there. The homes where I attended birthday parties, slumber parties, and was babysat were gone. And I was 100 miles away, using social media to get additional information to pass along to my parents. In the end my family was very lucky; our house survived, and my asthmatic father was able to stay out of the smoke zone an extra week.

The question that I was asking myself as we navigated the days after the fire was, as most of us do, what's next? It's a question no one expects to ask, even for people who, like me, grew up in the land of fire danger signs, very few legal fireworks, and a separate and recognized "fire season." I imagine it's the same for people growing up in lowlands near rivers or levees; all the preparation in the world for a catastrophic flood doesn't actually prepare you for what your life looks like when the water rises.

Modern life has some protective requirements that help, like homeowners insurance and disaster insurance (usually specific to the types of disasters in the geographic area), but it's one thing to know that you have the insurance and another to know how to get help from that insurance in the panicked moments while the dust is settling. Certain kinds of insurance are even required by law, making it easier to navigate the next steps. Luckily for the vast majority of people, their insurance companies have hotlines and general information lines that people can call to get that information. When a whole community is affected by a disaster like a flood, fire, or earthquake, relief organizations can also offer some of this direction. Where the insurance is required by law, cities may be able to provide that direction.

There are other purely legal protections for people who have been victimized by a natural disaster. What many people don't know is that many states have laws and statutes that are applicable only during the time of a declared emergency. In the state of California, the criminal statutes applicable to someone who is caught breaking into a building or home is different if the building or home is within the zone of a declared emergency. Laws specific to disaster or emergency zones usually have harsher penalties as well. This is not only to deter citizens from taking advantage of empty disaster zones but also to reflect the additional danger on law enforcement and emergency personnel who must respond to all reports of individuals in a disaster zone and put themselves at personal risk every time they respond. They also aim to discourage vigilant behavior from neighbors and homeowners around the evacuation area. These laws tend to be enforced only as long as evacuation orders are in place.

Disaster-specific laws do not target only people seeking to commit crimes on purpose. There are also laws and statutes passed to make sure that disaster victims do not also have to worry about abnormally raised prices on necessities. "Price gouging" can be a common tactic by landlords, grocers, and even gas stations that take advantage of desperate people needing to rent homes, buy food and water, or gas up to leave a disaster zone. These laws generally do not have accompanying harsh criminal penalties. They are less about creating harsh penalties for causing danger to emergency personnel or other citizens and more about discouraging opportunists from taking advantage of a natural disaster. The amount of time these laws tend to be enforced will vary dependent on the scope of the disaster and the amount of opportunistic behavior that is being reported.

So let's get back to that most important question anyone who has experienced a disaster has to ask himself or herself, "What do I do now?" The question is especially important because it will never have only one answer. The first step will be making sure to stay safe, and that's the easy part. As for those harder steps after that? That's trickier. What is right for each of us may be different, but we can at least take comfort in knowing that there are laws and policies that can protect us in times of disaster.

Eloise Merrifield grew up in California acutely aware of fire season every year after a small Independence Day grass fire during her childhood threatened her family home. An attorney who now works as a negotiator for a labor union, Ms. Merrifield previously had a criminal practice and was appointed defense counsel for clients accused of evacuation zone–specific crimes during the Valley Fire of 2015. A native of Sonoma County, Ms. Merrifield now lives and works in Sacramento.

Pele Says Hello
Chloe Olewitz

Pele was the first Hawaiian I met. Everywhere I went I heard about the goddess living in the volcano down the road. I learned how the sea winds changed with Pele's moods, shifting the plume of smoke where the lava flows from into the Pacific and texturing the island air. I learned two of Pele's best-known names: Pelehonuamea, she who shapes the sacred land, and Ka wahine 'ai honua, the woman who devours the land.

As Pele is revered for shaping the land, she is also credited with its destruction; she consumes land that is hers and births new land back into existence. And so we have Hawaii.

Pele has long lived in the Halema'uma'u Crater deep within Kilauea's summit caldera. But Pele doesn't just live in the volcano; Pele is the volcano. She is the rock of the island itself, as she is the lava red, yellow, spewing, stringed, slow, and dry. She is the foundation connecting lush green mountains to dense, wet jungle, linking flourishing farmland to endless ocean expanse.

My Own Story

On a bright January afternoon, I left my clothes in a heap on the black sand of Kehena Beach and dove into the sea with the rhythm of the weekly drum circle pounding behind me. I am a strong swimmer, but it was only by accident that I found myself in a depth of ocean beyond where I could stand. I swam in place, watching the tiny revelers drum on the faraway shore. I bobbed with the waves as they passed and laughed with the swimmers splashing around me.

When I decided to head toward the shore, I found that I couldn't get anywhere. The current was too strong and I was caught; the wills of the ocean and the moon and the earth pushed against each other, freezing my body where it was. I wasn't scared, but I was stuck.

"Ok, Pele," I said aloud. "I'll stay a little longer."

I accepted that I would return to land when Pele permitted me to, and I kept swimming. The black sand sparkled with millennia of volcanic memory along the beach. I had stopped trying to get to the shore because fighting felt futile and I was fine where I was.

Neither my brain nor my limbs were involved in the decision making when my body eventually started moving in the direction of the beach. It wasn't me; it was Pele. I felt her plant her big, strong, ocean-fingered hands on the cheeks of my behind, lifting me out of the water and depositing me on her shores.

After hours treading water I squished my toes into the sand and felt my feet balance on the earth. I bowed my head low and faced the open ocean, smiling: "Thank you, Pele."

Pele Speaks

In May 2018, Kilauea's steady flows erupted anew with volcanic activity. The mainland news narrative focused on the destruction and loss of property; photos of families evacuating their homes; and headlines detailing the ways manufactured neighborhoods with generic names were being swallowed up whole by the flows. But for native Hawaiians, the volcanic activity was neither surprising nor distressing. It was just Pele.

For the short time I lived on Hawaii, my world was imbued with spirit, with mana, and fire-fueled by Pele's whims. I am a white woman from New York City. I am neither a Hawaiian resident nor native Hawaiian. But I bowed down to the goddess while I rested on her back, and I bowed down to her from the mainland many years later, watching her spirit flow forth from the fissures in her skin.

Life in Hawaii is built atop a reverence for the goddess with whom all Hawaiians cohabitate, on whose earthly body they pass their years. If Pele hungers or if she rages, if she wants for land, the land was only ever Pele to begin with. "Tūtū Pele," grandmother, they call her, "this is your land, take it."

Pele in Sight

Hawaii Volcanoes National Viewing Park stops at a certain point. The National Park Service erects barricades to delineate the official viewing area. Hopping the fence is illegal but it is done, particularly at four in the morning with the blessing and guidance of a native Hawaiian or two. We were warned the walk across the desolate lava fields would take up to two hours. Bring sweaters, we were told, and water. Bring flashlights.

Because I continue to be raised by spiritual, goddess-worshipping women, I was prepared for devotion to the feminine divine. I brought Pele an offering as best as I knew how: a fresh banana leaf I'd found loose on the ground that morning, the dried husk of a flower from a fruit-bearing tree that had fallen hard on the roof of my hut the week before, and a packet of sugar. I stuffed my gifts into my pockets and set out across the hard black earth, with my flashlight illuminating a path in the pure darkness that spread out all around us.

I have been described as agile and surefooted. I am not clumsy. But within five minutes of our excursion beyond the official park fence, I tripped so violently that everything went flying from my pockets and my hands. My flashlight clicked itself off. I was a pancake laid flat on the ground. Shaken, I picked up my pieces, stuffed my pockets, dusted off my knees, and hurried to catch up with the rest of the group.

Not three steps on, I was again splayed out on the earth. I stopped there in a heap on Pele's back and I heard her demand. We laughed as I began to make my offering. Pele would wait no longer for her gift. I positioned the fruits and the flowers there where I knelt and I touched my palms to the lava. I strung together a prayer.

"I hear you, Tūtū Pele," I whispered. "You can have it. Yes, right away. This is yours, anyway. Take it."

Chloe Olewitz is a freelance writer from New York City. Her creative nonfiction and journalism have been published in Playboy, Roads & Kingdoms, i-D, Brooklyn Magazine, Athleta Magazine, Gigantic Sequins, *and more.*

Some Confessions of a Lifelong Storm Chaser
Lane Ponsart

In 1996 a certain movie was released to the big screen you may have heard of: *Twister!* Bill "The Extreme" Harding had made a career-shaking decision to leave the dusty off-roads of chasing tornadoes with his soon-to-be ex-wife Jo and their motley crew of weather-loving misfits. He headed for the cultured, urban, stable future work as on-camera meteorologist for a television news station and making a new life, a normal life, with his future Mrs. Harding, Dr. Melissa Reeves.

Twister captured the hearts and minds of thousands of future storm chasers. Many credit the movie as their sole inspiration to enter the world of intercepting violent weather, while those of us already storm chasing also watched and rewatched the blockbuster with cult-like adoration, unable to breathe some moments, cheering with the lungs of lions at others.

It hit the screens at a time in my life when I was burning out from a profession that, while I was exceptionally good at, had lost its former glory and was ultimately soul-sucking. Worse, to stay at the top of my game in that field, I had been giving up my one true, lifelong love: weather. *Twister* did not mark the beginning of the big chase for me. However, by 1996, pursuing money was a top priority no more, and after seeing *Twister*, every job, even every place I have chosen to live since, has been a means to an end for my lifelong pursuit of wild weather. Bill, Jo, Dusty, and crew helped jolt me back to my senses. Life is too short, not to chase one's dreams.

You might have read that last paragraph and thought that it sure sounds like a closer. But if I stopped now, where would you get to hear of some of my favorite personal stories?

Let me begin by stating some things maybe not so obvious. Most storm chasers are not ambulance chasers. We don't go around looking for death and destruction, even though there is plenty of it with extreme weather. Most of us do not have a degree in meteorology, or even work in the field. But it is probably safe to say that most of us have some interest in science, at least the science of weather!

How did it start for me? Water, meet heaven. Have you ever watched as water goes round and round a drain and found yourself losing a bit of time transfixed while it spins and spins and spins? I guess one could say that my very first chasing began as a toddler, because that was my favorite activity. I was gaga goo goo all over that.

I was driving westbound along Highway 183 in central Texas on this pitch-black night, illuminated only briefly by flashes of lighting and some hints that civilization was somewhere nearby when the base of clouds picked up a touch of color from some distant small town somewhere. The storm was on its way to being a big-time tornado, and I was chasing this one solo.

I had no onboard radar back then. My cell phone was barely a glorified pager that could sometimes double as a talking device, signal permitting. While driving the curvaceous roads of the Texas Hill Country, I was lucky just to flip through the few working channels on my NOAA weather radio.

Finally! A hill a few miles from a town with at least something that could pass for a view, despite the black, black dark of deep night. Thick cedar trees were all around. The Hill Country is more aptly known as Flash Flood Alley than tornado alley, and navigating this HP supercell in the dark, alone, meant the last place I wanted to be was down in some valley. So this tree-covered hill it was.

I park. But soon I was not alone. Turns out several other members of a Texas chase team I would later join up with also chose this spot to stop. Fortunate, as what was to come would make all of the hairs on our collective necks stand straight up.

Still dark. Very dark. The rain had since stopped. Quiet. Too quiet. Then, out of nowhere, that telltale sound of a locomotive. Louder and louder and louder still. The wind began picking up a little as we all locked eyes with one another in between turning our attentions to where the sound was coming from and attempting to get a lay of the land for anything that might pass for shelter. I could feel my racing heart leap up into my throat, choking off any chance to blurt out words as that devastating sound closed in on our location, rounding the corner, overtaking the tracks hidden by the thick forest all around us until it was just too late.

What a night! We followed that parent supercell as a group for at least another hour, chaser lights glaring as we drove through the nearest town with its tornado sirens blaring, trying to catch up with this fast-moving monster going at least 60 miles per hour. That was our speed, in 40-mile-per-hour zones. You see, the storm didn't have to worry about navigating roads, stop signs, tree limbs, and the like. Most chases actually end in a bust, and I wouldn't trade that night for anything.

Some of my very best "catches" have actually been nothing more than my being in the right place, at the right time, knowing what I was looking at and looking for. Hence, lifestyle can help. One has to be somewhat flexible about things if one wants to be a storm chaser and not just a "chaser." Oh, I'm that, too. Lots of enjoyment in kicking back in a lounger watching others intercept storms over livestreams, or watching Mr. Jim Cantore himself on The Weather Channel.

Yes, severe weather is often very tragic, and I've seen it up close and personal all too often. I have been in those communities as a tornado has wrapped stop signs around itself and hurled cars into bedrooms as children and parents huddled in their designated storm shelter, and as huge hail blasted holes the size of bowling balls into the roofs of well-built homes and crushed the cars outside with the force of the softball-sized meteors traveling over 100 miles per hour that they are.

Once while chasing inside the core of a hurricane, a brief spin-up crossed the road right ahead of me, tossing vehicles. During another hurricane making landfall, a waterspout formed within 50 yards right before my eyes while I was standing out on the balcony of our hotel room, took direct aim at us, and lifted only within moments of impact. Both of those events were a wee bit too close for comfort. I like to keep a little more distance, you know. But then, weather does whatever it wants to. Wouldn't trade it for anything in the world.

Lane Ponsart is a storm chaser from Austin, Texas, who forecasts and intercepts hurricanes, tornadoes, floods, and more primarily in the United States. He works full-time as a storm restoration specialist in the building industry and volunteers regularly for several weather safety organizations such as Skywarn and CFHC. When not immersed in weather-related activities, Lane also enjoys board games, virtual reality, and reading and writing about economics and politics.

4 Profiles

Much can be learned about the topic of natural disasters in a review of individuals and organizations that have played an important role in the field over the years. This chapter contains brief sketches of some of those individuals and organizations. Given the number of fields encompassed by the title "natural disasters," the number of possible subjects for such sketches is very large indeed. The items suggested for this chapter, then, have been selected to provide an overview of the range of individuals and organizations whose primary interest has been the overall field of natural disasters or of some specific type of such events.

American Red Cross

The history of the American Red Cross, and its international agency, Red Cross and Red Crescent, is one of the great stories of humanitarian aid for those suffering from natural or human-made disasters. That story begins in 1859, when Swiss businessman Henry Dunant was motivated to provide medical assistance to the wounded in both sides of the battle between Franco-Sardinian and Austrian troops clash at the Battle of Solferino. Seventeen years later, a committee formed by Dunant and four colleagues created the International Committee

---

Charles Richter, the California physicist who invented the Richter scale in 1935, in his seismology laboratory in Pasadena, California, 1972. The Richter scale is used worldwide to measure the magnitude of earthquakes. (Bettmann/Getty Images)

of the Red Cross, whose flag is the reverse of the Swiss flag. A year later, in 1864, 10 nations signed the First Geneva Convention guaranteeing medical assistance to military combatants and individuals providing those services.

In 1881, American nurse Clara Barton set out to form a national chapter of the International Red Cross, a year before the United States itself ratified the Geneva Convention. The organization's first chapter was established in Dansville, New York, in August of that year, and a month later, the organization provided its first rescue services to victims of widespread forest fires in Michigan. Other early events at which the Red Cross provided relief services were the Johnstown flood of 1889, the hurricane that struck the Sea Islands off South Carolina in 1893, survivors of the Turkish genocide of Armenians in 1896, and the late stages of the Spanish-American War in 1898.

Today, the American Red Cross responds to some type of disaster every eight minutes. These disasters range from simple home fires to widespread natural disasters that cover multiple states. The major services offered by the organization include the following:

- Overnight shelter and meals for individuals who have lost their own housing in a disaster
- Emergency supplies ranging from toothbrushes and toothpaste to shovels, rakes, and tarps
- Medical and mental health volunteer workers who travel to a disaster site and provide first aid, prescription medication services, dental attention, replacement eyeglasses, and other services
- Meals provided both to individuals housed in shelters and to those remaining in their homes by way of food delivery vehicles
- Volunteer workers who provide all types of physical services to displaced survivors and their properties

- Emergency vehicles used to transport injured individuals and the meals, medical supplies, and other materials needed by injured, stranded, or otherwise incapacitated individuals

The Red Cross also provides services that may not be directly related to disaster relief. For example, its blood donation project now provides about 40 percent of all the blood products used in the United States. The service was first provided in the 1940s for use with military personnel. That effort eventually resulted in the collection of more than 13 million pints of blood. The Red Cross also responded to other military-related needs during the war, such as enrolling more than 100,000 nurses for military service, shipping about 300,000 tons of personal supplies overseas, and preparing 27 million food and supply packages for American personnel and prisoners of war.

Training and certification programs continue to be an important part of Red Cross services. Today the organization offers such programs in the fields of first aid, cardiopulmonary resuscitation (CPR), automated external defibrillation, basic life support and CPR for health care providers, babysitting and childcare, swimming and water safety, lifeguarding, training and testing in certified nurse assistant positions, and instructor training in lifesaving skills.

Americares

Americares is a U.S.-based relief organization that grew out of an event that occurred during the Vietnam War. In April 1975, a planeload of Vietnamese orphans crashed in the jungle near the city of Tan Son Nhut, killing a third of the children and leaving the remainder badly injured. When the U.S. military said that it could not send aid or rescue assistance for more than a week, the leader of a paper manufacturing operation, Robert C. Macauley, and his wife mortgaged their home in order to rent a Boeing 747 airplane. The plane was used to fly the survivors of the crash to safety in California.

When word of the Macauleys work began to spread, they were asked to carry out similar operations for stranded and/or injured men, women, and children around the world. Americares grew out of those efforts. The organization was formally incorporated in 1979 as a 501(c)(3) organization. As of 2017, Americares was the 10th-largest charitable organization in the United States, with revenues of $915 million. In addition to its home office in Stamford, Connecticut, Americares has country offices in El Salvador, Haiti, India, the Philippines, Nepal, Liberia, and Tanzania. Overall, it provides some type of aid to more than 160 countries around the world.

Americares supports four major relief and aid programs: emergency services, access to medicine, clinical services, and community health. The organization's approach to emergency services consists of three phases: ready, respond, and recovery. The first stage involves the pre-positioning of supplies needed for a disaster, guidance for communities in preparation for such events, and training of personnel for dealing with a disaster. The respond phase consists of immediate marshaling of personnel and resources at the site of a disaster. In the recovery phase, Americares remains in a country for months or years, during which it assists in rebuilding hospitals and clinics and addressing other health needs of the community.

The Access to Medicine arm of Americares aims to provide free medicines and medical suppliers in countries where such materials are in otherwise short supply. It also includes training of medical personnel and education for the general community about health issues. As of 2016, Americares supported all types of health services in 91 countries, working with 7,125 local health care partners on a total of 86 specific projects with a total aid package valued at $632 million.

Disaster Research Center (University of Delaware)

The University of Delaware's Disaster Research Center (DRC) was founded in 1963 at the Ohio State University by three scholars interested in better understanding human responses to major natural and technological disasters. The concept for the center developed during the time when the U.S. government was concerned about the possibility of nuclear attacks and the possible effects of those attacks on civil society. Its early funding was obtained by the federal government's interest in learning more about this eventuality.

Research programs at DRC are classified into five major categories: infrastructure risk management, public health, protective actions, warning and risk perceptions, and response. Some examples of research conducted in these areas of resilient warning systems for tornadoes and flash floods are dynamic integration of natural, human, and infrastructure systems for hurricane evacuation and sheltering; promoting community resilience in New York City after Hurricane Sandy; Haiti earthquake, the forgotten aspects of evacuation; Tohoku earthquake and tsunami, post-earthquake fires; northwest China extreme weather disaster, interagency coordination response; Moore, Oklahoma, tornado response and recovery; and post-Nepal earthquake infant feeding, maternal vulnerability, and well-being.

DRC offers programs at both the undergraduate and graduate levels. The former consists of a BA concentration in the area of emergency and environmental management. A much broader group of options is available at the graduate level, where students can work toward a master's degree in disaster science and management, civil engineering, sociology, and emergency managements. PhD programs in disaster science and management, civil infrastructure systems, and sociology are also available. Graduates of a DRC program most commonly take jobs in academia in disaster-related fields or with federal or state disaster relief organizations.

One of the DRC's most important features is the E. L. Quarantelli Resource Collection, named after one of the center's founders. The collection currently consists of more than 125,000 books, monographs, research reports, documents, and other publications, many of which are not available from any other source. Of special interest is a directory of all publications produced at DRC from its founding in 1963 to the current date. More than 500 titles are listed in the directory, all of which can be accessed from the university library.

Earthquake Engineering Research Institute

The Earthquake Engineering Research Institute (EERI) was founded in 1948 as an offshoot of an earlier Advisory Committee on Engineering Seismology of the U.S. Coast and Geodetic Survey. Members of the committee became frustrated at the government's unwillingness to adopt its suggestions and decided to form an independent organization. An initial meeting of those interested in such a project consisted of 16 members from a variety of fields, such as engineering, geoscience, building administration, and architecture. The original bylaws required, more specifically, that EERI members come from at least three fields: professional practice, teaching and research, and government regulation. The primary purpose of the organization was to discover the reasons that buildings crumble and fall during an earthquake and what can be done to prevent such disasters.

At its founding EERI decided that its ultimate goal was to have its own research laboratory. That goal was never achieved, and the organization today serves primarily as a clearing house for research results from projects conducted at a wide variety of academic and governmental laboratories. The organization has shared office space with the Seismological Society of America since 1973 and is currently located in downtown Oakland, California. In 1984, the institute began publishing a quarterly journal, *Earthquake Spectra*, which remains in print today. The journal carries information on recent research and other topics of interest to specialists in the field. In 1966, the organization also began publishing a monthly newsletter focusing on association news, employment opportunities, a calendar of coming events, and related topics. In 2013, EERI initiated yet another new publication, a bimonthly online newsletter, *The Pulse of Earthquake Engineering*. Again, the publication has focused on recent earthquake news, as well as information about the association.

An important aspect of EERI's work is projects it sponsors, manages, and coordinates. Some of these projects have dealt with topics such as Learning from Earthquakes; the Concrete Coalition; Mitigation Center Earthquake Scenarios; Confined Masonry Network; Earthquake Clearinghouses; School Earthquake Safety Initiative; and the Friedman Family Visiting Professionals Program. (For detailed information about these projects, see https://www.eeri.org/eeri-projects-overview-and-search/.) Some of the work carried out by EERI occurs through one of 14 regional chapters, which give members an opportunity to get together and discuss problems of mutual interest. Those chapters are located in Alaska, British Columbia, the Great Lakes region, the District of Columbia region, New England, New Madrid, New York and the Northeast, northern California, Oregon, Sacramento, San Diego, Southern California, Utah, and Washington State. The association also sponsors 78 student chapters around the world, including groups in Canada, Chile, Dominican Republic, Egypt, England, India, Italy, Malaysia, Mexico, Pakistan, Peru, Puerto Rico, Romania, and Turkey.

EERI's Legislation Action Center provides information to members about legislative activity relating to earthquakes and earthquake safety. The center also develops and publishes white papers on a variety of policy issues, such as "Mitigation of Nonstructural Hazards in Schools," "Creating Earthquake Resilient Communities," "National Earthquake Hazards Reduction Program," and "Improve Reliability of Lifeline Infrastructure Systems."

Federal Emergency Management Agency

The Federal Emergency Management Agency (FEMA) was established in 1979 by President Jimmy Carter in Executive

Order 12148. Carter's order revoked all or part of a dozen earlier executive orders creating a number of agencies designed to assist Americans before, during, or as a result of natural or man-made disasters. Some of the agencies and authorities subsumed in the executive order were the National Fire Prevention and Control Administration; National Academy for Fire Prevention and Control; Emergency Broadcast System; and Federal Flood Insurance Act of 1956, National Flood Insurance Act of 1968, and Flood Disaster Protection Act of 1973. FEMA was also provided with a number of new responsibilities in the order. The origin of the federal government's role in disaster management actually dates back to a piece of legislation passed in 1803 that provides financial assistance to a New Hampshire town that had been devastated by fire.

The agency's current mission is to "coordinate the federal government's role in preparing for, preventing, mitigating the effects of, responding to, and recovering from all domestic disasters, whether natural or man-made, including acts of terror." Among the specific areas for which FEMA now has responsibility (taken from the 2018 Organizational Chart) are Resilience, Federal Insurance and Mitigation, National Preparedness, Response and Recovery, the U.S. Fire Administration, and Faith-Based and Neighborhood Partnerships. In 2017, the agency announced a five-year strategic plan developed with the assistance of state, local, tribal, and territorial governments; nongovernmental organizations; the private sector; and FEMA employees from all parts of the agency. The three overarching goals of that plan are designed to help FEMA build a culture of preparedness, ready the nation for catastrophic disasters, and reduce the complexity of FEMA. (For details of the plan, see https://www.fema.gov/media-library-data/1533052524696-b5137201a4614ade5e0129ef01cbf661/strat_plan.pdf.) At one time an independent agency, FEMA was moved to the new Department of Homeland Security in 2003, following the creation of that agency.

Although FEMA is probably best known for its post-disaster recovery programs, it also has other tasks designed to reduce the risk of natural and man-made disasters. As one example, FEMA's Project Impact was created to help individuals and communities build structures that are better able to survive disasters. The project has been demonstrated to reduce losses resulting from flooding and other disasters. Another example is the U.S. Fire Administration's Fire Is Everyone's Fight™ program, which makes available a variety of educational materials about fires in the form of media tool kits, pictographs, stock photos, videos, and B-rolls.

In the event of a disaster, FEMA acts as the coordinating agency for all federal agencies with specific types of assistance. Those agencies are responsible for 15 major aspects of a disaster (with responsible agency(ies) in parentheses): Transportation (Department of Transportation), Communications (National Communication System), Public Works and Engineering (U.S. Army Corps of Engineers, Department of Defense), Fire Fighting (U.S. Forest Service, Department of Agriculture), Information and Planning (FEMA), Mass Care (American Red Cross), Resource Support (General Services Administration), Health and Medical Services (U.S. Public Health Service, Department of Health and Human Services), Urban Search and Rescue (FEMA), Hazardous Materials (Environmental Protection Agency), Food (Food and Nutrition Service, Department of Agriculture), Energy (Department of Energy), Public Safety and Security (Department of Homeland Security, Department of Justice), Long-Term Community Recovery and Mitigation (Department of Homeland Security, Emergency Preparedness and Response, FEMA), and External Affairs Annex (Department of Homeland Security, FEMA).

The first step in mobilizing FEMA to deal with a disaster is for the president to declare a national disaster following an earthquake, flood, forest fire, landslide, or some other catastrophic event. This step usually follows an attempt by local and/or state governments to deal with the disaster. If state and local resources are not adequate to adequately resolve results of the disaster, FEMA may be notified, after which the agency recommends to the president the use of federal resources or not. At the point, the agency can begin to place into motion its (often complex) series of responses, depending on the type of disaster, the response of other stakeholders, and other factors. The types of aid provided tend to fall into three general categories: housing, medical, and property. FEMA is usually able to provide temporary housing (e.g., trailers) for individuals and families who have lost their own lodging. The agency can also make grants for individuals to repair or rebuild their homes. Medical assistance normally comes in the form of immediate aid, such as volunteer physicians, dentists, pharmacists, and other specialists, to deal with medical problems. Property loss can be handled with storage, transport, and replacement of physical property lost in a disaster. It may also be dealt with by the rebuilding of roads, bridges, sewer lines, and other types of infrastructure. Debris removal may also be a feature of property assistance.

FEMA has often been the subject of criticism for its failure to act quickly enough or with adequate resources. Its role in dealing with Hurricane Katrina in 2005 and Hurricane Maria in 2017 is just two examples of such problems. In both cases, critics argued that the agency was not adequately prepared to handle disasters of the size of these two events, was too slow to move aid to individuals and communities who needed it, did not sufficiently make use of individual agencies responsible for certain functions, and, in general, did not efficiently carry out the response the agency was expected to provide. One attempt to deal with purported FEMA shortcomings was the Post-Katrina Emergency Management Reform Act of 2006. That act attempted to rectify some of the failures for which FEMA was criticized in its handling of the hurricane. Those changes included paying greater attention to people with disabilities, developing systems for locating family members who have been separated from each other, improving the system for transporting individuals who have been displaced by a disaster, and devising systems for working one on one with problems faced by survivors of a disaster.

Tetsuya Fujita (1920–1998)

A number of scales have been devised over the years to describe the wind speed in a tropical storm, tornado, or other extreme weather event. The system most widely used of these systems for tornadoes is some form of the Fujita Tornado Scale, first announced by Japanese American meteorologist Tetsuya Fujita in 1971. That scale has undergone a number of revisions; the form in which it most commonly occurs is called the Enhanced Fujita Scale. The scale is used for wind speeds and the damage they cause from EF-0 ("light," 65–85 miles per hour) to EF-5 ("incredible," more than 200 miles per hour). Fujita was also the discoverer of *microbursts*, sudden, very strong but short-lived, downflows of air from a thundercloud. Fujita identified these previously unknown wind patterns in 1975 while studying the crash of Eastern Airlines Flight 66 at New York's JFK airport. He was able to later show that other previously unexplained air accidents resulted from the same phenomenon.

Fujita was born on October 23, 1920, in Kitakyushu City, on the southernmost island of Kyushu, Japan. His parents were Tomojiro and Yoshie; both of whom were teachers when they first met. After completing his secondary education in the small town of Nakasone, he matriculated at Meiji College in Fukuoka, Kyushu, in 1941. He had originally planned to attend Hiroshima College on the main island of Honshu but changed his plans at the urging of his father. That decision was crucial, since Fujita would almost certainly have been killed during the first atomic bombing of the city of Hiroshima in 1945. As it was, he survived the second atom bombing on Nagasaki when the U.S. Air Force changed its target (from a point near Meiji) because of weather conditions.

Fujita graduated from Meiji in 1943 with a degree in mechanical engineering. A year later, he was invited by the school to become an assistant professor of physics. (The institution had by that time changed its name to the Kyushu Institute of Technology.) Over the next two years, Fujita had the opportunity to study a number of examples of wind patterns following bombing events and severe storms. One of the most important of these experiences occurred while he was observing a thunderstorm at Mount Seburiyama. From his study of the event, he had the first glimmers of a weather pattern that involved a downward flow of cold air with a surrounding envelope of warm air, the basic principle behind downbursts. In a fortuitous act of hope, Fujita sent a copy of his report of the thunderstorm to Horace Byers, then professor and chair of the University of Chicago meteorology department. Byers responded favorably to Fujita's communication, and the exchange established a long-term relationship between the two men.

In the meantime, Fujita continued his doctoral studies in Tokyo, working on a thesis "Analytical Study of Typhoons." The thesis was approved in 1953, and Fujita was awarded his doctorate. Within a matter of months, Byers had offered, and Fujita had accepted, a job in Chicago as a research associate in the meteorology department. He was later (1956) named director of the department's Mesometeorology Research Project, associate professor of geophysical sciences in 1962, and professor in 1965. From 1964 to 1987, Fujita also served as director of the Satellite and Mesometeorology Research Project and as director of the Wind Research Laboratory from 1988 until his death. On his retirement in 1990, Fujita was named Charles Merriam Distinguished Service Professor. Fujita died in Chicago on November 19, 1998. In recognition of his many accomplishments in the field, Fujita has often been called "Mr. Tornado."

Fujita was recognized with a number of honors and awards during his lifetime, including the National Aeronautics and Space Administration's Public Service Medal (1979); the

Vermeil Gold Medal of the French National Academy of Air and Space (1989); Order of the Sacred Treasure, Gold and Silver Star (1991); Clarence Leroy Meisinger Award of the American Meteorological Society (1967); and Award of Outstanding Contribution to Applied Meteorology of the American Meteorological Society (1988). In 2007, the National Weather Association created the Dr. T. Theodore Fujita Research Achievement Award in recognition of achievements in operational meteorology. In 1997, Fujita was personally decorated by Japanese prime minister Kaifu and blessed by Emperor Akihito.

Landslides Hazards Program

The Landslides Hazards Program (LHP) is a division of the U.S. Geological Survey (USGS). It was created as part of the Disasters Relief Act of 1974 (the "Stafford Act"). The LHP partners with other organizations to determine where landslides and mudslides are likely to occur, what size and speed they may have, and what can be done to avoid or mitigate the effects caused by such events. To achieve this objective, the LHP works with nearly four dozen institutional and organizational partners, such as the Arizona Geological Survey, Bureau of Indian Affairs, CAL FIRE, Chinese Academy of Sciences, Colorado School of Mines, Coweeta Experimental Forest, Elliott State Forest, Istituto di Ricerca per la Protezione Idrogeologica (Italy), Kyoto University (Japan), Mesa County (Colorado), National Park Service, Portland State University, Sound Transit, U.S. Army Corps of Engineers, University of Bologna (Italy), University of Lausanne (Switzerland), University of Puerto Rico at Mayagüe, and the Washington Geological Survey.

In addition to its Emergency Assessment of Post-Fire Debris-Flow Hazards program, designed to estimate the probability of the occurrence and characteristics of landslides, LHP has developed a Flash-Flood and Debris-Flow Early-Warning

System that predicts the risk of flood and debris flow in regions where recent forest fires have occurred. In addition to these functions, LHP has an extensive educational function. A major feature of that element is basic information about landslides for state geologists and geological surveys and for the general public.

Possibly the most complete description of the LHP can be found in a special report issued in 2003 outlining the key elements of a national strategy for identifying landslide risks in the United States and methods for the mitigation and relief of such events.

Giuseppe Mercalli (1850–1914)

Mercalli is best known today for his invention of a scale for expressing the intensity of an earthquake. Earthquake scales are generally one of two types; the first, like Mercalli's, is based on its observable effects on humans and the environment. The second measures Earth movements. Scales of the first type are, of course, somewhat objective but very useful in indicating the damage done by a tremor. The latter are more objective but not always as helpful to a person wanting to know how destructive an event has been. Mercalli's scale was a modification of an earlier device invented by Italian seismologist Michele Stefano Conte de Rossi and Swiss scientist François-Alphonse Forel in the late 19th century. Mercalli actually devised two scales, the first of which (1883) consisted of 6 levels of intensity and the second (1902) 10 levels. The Mercalli scale has been modified numerous times since its invention, most importantly in 1931 by American seismologists Harry Wood and Frank Neumann. That revision differs from the original Mercalli scale in terms of the detail with which each level is described.

Giuseppe Mercalli was born in Milan on May 21, 1850, to Carlo and Carolina (De Simone) Mercalli, the third son of five children. Mercalli was educated at home before enrolling at the Monza Seminary in Milan. There he studied for the priesthood and came under the tutelage of Antonio Stoppani, then one of the most highly respected geologists of his day. He was ordained in 1874 and chose to begin a career in research and teaching rather than working as a religious adviser. Mercalli's first teaching assignment was as professor of natural sciences at his alma mater, the Monza Seminary. After some years there, he came under suspicion of being too liberal for the institution and was dismissed from his post. His career was salvaged, however, when the Italian government provided him with an appointment as professor at the Domodossola lyceum. He then moved to the Reggio di Calabria, a position he sought because of its vulnerabilities to earthquakes. By this time, the topic had become one of primary interest to Mercalli for both his research and teaching assignments.

In 1892, Mercalli applied for the post of mineralogy and geology at the University of Catania but did not obtain the job. Instead, he took a position as high school teacher at the Regio Liceo ("royal high school") Vittorio Emanuele in Naples, where he remained until 1911. In that year, he was appointed director of the Istituto Nazionale di Geofisica e Vulcanologia, near the famous volcano Mount Vesuvius, where he spent the rest of his life. He died in Naples on March 19, 1914, under somewhat mysterious circumstances. At first, his death was reported to have occurred when he was burned to death as the result of an overturned oil lamp in his home (*New York Times*, March 19, 1914). A few days later, however, Italian police announced that his death was more likely the result of a robbery, in which he was strangled, coated with oil, and then set afire.

In addition to his teaching responsibilities, Mercalli was a prodigious writer on scientific topics, having produced about 150 peer-reviewed papers during his life. Probably the most important of these works were the monograph *I vulcani attivi della Terra* (*The Active Volcanoes of the Earth*) and additional monographs on specific earthquakes at Casamicciola (1883), the Pontine Islands (1892), Messina (1908), Stromboli (1888),

Lombardy (1884), Lecco (1887), and Andalusia (1897). He also served as editor of *Notizie vesuviane* (*Vesuvian News*) from 1901 to 1907.

National Integrated Drought Information System

Drought is a normal, recurrent aspect of weather patterns in the United States. That trend is especially true in the western part of the country, where serious droughts occur at least a few times in every decade. In the mid-1930s, for example, drought covered at least 60 percent of the land area of the country. Since 2000, about 30 percent of all land area was designated as being in "severe" or "extreme" drought.

In June 2004, the Western Governors' Association issued a report called "Creating a Drought Early Warning System for the 21st Century." The report called for congressional action to create an agency that could "improv[e] collaboration among scientists and managers to enhance the effectiveness of observation networks, monitoring, prediction, information delivery, and applied research and to foster public understanding of and preparedness for drought." The Congress responded to that recommendation by passing the National Integrated Drought Information System (NIDIS) Act in 2006. The act created an interagency, multiple-partner approach to the study of drought and development of programs to deal with such conditions. The agency was to act under the general supervision of the National Oceanic and Atmospheric Administration (NOAA).

NIDIS programs fall into three general categories: planning and preparation, education, and recovery. The planning and preparation rubric, in turn, consists of three major activities: regional meetings, tabletop exercises, and webinars. Some of the programs in the first category have been workshops on Western States Drought Coordinators and Emergency Managers Meeting (2015, in Seattle), Drought Impacts Monitoring Meeting (2013, in Tucson, Arizona), Building a Sustainable Network of Drought Communities (2011, in Chicago), and Status of Drought Early Warning Systems in the United States (2008, in Kansas City, Missouri). Tabletop exercises are gaming events in which participants consider hypothetical drought events for which they must develop a response to drought conditions. Events in the webinar series have been programs on "Using NASA Tools to Manage Drought"; "The Missing Piece, a Discussion of the Arizona DroughtWatch Program"; "Colorado Water Conservation Board's Approach to Impacts Assessment"; and "Citizen Science Observation Networks."

The education arm of NIDIS includes programs for the general public and for students and teachers. Some products that have been included in the former include "Drought Preparedness and Water Conservation," "Understanding Drought (a training video)," and "Reducing the Impact of Disasters through Education," an online program focusing on basic drought information and links to helpful websites. The recovery section of the NIDIS program provides links to resources dealing with both short-term and long-term drought relief and recovery, such as the Farm Service Agency, Rural Development Program, Emergency Watershed Protection Program, Endangered Species Act, Risk Management Agency, Wetlands Reserve Program, and Conservation Technical Assistance Program.

An important feature was added to NIDIS in 2016 when former president Barack Obama created the National Drought Resilience Partnership, a partnership of seven federal agencies to help communities, businesses, farmers and ranchers, and other individuals to better prepare for and deal with the consequences of drought. The agencies involved are the U.S. Department of Agriculture, National Oceanic and Atmospheric Administration, Department of the Interior, Assistant Secretary of the Army for Civil Works, Federal Emergency Management Agency, Environmental Protection Agency, and U.S. Department of Energy.

Natural Hazards Center (University of Colorado)

The Natural Hazards Center (NHC) at the University of Colorado was established in 1975 following a two-year project by a group of social scientists at the university designed to determine the then current state of natural disaster research in the United States. The center was originally called the Natural Hazards Research and Applications Information Center, a name reflecting its two main missions: (1) to develop a rational basis for determining how best to spend taxpayer dollars on hazard research and (2) to develop a better system for deciding how to spend research dollars on hazards research. Today, the center's mission has expanded to include technological and human-caused disasters, as well as natural disasters. It includes all disasters in its agenda and uses a multidisciplinary approach to problem solving. Researchers at the center currently come from a variety of fields, including computer science, behavioral science, environmental studies, women and gender studies, anthropology, communication, geography, information science, architecture and planning, sociology, and education.

An overview of the types of research undertaken at the center is reflected in titles of some current projects, such as "Safer, Stronger, Smarter: A Guide to Improving School Natural Hazard Safety—Webinar Development"; "Demographic and Health Disparities in Recovery from Hurricane Katrina"; "The Risk Landscape of Earthquakes Induced by Deep Wastewater Injection"; and "A Risk-Informed Decision Framework to Achieve Resilient and Sustainable Buildings That Meet Community Objectives."

The center produces three regular publications for specialists in the field and the general public. "Natural Disaster Hazards Research" provides summaries of latest research, news of NHC events, new web resources, conferences and events, a jobs listing, and current educational resources sponsored by the center. "Natural Hazards Observer" is a monthly publication that focuses on current research in the field, much of which is understandable to the general public, as well as useful to specialists in the field. "Research Counts" is an online publication that provides information on current and recent research projects, lessons learned from disasters, and suggestions for new questions to be studied. The articles represent a wide variety of disciplines and are intended for the general public. The center website also contains a searchable database of publications on natural disasters, HazLib. The database can be accessed at http://hazlib.colorado.edu/.

An item of particular interest on the NHC website is its Quick Response Reports. These reports are produced by researchers who travel to the site of a disaster as soon after it occurs as possible. The reports take the form of a traditional scientific article that contains "perishable" data that can be used for researchers in their later studies of such events. The center has recently joined with Columbia University Press in the publication of a new series on Society and the Environment. The first two books in the series are to be *Underwater: Balancing Flood Risk and Real Estate Value in America's Coastal Cities* and *The Plant that Really Pollutes*.

Christopher G. Newhall (1948–)

Newhall is an American volcanologist who, with colleague Stephen Self, devised the Volcanic Explosivity Index (VEI 7), a mechanism for expressing the intensity of a volcanic eruption. They developed the system in 1982, while both were working at the University of Hawaii. It was based on a study of severe volcanic eruptions that have occurred in recorded history and has been used as a possible guide for future severe volcanic events. The VEI scale consists of eight categories, ranging from 0 (no eruption at all) to 8 (very large). These categories are defined by the amount of material ejected during an eruption, ranging from 0.0001 cubic kilometers of material at the lowest range of the scale to 1,000 cubic kilometers at the upper end of the scale. In their original paper on the topic, Newhall and Self used specific examples of historic volcanic eruptions to illustrate each category on the scale.

Christopher G. Newhall was born in Quincy, California, on October 30, 1948. He attended the University of California at Davis, from which he received his BS and MS degrees in 1970 and 1977, respectively. From 1970 to 1972 and from 1974 to 1976, Newhall served as a Peace Corp volunteer in the Philippine Islands. His assignment there was to teach geology at Aquinas University in Legazpi City in the province of Albay. On his return to the United States, he matriculated at Dartmouth College, from which he received his PhD in 1980. From 1977 to 2005, Newhall served with the Volcanic Hazards Program of the U.S. Geological Survey, while simultaneously working as affiliate professor in the Department of Earth and Space Sciences at the University of Washington. He also took a year off from 1991 to 1992 to serve as a volunteer visiting professor at the University of the Philippines. In 2008, he accepted an appointment at the newly created Earth Observatory of Singapore of the Nanyang Technological University. He has said that his primary mission as a volcanologist is to help people to live safely around volcanoes.

On his retirement from Nanyang, Newhall returned to the Philippines, where he created the Mirisbiris Garden and Nature Center. His partner in this project was his wife Glenda, whom he had met in 1970 while both were serving in the Peace Corps. Glenda had been a teacher and nurse before their return to the islands and now puts those skills to work in helping individuals and families in the region around the gardens. The Newhalls say that the purpose of the gardens is to provide a welcoming place where people can learn more about nature and find a place of peace and relaxation there. They also provide a livelihood for residents of the area, including assistance to 15 local boys and girls in their college educations.

Office of Wildland Fire

The Office of Wildland Fire (OWF) was created in 2001 as the Office of Wildland Fire Coordination (OWFC) by Secretarial Order 3219 by the secretary of the Interior. The mission of the office was to develop aggressive planning efforts to deal with the growing problem of fires in the wildland-urban interface.

OWF's programs are developed and implemented by an extensive and somewhat complex combination of governing agencies, including the Wildland Fire Leadership Council; Federal Fire Policy Council; Fire Executive Council; Fire Management Board; U.S. Forest Service Fire and Aviation Management; Wildland Fire Offices of the Bureau of Indian Affairs, Bureau of Land Management, U.S. Fish and Wildlife Service, and National Park Service; and the National Wildfire Coordinating Group.

OWF carries out its mission by providing oversight on a number of programs carried out by a variety of federal agencies. Those programs include Aviation, Community Assistance, Fuels Management, Government-to-Government Consultations, International Coordination, Performance Measures, Safety/Risk Management, Science, Smoke Management, Wildfire Suppression, Wildland Fire Information and Technology, Wildland Fire Policy, Wildland Fire Preparedness, and Wildland Fire Resilient Landscapes. The office provides information about its activities and wildland fires, in general, by means of a variety of formats, including press releases, an OWF Twitter account, fire season key messages, direction to wildland fire leadership, monthly significant wildland fire potential outlook, incident management situation report, and archives of past news items.

Charles F. Richter (1900–1985)

Richter was the inventor of a scale to measure the magnitude, or intensity, or an earthquake. Efforts to describe the "size" of an earthquake date back to at least 1873 when Italian seismologist Michele Stefano Conte de Rossi and Swiss seismologist François-Alphonse Forel developed a 10-level scale for expressing the intensity of an earthquake. The scale ranged from a low of 1, a tremor that could barely be felt by an individual, to 10, an "extremely high-intensity tremor." That system depends almost entirely on subjective reports about the way people experienced an earthquake. One of the most significant improvements on the Rossi–Forel system was that invented by American seismologist Charles F. Richter in 1935.

Richter's scale was based on a more objective measure of earthquake intensity, the amount by which a seismograph, or group of seismographs, measures the displacement of the ground during a tremor. He also used a 10-level system but a more sophisticated one. The difference between two levels on the scale was a logarithmic number. That is, a tremor with a Richter number of 2 was 10 times greater than one with a number of 1, and a quake with a Richter number of 6 was 100 times greater than one with a number of 4. Since its introduction, the advantages and disadvantages of the Richter scale have become more obvious, and a variety of modifications have been proposed to make it even more useful for expressing the magnitude of an earthquake.

Charles Francis Richter was born on April 26, 1900, in the small town of Overpeck, Ohio, north of Cincinnati. His mother later reported that he was born Charles Francis *Kinsinger*, later changed to *Richter*, that being her maiden name. His parents, Frederick William Kinsinger and Lillian Anne Richter, were eventually married and divorced twice. Richter was homeschooled by his mother, who had been a teacher prior to her marriage. In 1909, he moved to Los Angeles with his mother, older sister, and maternal grandfather, Charles Otto Richter. There he attended Los Angeles High School, which was affiliated with the University of Southern California (USC). On graduation, he then matriculated at USC but remained there only one year. He then transferred to Stanford

University, where he planned to major in chemistry. After a time, he realized that he was more interested in physics, for which he earned his bachelor's degree in 1920. Richter's post-Stanford years were marked by a period of mental and emotional issues that at one time became serious enough for his stay in an institution for about a year. Once recovered, he took on a series of odd jobs that would not normally be associated with a Stanford graduate, such as messenger boy at the Los Angeles County Museum and a warehouse worker for the California Hardware Company.

In 1923, Richter was able to begin his graduate studies at the California Institute of Technology (Caltech). He received his PhD in theoretical geophysics from Caltech in 1928 but had made an important career move one year earlier. In 1927, he had been invited to join the staff of the newly established Seismological Laboratory of the Carnegie Institution of Washington in Pasadena, California. The lab was one of the first and probably most prestigious centers for seismological research in the United States and, perhaps, the world. It was at the Seismological Laboratory that Richter, along with his colleague, Beno Gutenberg, developed the magnitude scale that continues to carry his name. When Carnegie discontinued funding for the Seismological Laboratory, Richter and Gutenberg were named assistant professors of seismology at Caltech. He was later promoted to associate professor (1947), full professor (1952), and, on his retirement, professor emeritus (1970). Of the two books he wrote, the best known and most popular was *Elementary Seismology*, published in 1958.

Shortly after his retirement, in 1971, Richter joined with Caltech emeritus professor of mechanical and electrical engineering Frederick C. Lindvall to form a consulting firm, Lindvall-Richter, which specialized in earthquake hazards and seismic engineering. Richter died of congestive heart failure on September 30, 1985, in Pasadena, California. Richter was awarded the second Medal of the Seismological Society of America, and the seismological laboratory at which he worked has been renamed in his honor. The Charles F. Richter Early Career Award of the Seismological Society of America has also been named in his honor.

Seismological Society of America

The Seismological Society of America (SSA) was formed in August 1906 in response to the earthquake that had devastated San Francisco in April that year. The organization was formed as a result of one of the recommendations made by the state committee established to study the tremor. The stated objectives of the new organization were "to mold public opinion, to advise wisely, to set forth the truth, and to provide funds for research and investigation" (Byerly 1964). Members of the original group came from a variety of fields, such as astronomy, geography, mathematics, geology, and meteorology, although there were no professional seismologists or geophysicists among them—those fields not having existed at the time.

As was to be expected, much of the early work of the SSA was conducting research on earthquakes. One early proposal, for example, was for the setting of markers along the San Andreas Fault, the origin of the San Francisco and many later earthquakes. As memories of the San Francisco tremor began to fade, interest in the committee decreased, with often few more than a handful of members present at annual or other meetings. Renewed interest in the work of SSA developed in 1925 with the giant earthquake at Santa Barbara on January 29 that year. SSA members once more became interested in the society's goals and activities, and financial support from outside organizations began to make original research more readily available.

In 1911, the society decided to create a journal to carry out its mission to encourage research and make its results known to professionals and the general public. One part of that journal, the *Bulletin of the Seismological Society of America* (*BSSA*), was a section called "Seismological Notes," which carried descriptions of individual earthquakes, primarily in the United States. It was later expanded to include reports of major earthquakes around the world. *BSSA* has continued to be published on a bimonthly basis ever since.

In 1926, the first (and only) section of the SSA was formed at the Carnegie Institution in Washington, D.C. The group was established to deal with the special problems and issues of earthquakes in the eastern United States and Canada, as well as interplate seismology. One reason for developing the new organization was simply the cost and inconvenience of traveling to California in order to attend meetings of the SSA itself. The separate group continues to exist today, still the only subsection of the SSA. The section began publishing its own separate journal in 1929, *Earthquake Notes*. The publication was at first very simple in its concept, such as notes from individual members and reports on section activities. In 1987, *Notes* was reinvented as a new publication, *Seismological Research Letters* (*SRL*), which is still published today. *BSSA* and *SRL* constitute the primary publications of SSA, the former aimed at specialists in the field and the latter aimed at both specialists and members of the general public who are interested in the field of seismology.

The major part of SSA's activities consists of general meetings it sponsors or cosponsors. For example, in 2018, it conducted or took part in the 2018 annual meeting, "Seismology of the Americas"; the First Conference on Earthquakes and Tsunamis, in Oaxaca, Mexico; a forum on infrastructure, in Stillwater, Oklahoma; the 36th annual meeting of the European Seismological Commission; a workshop on induced seismicity in Banff, Canada; and the fall meeting of the American Geophysical Union.

The association has six levels of membership—regular, student, affiliate, emeritus, developing country, and corporate—ranging in cost from $25 to $1,000 a year. It sponsors a number of honors and awards to outstanding individuals in the field of seismology, including the Harry Fielding Reid Medal,

Charles F. Richter Early Career Award, Frank Press Public Service Award, Distinguished Service Award, Bruce Bolt Medal, Student Presentation Awards, Eastern Section—SSA JSA Award, and William B. Joyner Memorial Lecture.

Stephen Self (1946–)

All fields of natural disasters now have some type of "intensity" measurement. When an earthquake (volcanic eruption landslide, hurricane, tornado, etc.) occurs, researchers want to have some reliable method for expressing how "intense" it was. The quotation marks around "intense" mean that that property can be expressed in various ways (e.g., damage to buildings or shaking of the ground) with different kinds of scales. For volcanic eruptions, the scale currently used is the Volcanic Explosivity Index (VEI), invented in the early 1980s by Stephen Self and Christopher Newhall, both then at Dartmouth College, in Hanover, New Hampshire. The scale uses a measure of the amount of tephra (the debris expelled by a volcano) to express how intense an explosion is. It has nine categories, running from 0 ("effusive") to 8 ("mega-colossal"). The criteria for these categories are less than 10,000 cubic meters of tephra for VEI0 to more than 1,000 cubic kilometers for VEI8.

Stephen Self was born in London, England, on October 26, 1946. He attended Leeds University, in the United Kingdom, from which he received his BSc degree (with honors) in 1970. He then continued his studies at Imperial College, in London, where he earned his PhD in 1973. He served as postdoctoral fellow at Victoria University, in Wellington, New Zealand, from 1974 to 1976. His first work assignments were as a NASA research fellow at Dartmouth and the Goddard Institute of Space Sciences from 1977 to 1979. He was then appointed assistant professor at Arizona State University, where he served from 1979 to 1983, and as associate and full professor at the University of Texas at Arlington from 1983 to 1990.

In 1990, Self accepted an appointment as professor at the University of Hawaii at Manoa, in Honolulu, where he remained until 2001. He then became professor at the Open University, Milton Keynes, United Kingdom, where he held the chair in volcanology from 2001 to 2008. He has retained the title of visiting research professor at the Open University from 2008 to the present day. In 2008, Self returned to the United States, where he took the position of senior volcanologist at the U.S. Nuclear Regulatory Commission. He held that post until his retirement in 2017. Self also holds positions as affiliate professor at Washington State University (2011–present) and the University of California at Berkeley (2012–present).

Self has been an invited speaker at many conferences and conventions in countries around the world, including Australia, Brazil, Germany, Iceland, Italy, Japan, United Kingdom, and, of course, the United States. He is a fellow of the American Geophysical Union, Geological Society of America, and The Geological Society of London and a member of the International Association of Volcanology and Chemistry of the Earth's Interior, The Open University Geological Society and Volcanological Society of Sacramento.

United Nations Office for Disaster Risk Reduction

The United Nations Office for Disaster Risk Reduction is an entity created in December 1999 in accordance with General Assembly resolution 54/219. The office is most commonly referred to by acronym UNISDR (United Nations International Strategy for Disaster Reduction), designating the general plan for disaster risk reduction adopted by the General Assembly in that resolution. Resolution 54/219 created UNISDR as a successor to the secretariat of the International Decade for Natural Disaster Reduction (IDNDR), with the goal of providing an ongoing UN organization for accomplishing the objectives adopted by the IDNDR final reports. In 2001, UNISDR's mandate was expanded to include all organizations and activities within the UN purview for dealing with natural disasters and the risk associated with them.

Two documents that currently define the mission of the UNISDR are the Hyogo Framework for Action, adopted in 2005, and, its successor, the Sendai Framework for Disaster Risk Reduction, 2015–2030, adopted in 2015. Both documents laid out a group of "priorities for action" that define the UN's approach to aiding nations and regions in their efforts to ameliorate the effects of natural disasters, such as earthquakes and tsunamis, forest fires, landslides, and drought. The four guiding principles from the Sendai document, for example, are "understanding disaster risk," "strengthening disaster risk governance to manage disaster risk," "investing in disaster risk reduction for resilience," and "enhancing disaster preparedness for effective response and to 'build back better' in recovery, rehabilitation and reconstruction."

The specific activities of UNISDR are categorized under five major headings: coordination, campaigning, advocating, informing, and monitoring. "Coordination" primarily involves the conduct of "platforms," meetings held for the exchange of information and ideas at the global, regional, and national levels. The regional platforms are focused on Africa, the Americas, the Arab states, Asia, Europe, and the Pacific. National platforms have been developed for each of the member states of the United Nations.

The "campaigning" activity of UNISDR is designed to educate governments and the general public about the risks of natural disasters and methods for preparing for, dealing with, and recovering from such events. Campaign programs designed for 2018, for example, included "Making Cities Resilient," "Safe Schools and Hospitals," and the "International Day for Disaster Reduction." "Advocating" includes activities that focus on specific aspects of natural disaster risk reduction, such as adaptation to climate change, education about natural disasters and risk reduction, consideration of gender-related issues, and the role of natural disaster risk reduction in campaigns for sustainable development. The goal of "informing" is carried out through a variety of educational tools by which information about natural disaster risk reduction can be distributed, including a biennial Global Assessment Report, a summary of the status of disaster risk reduction for the preceding two years; PreventionWeb, an online resource with information about a host of disaster-related topics; terminology, a web page containing a glossary of disaster-related terms; a library of more than 10,000 publications, multimedia products, and other educational resources; UN resolutions and reports; and a collection of photos and videos dealing with disaster risk reduction. The "monitoring" function of the UNISDR agenda includes a variety of activities through which the agency follows up on the effectiveness of its programs in achieving the goal set out in the Sendai Framework.

An important feature of UNISDR's work is the mechanisms by which it works with other agencies around the world of all types. It coordinates its activities, for example, with regional platforms in the six major regions of the world mentioned earlier; with other UN organizations and agencies; with international financial institutions; with civil organizations, such as Youth Beyond Disasters, Disability-Inclusive DRR Network, and the Animals in Disasters Initiative; with the media; and with children and youth groups worldwide.

The UNISDR website is a treasure chest of publications on virtually every aspect of disaster risk reduction, including annual reports, documents related to the Sendai Framework, recommendations for good practices in the field, conference proceedings, and special reports on specific topics, such as wildfire hazard, coastal erosion hazard, sea-level rise, landslide hazard, direct and indirect economic impact, citizens' participation and crowdsourcing, marginalized and minority groups, and health aspects and risk assessment.

Alfred Wegener (1880–1930)

Although trained as an astronomer, Wegener is probably best known today as an early proponent of the theory of continental drift, the hypothesis that, at some time in the distant past, all land mass on the face of Earth was concentrated in a single continent. Wegener called that land mass *Urkontinent*, more commonly known today as *Pangea* ("all Earth"). Wegener based his hypothesis on a handful of basic facts about the geography, geology, and biology of existing continents. First, and perhaps foremost, he noticed that the boundaries of the continents appear to fit together, almost as neatly as the pieces in a jigsaw puzzle. This idea was by no means the first time such a hypothesis had been expressed. It was almost certainly, however, the first piece of evidence: the continents simply look as if they had once been a single unit.

A second piece of evidence came from a study of fossils from continents. Wegener noted that fossils from South America, for example, were sometimes strikingly similar to those of Africa. That fact could be explained, he said, by assuming that the two land masses had at one time been joined to each other so that animals and plants could move easily back and forth between the two regions. A third consideration, Wegener said, was the similarities that occur *within* continents. For example, the Appalachian Mountains of eastern North America are geologically very similar to the Scottish Highlands, and the rocky strata that make up the Karroo system of South Africa are a good match with the Santa Catarina Mountains in Brazil. Finally, the study of ancient glacial actions suggests that those landforms all had a common origin and a common history. The types of glacial deposits and rock striations found today can almost certainly not be explained by any theory that demands the existence of separate continents at some distant point in the past.

Wegener's theory went essentially nowhere. Some colleagues simply rejected his ideas as too fanciful, but the most serious problem was one of cause and effect. By what force(s) were the huge land masses that make up continents able to slide across Earth's surface? Wegener suggested some rather unlikely answers to that question but, in the end, was unable to find a reasonable explanation for the phenomenon. Indeed, it took nearly a half century for such answers to develop, largely through the efforts of multiple researchers.

Alfred Wegener was born in Berlin on November 1, 1880, to Richard and Anna Wegener. Richard was an evangelical preacher and a teacher of classical languages at the Berlinisches Gymnasium zum Grauen Kloster, an evangelical school in the suburbs on Berlin, while Anna was a housewife, largely responsible for raising Alfred and his four older siblings. Alfred attended the Köllnisches Gymnasium in Berlin, from which he graduated with a "best in class" honor. In 1899, Wegener enrolled at the University of Berlin, signing up for courses in analytical geometry and calculus, chemistry, physics, and "practical astronomy," the last of these being the field in which Wegener was actually most interested. At the end of his first year at Berlin, Wegener decided to attend summer school at the Ruprecht-Karls University at Heidelberg. There he enrolled in much the same course schedule as he had just completed at Berlin. The one exception was a course in meteorology, which he was under the impression would be another course on astronomy. As his biographer has pointed out, however, the primary fields in which Wegener concentrated during the summer session were sabre fencing and beer.

In the fall of 1900, Wegener returned to Berlin, where he continued his studies in the physical sciences, at, of course, a higher level than before. At the end of this academic year, Wegener and his brother Kurt again chose to spend the summer in academic studies, this time at the University of Innsbruck. There they signed up for courses in botany and field geology, while planning to spend much of their free time exploring the region around Innsbruck. In the fall of 1901, Wegener returned to Berlin, where he remained until he earned his PhD in astronomy in 1905.

By the time Wegener had completed his doctoral studies, he had come to the conclusion that a career in astronomy was a dead end, in that everything in the field had essentially been done. As a consequence, the first job he had after graduation from Berlin was at the Royal Prussian Aeronautical Observatory, where he worked as technical assistant on problems in meteorology. (Joining him in his work was his brother Kurt, who had majored in meteorology in his own university studies.) The brothers soon settled on balloon ascents as an approach to learning more about Earth's atmosphere and the development of weather patterns. Less than a year after beginning their research, the Wegener brothers set a world's record for inflight time of a balloon, 52.5 hours, from April 5 to April 7, 1906.

In the middle of his work on balloon explorations, Wegener was offered another opportunity that appealed to his sense of adventure: a trip to Greenland to explore the last remaining parts of the island that had not been studied. Although the 1906 expedition was focused primarily on a study of the native Inuit population, Wegener found time to establish the first meteorological station on the island, where he used balloons and kites to learn more about the regional atmosphere. The 1906 expedition turned out to be the first of four such trips to Greenland, probably the most rewarding research studies he undertook during his life. He was part of three later expeditions also, in 1912–1913, 1929, and 1930–1931.

Wegener's work in Greenland was sufficiently impressive for the University of Marburg to offer him a post as privatdozent in 1909. His assignment there was to offer courses in astronomy and meteorology. It allowed him time also to write his first major work, a textbook on meteorology, *Thermodynamik der Atmosphäre* (*Thermodynamics of the Atmosphere*), soon to become a standard in the field. His early years at Marburg also marked his first interest in the history of Earth's continents that was to lead to his hypothesis about continental drift. After serving as an infantry officer in the German army during World War I, Wegener returned to civilian life and accepted a position as director of the meteorological research department at the

German Marine Observatory at Gross Borstel near Hamburg. He remained in that post until 1924, when the University of Graz created a new professorship specifically for him in meteorology and geophysics. He held that post until his death in 1930.

Wegener died during his last expedition to Greenland in the village of Clarinetania.

World Weather Attribution

For many years, scientists have been interested in the question as to whether global climate change can be correlated with specific natural disasters, such as a specific flood or storm. By the mid-2010s, the scientific community had come to the conclusion that, yes, such connections can be made in certain specialized instances, most commonly, severe weather events. World Weather Attribution (WWA) was founded in 2014 to pursue this goal, conducting research to show how specific weather disasters can be explained at least in part by climate changes.

WWA is a partnership of six organizations: the Environmental Change Institute, University of Oxford; Royal Netherlands Meteorological Institute, in de Bilt, Netherlands; Laboratoire des Sciences du Climat et de l'Environment, Gif-sur-yvette Cedex; Princeton University, Princeton, New Jersey; National Center for Atmospheric Research, Boulder, Colorado; and the Red Cross Red Crescent Climate Centre, The Hague, Netherlands. Research conducted at these institutions and organizations is compiled, summarized, and distributed by WWA. The purpose of this work is to help researchers, decision makers, and the general public develop a more concrete understanding about the relationship between climate change and specific extreme weather events, with the goal of improving planning for such events in the future.

Reports released thus far have dealt with five types of weather events: cold spells, drought, extreme rainfall, heat waves, and storms. Examples of this research are studies of a cold winter in North America from December 2017 to January 2018, extreme cold in southeast Europe in 2017, extreme rainfall in Japan in 2018, water shortage crisis in Cape Town in 2018, devastating rains in Kenya in 2018, and unusually high temperatures at the North Pole in 2016. The WWA website offers a database that can be searched by regions of the world, types of disaster, and year. It also contains a list of articles dealing with specific climate change/severe weather events produced by WWA researchers.

Zhang Heng (78–139 CE)

Zhang Heng (also Chang Heng) was a Chinese polymath who made contributions to the fields of astronomy, ethnography, geography, hydraulics, mathematics, mechanical engineering, poetry, and seismology. He is sometimes referred to as the Da Vinci of ancient China. Zhang is probably best known today as the inventor of one of the earliest seismoscopes, a device similar to a seismograph. A seismoscope differs from a seismograph in that it can detect ("scope") a tremor but makes no permanent record ("graph") of the event. Zhang's invention (known as a Di Dong Yi) consisted of a cylindrical metal urn within which hung some type of pendulum apparatus, the exact details of which have been lost. The pendulum was very sensitive to vibrations and, when activated, swung back and forth until it came into contact with one of eight balls arranged around the inside of the urn. The ball thus disturbed then fell out of a hole in the urn into the mouth of one of eight dragons arranged around the base of the device. The sound made by the ball falling into the dragon's mouth alerted an attendant that a movement had occurred within Earth's crust. The device was unable to predict an earthquake, although it was able to predict the direction in which such an event had occurred. (For a reconstruction of

Zhang's seismoscope, see http://hua.umf.maine.edu/China/astronomy/tianpage/0012ZhangHeng6539w.html.)

Zhang was born in 78 CE, the third year of the reign of Emperor Zhang of the Eastern Han Dynasty, in the town of Xi'E in Nanyang Province. Zhang's father died when he was 10 years old, after which he was raised by his mother and grandmother. At the age of 16, he left home to begin his studies in the capital of the empire, Chang'an, and, soon after, at the Imperial University in Luoyang. At the conclusion of his studies at Luoyang, he was offered appointments in the imperial government as an imperial secretary, which he declined. He then returned to his home town, where he took the position as "officer of merit," in which he served as "master of documents." During his stay in Xi'E, he devoted much of his time to the writing of poetry, producing three of the most famous works of the time during that period.

In 112 CE, Zhang was summoned to the court of Emperor An, who was especially interested in his work in mathematics and the sciences, and was appointed Zhang court astronomer, a post he held until An's death in 125 CE, and then through the reigns of An's successors, the emperors Shao and Shun. Zhang also served Emperor An as a Prefect of the Majors of Official Carriages, a somewhat modest position in which he was responsible for accepting gifts to the emperor through either the northern of southern gates of the palace. During his years under An and his successors, Zhang produced a number of striking technological developments, including

- a book, *Ling Xian*, summarizing astronomical theories of the time;
- a book, *Suan Wang Lun*, describing the current general theory of mathematics;
- an improved version of the clepsydra, a device for keeping time;

- a water-powered armillary sphere, a device used to represent the celestial sphere;
- a device powered by a waterwheel that pumped a bellows to operate a blast furnace for the production of pig iron and cast iron;
- an odometer, sometimes said to be the first machine of its kind ever built;
- a south-pointing chariot, designed without the use of magnetic materials, to indicate directions (hence its name).

In addition to his inventions, Zhang made a number of contributions to mathematics, perhaps the most memorable of which was his calculation of the value of the constant pi. His value, 3.1724, is a good approximation of today's accepted value of 3.14159265359 . . .

By 136 CE, Zhang resigned his post with the imperial government. His decision was based largely on the complexities of court intrigues in which he had become involved. Zhang accepted the post of administrator in the city of Hejian in Hebei Province, where he is said to have earned the respect of the populace by being "tough on crime." He retained the office for only two years before deciding to retire and return to his hometown. In 139 CE, Zhang was summoned once again to return to the imperial household, where he was made master of writing. He died in Luoyang shortly after accepting this appointment.

Zhang received a number of memorial accolades on his death. He has been remembered today by the naming of an asteroid (1802 Zhang Heng), a lunar crater (Chang Heng), a mineral (zhanghengite), and a Chinese research satellite (Zhangheng-1).

Reference

Byerly, Perry. 1964. "General History of the Society." *Bulletin of the Seismological Society of America.* 54(6): 1723–1741.

5 Data and Documents

One way of having a better understanding of natural disasters is by examining data and documents relating to that issue. The data provided here all come from federal reporting agencies: the National Oceanic and Atmospheric Administration, the U.S. Geological Survey, and the National Weather Service. The documents included here are all excerpts from laws, court cases, reports, and guides related to natural disasters.

Data

Table 5.1 lists, in order of severity, the 10 most deadly tornadoes in recorded history in the United States.

Table 5.1   Deadliest Tornadoes in U.S. History

Date	Location	Deaths
March 18, 1925	Tri-State (MO/IL/IN)	695
May 6, 1840	Natchez, MS	317
May 27, 1896	St. Louis, MO	255
April 5, 1936	Tupelo, MS	216
April 6, 1936	Gainesville, GA	203
April 9, 1947	Woodward, OK	181
May 22, 2011	Joplin, MO	158

(Continued)

A supercell thunderstorm develops in Elbert County outside of Limon, Colorado, on May 8, 2017. (Drew Angerer/Getty Images)

Table 5.1   (Continued)

Date	Location	Deaths
April 24, 1908	Amite, LA; Purvis, MS	143
June 12, 1899	New Richmond, WI	117
June 8, 1953	Flint, MI	116

Source: "The 25 Deadliest Tornadoes." 2018. Storm Prediction Center. NOAA. http://www.spc.noaa.gov/faq/tornado/killers.html. Accessed on April 23, 2018.

Table 5.2 lists the 10 costliest tornadoes in recorded history in the United States. In addition to the date and location of the storm, its cost is listed in contemporary and 2018 dollars.

Table 5.3 lists the 10 tsunamis with the highest-recorded water height, in meters. A dash (–) indicates that no data are available. For explanation of damage data, see at end of table.

Table 5.2   Costliest Tornadoes in U.S. History since 1950

Date	Location	Actual Dollars	2018 Dollars
May 22, 2011	Joplin, MO	2,800,000,000	3,140,000,000
April 27, 2011	Tuscaloosa, AL	2,450,000,000	2,774,000,000
May 20, 2013	Moore, OK	2,000,000,000	2,160,000,000
April 27, 2011	Hackleburg, AL	1,290,000,000	1,450,000,000
May 3, 1999	Moore/Oklahoma City, OK	1,000,000,000	1,510,000,000
April 10, 1979	Wichita Falls, TX	277,841,000	964,364,000
May 6, 1975	Omaha, NE	250,603,000	1,173,800,000
June 8, 1966	Topeka, KS	250,000,000	1,944,000,000
May 11, 1970	Lubbock, TX	250,000,000	1,623,000,000
April 3, 1974	Xenia, OH	250,000,000	1,278,000,000

Source: "The 10 Costliest U.S. Tornadoes since 1950." 2018. Storm Prediction Center. NOAA. http://www.spc.noaa.gov/faq/tornado/damage$.htm. Accessed on April 23, 2018.

Table 5.3   Highest-Recorded Tsunami Water Height (meters)*

Date	Location	Water Height (m)	Deaths	Injuries	Damage**
July 10, 1958	Southeast Alaska	524.60	5	–	0.1
March 16, 1930	Krakatoa, Indonesia	500.00	–	–	–
May 18, 1980	Washington State	250.00	–	–	–
October 9, 1963	Vajont Dam, Italy	235.00	2,000	–	3
October 18, 2015	Ice Bay, AK	190.00	–	–	–
October 27, 1936	Lituya Bay, AK	149.35	–	–	1
1853	Lituya Bay, AK	120.00	–	–	–
June 20, 2017	Karrat Fjord, Greenland	90.00	4	9	1
September 9, 1936	Loen, Norway	74.00	73	–	1
April 7, 1934	Tafjord, Norway	62.30	41	–	–

Source: "Tsunami Events Search—Sorted by Date, Country." 2018. National Centers for Environmental Information. https://www.ngdc.noaa.gov/hazard/tsu_db.shtml. Accessed on April 26, 2018.

*Earthquake-caused unless otherwise indicated.

**Millions of dollars or

damage scale: 0 = none.

1 = limited (<$1 million).

2 = moderate ($1–$5 million).

3 = severe ($5–$24 million).

4 = extreme (<$24 million).

Table 5.4 provides basic data on the most severe weather and climate events in the United States during 2017, the most recent year for which data are available.

Table 5.4 Billion-Dollar Weather and Climate Disasters: Summary Stats, 2017

Type	Number	Percentage of All Events	Damage (billions of dollars)	Percentage of All Losses	Deaths
Drought	1	5.3	2.5	0.8	0
Flooding	2	10.5	3.2	1.0	25
Freeze	1	5.3	1.0	0.3	0
Severe storm*	9	47.4	18.1*	5.8*	3,535
Tropical cyclone	3	15.8	267.7	85.4	251
Wildfire	1	5.3	18.2	5.8	54
Winter storm	2	10.5	2.8	0.9	31
All disasters	19	100	313.5	100	396

Source: "Billion-Dollar Weather and Climate Disasters: Table of Events." 2018. National Centers for Environmental Information. https://www.ncdc.noaa.gov/billions/events/US/1980-2018. Accessed on April 28, 2018.

*Does not include cost statistics for the following: southeastern severe storms (March 2018).

The National Centers for Environmental Information has collected data for the cost in lives and dollars of the most severe weather and climate events in the United States from 1980 to 2017. These data are provided in Table 5.5.

Table 5.5 Billion-Dollar Weather and Climate Disasters: Summary Stats, 1980–2017

Type	Number	Percentage of All Events	Damage (billions of dollars)	Percentage of All Losses	Deaths
Drought	25	10.9	239.1	15.2	2,993*
Flooding	29	12.6	122.5	7.8	543
Freeze	9	3.9	29.3	1.9	162
Severe storm**	96	41.7	214.4**	13.7**	1,610
Tropical cyclone	40	17.4	862.0	55.0	3,469

Type	Number	Percentage of All Events	Damage (billions of dollars)	Percentage of All Losses	Deaths
Wildfire	15	6.5	54.3	3.5	238
Winter storm	16	7.0	46.4	3.0	1,044
All disasters	230	100	1,568.0	100	10,059

Source: "Billion-Dollar Weather and Climate Disasters: Table of Events." 2018. National Centers for Environmental Information. https://www.ncdc.noaa.gov/billions/events/US/1980-2018. Accessed on April 28, 2018.

*Deaths associated with drought are the result of heat waves. (Not all droughts are accompanied by extreme heat waves.)

**Does not include cost statistics for the following: southeastern severe storms (March 2018).

Table 5.6 illustrates the dramatic rise in earthquakes in certain selected states beginning in about 2011. Data for more recent years are currently not available.

Table 5.6   Recent Changes in Earthquake Activity in Selected States

State	2010	2011	2012	2013	2014	2015
Alabama	1	1	0	0	2	6
Alaska	2,245	1,409	1,166	1,329	1,296	1,575
Hawaii	17	34	40	30	26	53
Idaho	7	4	4	11	31	38
Iowa	0	0	0	0	0	0
Kansas	0	0	0	2	42	60
Nebraska	2	0	1	0	0	3
Nevada	38	86	22	34	161	172
Oklahoma	41	63	34	103	585	888
Texas	9	18	11	16	8	21
Utah	17	16	16	6	10	4
Wyoming	43	6	9	73	179	198

Source: "Earthquake Counts by State 2010–2015 (M3+). Counts Are as of March 10, 2016." U.S. Geological Survey. https://earthquake.usgs.gov/earthquakes/browse/stats.php. Accessed on April 16, 2018.

In Table 5.7, data for deaths resulting from severe weather events in the United States are shown from 1940 to 2017. Data for early years are incomplete since the National Weather Service did not collect the relevant information needed for the table. See notes following the table for more information on this point.

Table 5.7   Seventy-Eight-Year List of Severe Weather Fatalities

Year	Lightning	Tornado	Flood	Hurricane	Heat*	Cold*	Winter*	Rip Tides	Wind*
1940	340	65	60	51					
1941	388	53	47	10					
1942	372	384	68	8					
1943	432	58	107	16					
1944	419	275	33	64					
1945	268	210	91	7					
1946	231	78	28	0					
1947	338	313	55	53					
1948	256	140	82	3					
1949	249	212	48	4					
1950	219	70	93	19					
1951	248	34	51	0					
1952	212	230	54	3					
1953	145	515	40	2					
1954	220	36	55	193					
1955	181	126	302	218					
1956	149	83	42	21					
1957	180	191	82	395					
1958	104	66	47	2					
1959	183	58	25	24					
1960	129	47	169	65					
1961	149	51	93	46					
1962	153	28	53	4					
1963	165	31	41	11					
1964	129	73	142	49					
1965	149	296	188	75					

Year	Lightning	Tornado	Flood	Hurricane	Heat*	Cold*	Winter*	Rip Tides	Wind*
1966	110	98	56	54					
1967	88	114	53	18					
1968	129	131	57	9					
1969	131	66	445	256					
1970	122	72	131	11					
1971	122	156	68	8					
1972	94	27	555	121					
1973	124	87	178	5					
1974	102	361	111	1					
1975	91	60	127	4					
1976	74	44	193	9					
1977	98	43	210	0					
1978	88	53	125	36					
1979	63	83	121	22					
1980	74	28	82	4					
1981	66	24	84	0					
1982	77	64	155	0					
1983	77	34	204	22					
1984	67	122	126	4					
1985	74	93	166	30					
1986	68	15	94	11	40		69		
1987	88	59	70	0	38		30		
1988	68	32	31	9	41	17	55		
1989	67	50	85	38	6	121	63		
1990	74	53	142	0	32	13	48		
1991	73	39	61	19	36	13	45		
1992	41	39	62	27	8	14	59		
1993	43	33	103	2	20	18	66		
1994	69	69	91	9	29	52	29		
1995	85	30	80	17	1,021	22	17		84
1996	52	25	131	37	36	62	86		54
1997	42	67	118	1	81	51	90		75
1998	44	130	136	9	173	11	68		65

(Continued)

Table 5.7   (Continued)

Year	Lightning	Tornado	Flood	Hurricane	Heat*	Cold*	Winter*	Rip Tides	Wind*
1999	46	94	68	19	502	7	41		62
2000	51	41	38	0	158	26	41		51
2001	44	40	48	24	166	4	18		31
2002	51	55	49	51	167	11	17	43	45
2003	43	54	86	14	36	20	28	41	43
2004	32	35	82	34	6	27	28	32	42
2005	38	38	43	1,016	158	24	34	35	23
2006	48	67	76	0	253	2	17	23	40
2007	45	81	87	1	105	47	16	57	34
2008	27	127	82	12	71	44	21	68	70
2009	34	21	56	2	45	33	28	55	47
2010	29	45	103	0	138	34	21	64	33
2011	26	553	113	9	206	29	17	41	76
2012	28	69	29	4	156	8	34	42	104
2013	23	55	82	1	92	24	42	63	36
2014	26	47	40	0	20	43	42	57	55
2015	27	36	187	14	45	53	28	56	68
2016	38	18	126	11	94	31	30	58	46
2017	16	35	116	43	107	26	14	70	50
Total	9,365	7,635	8,058	3,391	4,086	887	1,242	805	1,234
10YA	27	101	93	10	97	33	28	57	59
30YA	44	69	85	47	134	30	40		

Source: "78-Year List of Severe Weather Fatalities." 2018. National Weather Service. http://www.nws.noaa.gov/om/hazstats/resources/weather_fatalities.pdf. Accessed on June 13, 2018.
Note: 10A = 10-year average; 30A = 30-year average.
*Empty cells = data not available.

Documents

Albers v. County of Los Angeles (1965)

"It's not my (our) fault. It was an act of God!" That argument appears over and over again in debates over natural disasters and the damages they cause to private or corporate landowners. One of

the classic cases in this debate is Albers v. County of Los Angeles, *decided in 1965. The case involves the development in the 1920s of a piece of property in Los Angeles County for the construction of private homes, summer residences, and a yacht club. Construction in the region went ahead in spite of the fact that geologists knew that the land was subject to landslides in prehistoric times but not within modern history. The depositing of about 175,000 cubic yards of fill by the county during road improvements in 1956 initiated a landslide that was continuing at the time of this case, causing the developed land to continue "moving slowly toward the ocean." Property owners in the area sued the county of Los Angeles for damages resulting from the landslide and were awarded a judgment in the total amount of $5,360,000 by the trial court. This judgment was affirmed and increased by the California Supreme Court in the case cited here. Part of the court's reasoning is as follows. The term* inverse condemnation *refers to a situation in which the government takes private property but fails to pay the compensation required by the Fifth Amendment of the U.S. Constitution, so the property's owner has to sue to obtain the required just compensation. (Triple asterisks, ***, indicate the omission of text.)*

The county's chief contention on appeal is that since the trial court's findings negated the possibility of a recovery on the grounds of negligence, nuisance or trespass, plaintiffs would have been unable to prevail had the defendant been a private individual whose actions were identical to those of the county herein; and that under prevailing authority there is no liability on the theory of inverse condemnation where, under the same facts, there would be no cause of action against a private individual.

* * *

[citing an earlier case:] "We are of the opinion that the right assured to the owner by this provision of the *[California]* constitution is not restricted to the case where he is entitled to

recover as for a tort at common law. If he is consequently damaged by the work done, whether it is done carefully and with skill or not, he is still entitled to compensation for such damage under this provision. This provision was intended to assure compensation to the owner, as well where the damage is directly inflicted, or inflicted by want of care and skill, as where the damages are consequential, and for which damages he had no right of recovery at the common law."

* * *

[1] From the foregoing analysis of the cases and other legal authorities it is apparent that we are not required to choose between two absolute rules, one of liability and one of nonliability, but are faced with a more limited issue. The question is not whether in all cases, a property owner should not be permitted to recover in an inverse condemnation action *** if a private party would not be liable for damages similarly inflicted, fn. 3 but whether there is or should be a qualification or limitation of that rule to the effect that the property owner may recover in such an action where actual physical damage is proximately caused to his property by a public improvement as deliberately planned and built, whether such damage is foreseeable or not.

To restate the question: The issue is how should this court, as a matter of interpretation and policy, construe article I, section 14, of the Constitution in its application to any case where actual physical damage is proximately caused to real property, neither intentionally nor negligently, but is the proximate result of the construction of a public work deliberately planned and carried out by the public agency, where if the damage had been foreseen it would render the public agency liable?

* * *

The following factors are important. First, the damage to this property, if reasonably foreseeable, would have entitled the property owners to compensation. Second, the likelihood of public works not being engaged in because of unseen and

unforeseeable possible direct physical damage to real property
is remote. Third, the property owners did suffer direct physical damage to their properties as the proximate result of the
work as deliberately planned and carried out. Fourth, the cost
of such damage can better be absorbed, and with infinitely less
hardship, by the taxpayers as a whole than by the owners of the
individual parcels damaged. Fifth, to requote Clement, supra,
35 Cal.2d page 642, "the owner of the damaged property if
uncompensated would contribute more than his proper share
to the public undertaking."

* * *

For these reasons we conclude that in the appeal of the county
the judgments should be affirmed on the ground that with the
exceptions stated in Gray, supra, and Archer, supra, any actual physical injury to real property proximately caused by the
improvement as deliberately designed and constructed *** is
compensable under article I, section 14, of our Constitution
whether foreseeable or not.

Source: *Albers v. County of Los Angeles*, 62 Cal.2d 250. [L. A.
No. 27930. In Bank. Jan. 22, 1965.]

Landslide Loss Reduction (1989)

*Like earthquakes, volcanoes, and tsunamis, landslides may occur
spontaneously as a result of natural conditions. But unlike many
types of natural disasters, the likelihood of a landslide may depend
to some extent on human activity, such as the clear-cutting of forest lands. In 1989, the Federal Emergency Management Agency
(FEMA) released a report reviewing the problems of landslides in
the United States and recommending actions that can be taken to
reduce the probability of such an event's occurring. The following
section is extracted from that report. (References have been removed.)*

A significant reduction in landslide losses can be achieved by
preventing or minimizing the exposure of populations and

facilities to landsliding; by preventing, reducing, or managing the actual occurrence of landslides; and by physically controlling landslide-prone slopes and protecting existing structures.

Subsidized insurance is not considered a loss-reduction technique because it does not prevent or reduce losses but merely transfers the loss to other segments of the population. Indeed, it may encourage lenders to develop hazardous lands because they are indemnified by uninvolved taxpayers. The insurance industry could become a strong promoter of hazards reduction if it would establish its rates to reflect relative risks. Most homeowners' insurance policies exclude coverage for ground movements, including landslides.

Preventing or Minimizing Exposure to Landslides

Vulnerability to landslide hazards is a function of a site's location, type of activity, and frequency of landslide events. Thus, the vulnerability of human life, activity, and property to landsliding can be lowered by total avoidance of landslide hazard areas or by restricting, prohibiting, or imposing conditions on hazard-zone activity. Local governments can accomplish this by adopting land-use regulations and policies and restricting redevelopment.

Land-Use Regulations

Land-use regulations and policies are often the most economical and effective means of regulation available to a community— particularly if enacted prior to development. However, where potentially hazardous land is privately owned with the expectation of relatively intense development and use, or where land optimally suited for development in communities is in short supply, there is strong motivation and pressure to use the land intensively. Land-use regulations must be balanced against economic considerations, political realities, and historical rights.

Various types of land-use regulations and development policies can be used to reduce landslide hazards. Responsibility for their implementation resides primarily with local governments, with some involvement of state and federal governments and the private sector.

Reducing the Occurrence of Landslides and Managing Landslide Events

Many landslides occur as a direct result of human activities. The excavation and grading associated with the construction of buildings, highways, transmission lines, and reservoirs can create conditions that will ultimately result in slope failure. The development and enforcement of codes for excavation, grading, and construction can prevent such landslides. A review of the state of the art and standards of performance of hillside and flatland urban development from the 1950s to the early 1980s is available in a training manual. This manual describes the mitigation of several geologic hazards: landsliding, subsidence, expansive soils, drainage, and earthquakes. The concepts and technical applications described in this book may be applied in short- or long-term planning regarding geologic risks anywhere.

Building and Grading Codes

Design, building, and grading codes are regulatory tools available to local government agencies for achieving desired design and building practices. They can be applied to both new construction and pre-existing buildings. In rare cases, such as those involving large offshore structures, the effect of landslides can be considered explicitly as part of the design, and the facility can be built to resist landslide damage. In some cases, existing structures in landslide-prone areas can be modified to be more accommodating to landslide movement. The extent to which this is successful depends on the type of landsliding to which the structure is exposed. Facilities other than buildings (e.g., gas pipelines and water mains) can also be designed to tolerate ground movement. Codes and regulations governing grading and excavation can reduce the likelihood that construction of buildings and highways will increase the degree to which a location is prone to landslides. Various codes that have been developed for federal, state, and local implementation can be used as models for landslide-damage mitigation. A fundamental concern with design and building codes is their enforcement in a uniform and equitable way.

Emergency Management

Emergency management and emergency planning contribute to landslide loss reduction by saving lives and reducing injuries. Such planning can also protect and preserve property in those cases where property is mobile or where protective structures can be installed if sufficient warning time is available. Emergency management and planning consist of identifying potential hazards, determining the required actions and parties responsible for implementing mitigation actions, and ensuring the readiness of necessary emergency response personnel, equipment, supplies, and facilities. An important element of emergency management is a program of public education and awareness informing citizens of their potential exposure, installation of warning systems, types of warnings to be issued, probable evacuation routes and times available, and appropriate protective actions to be taken.

A warning system may include the monitoring of geologic and meteorologic conditions (e.g., rates of landslide movement, snowmelt runoff, storm development) with potential for causing a catastrophic event or the placement of signs instructing people within a potentially hazardous area of proper procedures. Automatic sensors, located within landslide-prone areas, with effective linkages to a central communication warning facility and, thence, to individuals with disaster management responsibilities, are also sometimes used. Warning systems can be long-term or temporary-used only when high risk conditions exist or while physical mitigation methods are being designed and built.

Controlling Landslide-Prone Slopes and Protecting Existing Structures

Physical reduction of the hazard posed by unstable slopes can be undertaken in areas where human occupation already poses a risk, but where measures such as zoning are precluded by the cost of resettlement, value or scarcity of land, or historical rights. Physical measures can attempt to either control and stabilize the hazard or to protect persons and property at risk.

It is not possible, feasible, or even necessarily desirable to prevent all slope movements. Furthermore, it may not be economically feasible to undertake physical modifications in some landslide areas. Where land is scarce, however, investment in mitigation may increase land value and make more expensive and elaborate mitigation designs feasible.

Landslide control structures can be costly and usually require considerable lead time for project planning and design, land acquisition, permitting, and construction. Such structures may have significant environmental and socioeconomic impacts that should be considered in planning.

Precautions Concerning Reliance on Physical Methods

Although physical techniques may be the only means for protecting existing land uses in hazard area, sole reliance on them may create a false sense of security. An event of greater severity than that for which the project was designed may occur, or a structure may fail due to aging, changing conditions, inadequate design, or improper maintenance. The result could be catastrophic if the hazard zone has been developed intensively.

Design Considerations and Physical Mitigation Methods

When designing control measures, it is essential to look well beyond the landslide mass itself. A translational slide may propagate over great distances if the failure surface is sufficiently inclined and the shear resistance along the surface remains lower than the driving force. Debris flows can frequently be better controlled if mitigation efforts emphasize stabilizing the source area along with debris containment in the runout area. An understanding of the geological processes and the surface- and ground-water conditions, under both natural and human-imposed conditions, is essential to any mitigation planning. Some factors that determine the choice of physical mitigation are:

[The report then continues with an extended discussion of factors affecting the choice of physical mitigation techniques.]

Source: "Landslide Loss Reduction: A Guide for State and Local Government Planning." 1989. Federal Emergency Management Agency, 30-33. https://www.fema.gov/media-library-data/20130726-1440-20490-1637/fema_182.pdf. Accessed on June 12, 2018.

Florida Statute 501.160 (1993)

Hurricane Andrew struck the Bahamas and Florida between August 16 and 28, 1992. At the time, it was the most destructive storm ever to hit the state, causing 65 deaths and about $27.3 billion in property damage. In response to this disaster, Florida officials passed a number of new laws and implemented other regulations to deal with similar events in the future. One of the many issues covered by these new laws and regulations was price gouging. Price gouging is the practice of significantly increasing the price of goods and/or services because of scarcities caused by a natural disaster. The selections below are excerpts from Florida Statute 501.160:
"Rental or sale of essential commodities during a declared state of emergency; prohibition against unconscionable prices."

b) It is prima facie evidence that a price is unconscionable if:

1. The amount charged represents a gross disparity between the price of the commodity or rental or lease of any dwelling unit or self-storage facility that is the subject of the offer or transaction and the average price at which that commodity or dwelling unit or self-storage facility was rented, leased, sold, or offered for

rent or sale in the usual course of business during the 30 days immediately prior to a declaration of a state of emergency, unless the increase in the amount charged is attributable to additional costs incurred in connection with the rental or sale of the commodity or rental or lease of any dwelling unit or self-storage facility, or regional, national, or international market trends; or

2. The amount charged grossly exceeds the average price at which the same or similar commodity was readily obtainable in the trade area during the 30 days immediately prior to a declaration of a state of emergency, unless the increase in the amount charged is attributable to additional costs incurred in connection with the rental or sale of the commodity or rental or lease of any dwelling unit or self-storage facility, or regional, national, or international market trends.

(2) Upon a declaration of a state of emergency by the Governor, it is unlawful and a violation of S. 501.204 for a person or her or his agent or employee to rent or sell or offer to rent or sell at an unconscionable price within the area for which the state of emergency is declared, any essential commodity including, but not limited to, supplies, services, provisions, or equipment that is necessary for consumption or use as a direct result of the emergency. This prohibition is effective not to exceed 60 days under the initial declared state of emergency as defined in S. 252.36(2) and shall be renewed by statement in any subsequent renewals of the declared state of emergency by the Governor.

(3) It is unlawful and a violation of S. 501.204 for any person to impose unconscionable prices for the rental or lease of any dwelling unit or self-storage facility during a period of declared state of emergency.

[The law follows with exceptions to these restrictions and administration details.]

Source: "The 2018 Florida Statutes." 2018. Online Sunshine. http://www.leg.state.fl.us/statutes/index.cfm?App_mode=Display_Statute&URL=0500-0599/0501/Sections/0501.160.html. Accessed on June 7, 2018.

Floodplain Management Strategies (2005)

In 2005, the Federal Emergency Management Agency produced a study guide to improve the knowledge and skills of local officials responsible for administering and enforcing floodplain management regulations. It concluded this document with a list of four strategies that can be used in the protection of floodplains and reduction of flooding risks.

Strategy 1: *Modify Human Susceptibility to Flood Damage*

Reduce disruption by avoiding hazardous, uneconomic or unwise use of floodplains.

Tools include:

- Regulating floodplain use by using zoning codes to steer development away from hazardous areas or natural areas deserving preservation, establishing rules for developing subdivisions, and rigorously following building, health and sanitary codes.
- Establishing development and redevelopment policies on the design and location of public services, utilities and critical facilities.
- Acquiring land in a floodplain in order to preserve open space and permanently relocate buildings.
- Elevating or floodproofing new buildings and retrofitting existing ones.
- Preparing people and property for flooding through forecasting, warning systems and emergency plans.
- Restoring and preserving the natural resources and functions of floodplains.

Strategy 2: *Modify the Impact of Flooding*

Assist individuals and communities to prepare for, respond to and recover from a flood.

Tools include:

- Providing information and education to assist self-help and protection measures.
- Following flood emergency measures during a flood to protect people and property.
- Reducing the financial impact of flooding through disaster assistance, flood insurance and tax adjustments.
- Preparing post-flood recovery plans and programs to help people rebuild and implement mitigation measures to protect against future floods.

Strategy 3: *Modify Flooding Itself*
Develop projects that control floodwater.
  Tools include:

- Building dams and reservoirs that store excess water upstream from developed areas.
- Building dikes, levees and floodwalls to keep water away from developed areas.
- Altering channels to make them more efficient, so overbank flooding will be less frequent.
- Diverting high flows around developed areas.
- Treating land to hold as much rain as possible where it falls, so it can infiltrate the soil instead of running off.
- Storing excess runoff with on-site detention measures.
- Protecting inland development with shoreline protection measures that account for the natural movement of shoreline features.
- Controlling runoff from areas under development outside the floodplain.

Strategy 4: *Preserve and Restore Natural Resources*
Renew the vitality and purpose of floodplains by reestablishing and maintaining floodplain environments in their natural state.

Tools include:

- Floodplain, wetlands and coastal barrier resources or land use regulations, such as zoning, can be used to steer development away from sensitive or natural areas.
- Development and redevelopment policies on the design and location of public services, utilities and critical facilities.
- Land acquisition; open space preservation; permanent relocation of buildings; restoration of floodplains and wetlands, and preservation of natural functions and habitats.
- Information and education to make people aware of natural floodplain resources and functions and how to protect them.
- Tax adjustments to provide a financial initiative for preserving lands or restoring lands to their natural state.
- Beach nourishment and dune building to protect inland development by maintaining the natural flood protection features.

Source: National Flood Insurance Program (NFIP). Floodplain Management Requirements. A Study Guide and Desk Reference for Local Officials. FEMA480. 2005. Federal Emergency Management Agency. https://www.fema.gov/media-library-data/1481032638839-48ec3cc10cf62a791ab44ecc0d49006e/FEMA_480_Complete_reduced_v7.pdf. Accessed on July 10, 2018.

California Constitution (Article 1, Section 19) (2008)

Legal disputes over the effects of natural disasters are not uncommon. When they arise, they often involve complex legal issues that are not easily resolved. Who, for example, is legally and financially responsible for losses resulting from a forest fire that may or may not have been caused by some human action, such as the construction of electrical lines through the forested area? The state constitution allows owners of private property to sue utilities in the example cited here. They may receive up to 100 percent of the damages incurred in the fire. The following is the relevant section of the state constitution.

(a) Private property may be taken or damaged for a public use and only when just compensation, ascertained by a jury unless waived, has first been paid to, or into court for, the owner. The Legislature may provide for possession by the condemnor following commencement of eminent domain proceedings upon deposit in court and prompt release to the owner of money determined by the court to be the probable amount of just compensation. . . .

(e) For the purpose of this section: . . .

5. "Public work or improvement" means facilities or infrastructure for the delivery of public services such as education, police, fire protection, parks, recreation, emergency medical, public health, libraries, flood protection, streets or highways, public transit, railroad, airports and seaports; utility, common carrier or other similar projects such as energy-related, communication-related, water-related and wastewater-related facilities or infrastructure; projects identified by a State or local government for recovery from natural disasters; and private uses incidental to, or necessary for, the public work or improvement.

Source: "Article 1: Declaration of Rights." 2018. California Legislative Information. https://leginfo.legislature.ca.gov/faces/codes_displayText.xhtml?lawCode=CONS&division=&title=&part=&chapter=&article=I. Accessed on June 13, 2018.

Alfredo Mejia v. Citizens Property Insurance Corp (2014)

Damage resulting from sinkholes is the subject of an extensive history of litigation. Since the sinkhole activity is likely to be at

*least partly a "natural disaster," who pays for the disaster costs
to a property owner, even if the property is covered by typical
insurance policies? Courts have answered this question in various
ways, generally depending on the specific conditions of the case
presented. The following excerpt represents one way of interpret-
ing such issues. (Triple asterisks, ***, indicate the omission of
footnotes and other text.)*

Alfredo Mejia appeals a final judgment in favor of Citizens
Property Insurance Corp. following a jury trial on his insurance claim for damages to his home allegedly caused by sinkhole activity. The trial court erred in allocating the burden of
proof between the parties, and it erred in excluding evidence
that tended to impeach the credibility of an expert witness who
testified for Citizens. Accordingly, we reverse and remand for
a new trial.

Mejia owned a home that was insured under a policy issued
by Citizens. ***

The standard policy insured against risk of direct physical loss
to the property. It excluded, among other things, coverage for
loss caused by earth movement and settlement and loss caused
by sinkholes. Mejia, however, had paid an additional premium
for a Sinkhole Loss Coverage endorsement. *** This endorsement added sinkhole loss as a covered peril, and it stated that
the earth movement and sinkhole exclusions did not apply.

During the policy term, Mejia reported a claim for damage to his home. Citizens retained BCI, an engineering firm,
to evaluate the property for sinkhole activity. BCI investigated
and concluded that the damage was not caused by sinkhole
activity, and Citizens denied Mejia's claim. At trial on Mejia's
breach-of-contract claim, Citizens relied on testimony from experts, including an engineer from BCI, to argue that there was
no sinkhole activity and no structural damage to the property.
Mejia presented his own expert evidence that his home had suffered structural damage due to sinkhole activity.

Prior to trial, the court ruled that Mejia had the burden of
showing that the damage was caused by sinkhole activity during

the policy period. This was contrary to the jury instructions requested by Mejia, which required him to show only that his home was damaged while the insurance policy was in force and then shifted to Citizens the burden to show that the cause of the damage was not covered by the policy. Instructed otherwise pursuant to the pretrial ruling, the jury found that Mejia had not established by the greater weight of the evidence that his home had suffered physical damage caused by a sinkhole. Final judgment was thereafter entered in favor of Citizens, and this appeal followed.

Mejia argues on appeal, and we agree, that the trial court erred in allocating the burden of proof. In litigation involving an insurance claim, the burden of proof is assigned according to the nature of the policy. Without dispute, the insurance policy at issue here is an "all risks" policy. An all-risks policy provides coverage for "all losses not resulting from misconduct or fraud unless the policy contains a specific provision expressly excluding the loss from coverage." *** Consistent with the jury instruction requested by Mejia in this case, an insured claiming under an all-risks policy has the burden of proving that the insured property suffered a loss while the policy was in effect. The burden then shifts to the insurer to prove that the cause of the loss was excluded from coverage under the policy's terms. ***

Source: "Mejia v. Citizens Property Insurance Corp." 2014. District Court of Appeal. Florida. http://www.2dca.org/opinions/Opinion_Pages/Opinion_Pages_2014/November/November%2026,%202014/2D13-2248.pdf. Accessed on June 9, 2018.

Ladra v. New Dominion, LLC (2015)

Oklahoma is a state in which earthquakes have not traditionally been much of a problem. That situation changed in about 2009 when a sharp increase in the number of such events was reported in the state. The sudden appearance of quakes was soon given the name of an earthquake swarm. Many observers quickly *blamed this event on the increasing use of a procedure known as hydraulic fracturing (or fracking) for the recovery of oil and gas resources. Since that time, the best evidence suggests that the earthquakes were caused not by fracking but by the disposal of liquid wastes into empty deep wells. In any case, damage caused by the earthquake swarm has prompted a number of lawsuits by individuals and groups against agencies involved in fracking and/or waste disposal. One of the most important of these cases did not involve an actual award of damages but approval by the Oklahoma Supreme Court of such suits. That decision was significant because it, at least potentially, opened the door to a flood of damage suits by individuals and groups who claim to have been injured by the earthquake swarm. The following selection contains some of the most relevant of the Court's 2015 decision. (Triple asterisks, ***, indicate the omission of references and some other text.)*

I. Facts

Appellees operate wastewater injection wells in and around Lincoln County, Oklahoma, as well as other wells in central Oklahoma. Since approximately 2009, Oklahoma has experienced a dramatic increase in the frequency and severity of earthquakes.

On November 5, 2011, Appellant was at home in Prague, Oklahoma watching television in her living room with her family when a 5.0 magnitude earthquake struck nearby. Suddenly, Appellant's home began to shake, causing rock facing on the two-story fireplace and chimney to fall into the living room area. Some of the falling rocks struck Appellant and caused significant injury to her knees and legs, and she was rushed immediately to an emergency room for treatment. She claims personal injury damages in excess of $75,000.

Appellant filed this action in the District Court of Lincoln County to recover damages from Appellees, alleging that their injection wells—by causing, inter alia, the Prague earthquake—were the proximate cause of Appellant's injuries. Appellees objected to the court's jurisdiction and moved to dismiss. The district court dismissed the case on October 16, 2014, explaining that the Oklahoma Corporation Commission ("OCC") has exclusive jurisdiction over cases concerning oil and gas operations. Appellant filed with this Court a Petition in Error seeking review of the district court's order.

* * *

IV. Discussion

Oklahoma law vests in the OCC exclusive jurisdiction over "the exploration, drilling, development, production and operation of wells used in connection with the recovery, injection or disposal of mineral brines." *** Consequently, only this Court has jurisdiction to review, affirm, reverse, or remand any action of the OCC. ***

The OCC's jurisdiction is limited solely to the resolution of public rights. *** That is, the OCC "is without authority to hear and determine disputes between two or more private persons or entities in which the public interest is not involved." *** "The Commission, although possessing many of the powers of a court of record, is without the authority to entertain a suit for damages." *** Private tort actions, therefore, are exclusively within the jurisdiction of district courts. ***.

* * *

V. Conclusion

Allowing district courts to have jurisdiction in these types of private matters does not exert inappropriate "oversight and control" over the OCC, as argued by the Appellees. Rather, it conforms to the long-held rule that district courts have exclusive jurisdiction over private tort actions when regulated oil and gas operations are at issue. *** Because the Appellant properly brought the action in the District Court of Lincoln County, we reverse and remand for further proceedings consistent with the views expressed in this opinion.

Source: *Ladra v. New Dominion, LLC.* 2015 OK 53. 353 P.3d 529. 2015. Oklahoma State Courts Network. http://www.oscn .net/applications/oscn/DeliverDocument.asp?CiteID=476440. Accessed on June 9, 2018.

Earthquake Safety Checklist (2017)

The Federal Emergency Management Agency (FEMA) provides a good deal of helpful information to help citizens deal with natural disasters. One such item is a booklet called "Earthquake Safety Checklist." The main features of that booklet are reproduced here. Only the title and a few identifying sentences of each section are provided.

Have on Hand for Any Emergency Ideas for Home, Workplace, and Car

Because you don't know where you will be when an earthquake occurs, prepare a Disaster Supplies Kit for your home, work-place, and car. . . .

Bottled Water

Have commercially bottled water on hand for emergencies. Keep bottled water in its original container and do not open it until needed. Pay close attention to the expiration or "use by" date. Store water in plastic containers. . . .

Purifying Water

If bottled water is unavailable or you have questions about the quality of water, purify before drinking. Below are three ways to purify water: . . .

[Special materials to have readily available:]

- Portable, battery-powered radio or television and spare batteries. . . .
- First aid kit and manual. . . .
- Fire extinguishers. . . .
- Special needs. Keep a supply of special needs items, such as medications, extra eyeglasses, contact lens solutions, hearing aid batteries, items for infants (formula, diapers, bottles, and pacifiers), sanitation and hygiene items (moist towelettes and toilet paper), and any other items unique to your family's needs.
- Prepare customized emergency plans for people with disabilities in advance. . . .
- Tools. In addition to a pipe wrench and crescent/adjustable wrench (for turning off gas and water valves), you should have a lighter, a supply of matches in a waterproof container, and a whistle for signaling rescue workers.
- Important papers and cash. . . .
- Clothes. . . . Be sure to have one complete change of clothing and shoes per person, including the following: *[clothing recommendations follow]*
- Pet needs. Identify a shelter area for your pet, gather the necessary supplies, ensure that your pet has proper ID and up-to-date veterinarian records, and make sure you have a pet carrier and a leash. . . .

Home Preparedness

In the event of an earthquake, you may be instructed to shut off the utility services at your home. Teach responsible members of your family how to turn off the gas, electricity, and water at valves and main switches. Consult your local utilities if you need more information. . . .

Earthquake Hazard Hunt

You can identify potential dangers in your home by conducting an earthquake hazard hunt. Knowledge of the issues below and actions taken to mitigate them can decrease your risk of damage and/or injury from an earthquake. *[Some possible hazards are listed next.]* . . .

Family Earthquake Drill

It's important to know what to do for protection when your home starts to shake. By planning and practicing what to do before an earthquake occurs, you can condition yourself and your family to react correctly and spontaneously when the first jolt or shaking is felt. An earthquake drill can teach your family what to do in an earthquake. *[Components of an earthquake drill are listed next.]*

How to Ride Out the Earthquake

Limit your movements during an earthquake to a few steps to a nearby safe place. Stay indoors until the shaking has stopped and you are sure it is safe to leave. *[Suggestions follow in case one is indoors, outdoors, in a car, on public transportation, or trapped under debris.]* . . .

When the Ground Stops Shaking

Check for Injuries. . . .

Keep a battery-powered radio with you so you can listen for emergency updates and news reports. . . .

Be aware of possible tsunamis if you live in a coastal area. . . .

Do not use the telephone as telephone lines may be down and service limited. . . .

Wear shoes in areas near fallen debris or broken glass. . . .

If possible, put out small fires. If this is not possible, leave your home immediately, notify the fire department if possible, and alert your neighbors. . . .

Use a battery-powered flashlight to inspect your home. . . .

Be prepared for aftershocks. These secondary earthquakes are usually less violent than the main quake, but they can be strong enough to cause additional damage and weaken buildings. . . .

Check water and food supplies. . . .

Do not use your car, unless there is an emergency. . . .

Switch off electrical power if there is damage to your home's electrical wiring. . . .

Check the building for cracks and damage, particularly around chimneys and masonry walls. Leave immediately if it looks like the building might collapse. . . .

Check to see that water and sewage lines are intact before using the toilet. . . .

Do not touch downed lines or broken appliances. . . .

Check closets and cupboards. . . .

Clean up spilled medicines, bleaches, gasoline, and other flammable liquids. . . .

Check gas, electrical, and water lines, and check appliances for damage. . . .

Plan to Reunite

Post a message in clear view that states where you can be found. Take your Disaster Supplies Kit. List reunion points in case of separation. Such points may be the homes of neighbors, friends, or relatives; schools; or community centers.

Source: "Earthquake Safety Checklist." 2017. FEMA B-526. https://www.fema.gov/media-library-data/1510153676317-82124ab3b0a31ea239f60acc8d46c2ba/FEMA_B-526_ Earthquake_Safety_Checklist_110217_508.pdf. Accessed on February 18, 2019.

Assembly Bills 1857 and 2681 (California) (2018)

The state of California is situated on one of the most active earthquake faults in the United States. Most experts predict that another *earthquake, "the big one," is likely to occur with decades, if not years. Yet building codes covering high-rise buildings, some of the structures most susceptible to damage in earthquake, have not been updated in years and are thought by some to be inadequate to protect people and property from the destruction of such buildings. In 2018, Assemblyman Adrin Nazarian introduced "A Stronger Safer California"—Earthquake Resiliency Legislation consisting of two bills, AB 1857: Building Codes and AB 2681: Seismically Vulnerable Mapping. Excerpts from both bills are given here. (Triple asterisks, ***, indicate the omission of parts of the bills.)*

Assembly Bill 1857
Legislative Counsel's Digest

* * *

The California Building Standards Law provides for the adoption of building standards by state agencies by requiring all state agencies that adopt or propose adoption of any building standard to submit the building standard to the California Building Standards Commission (commission) for approval and adoption. This bill would require the commission to assemble a functional recovery working group comprised of certain state entities and members of the construction and insurance industries, as specified. The bill would require the group, by July 1, 2020, to investigate and determine criteria for a "functional recovery" standard following a seismic event, for all or some building occupancy classifications and to direct the commission to propose the appropriate building standards, as specified. The bill would require the commission to produce a document providing guidance to, among others, building owners and local jurisdictions regarding function recovery after a seismic event, in the event that new building standards are not in place by January 1, 2023, as specified. The bill would authorize the commission to issue regulations based upon the recommendations from the group. The bill would define "functional recovery" for purposes of these provisions ***

The people of the State of California do enact as follows:

SECTION 1. Section 18941.11 is added to the Health and Safety Code, to read:

18941.11. (a)__The Building Standards Commission shall assemble a functional recovery working group comprised of appropriate public and private sector entities, including, but not limited to:

[15 agencies to be included in the working group are listed here.]

Not later than July 1, 2020, the functional recovery working group shall do both of the following:

(1)__Investigate and determine criteria for a "functional recovery" standard for all or some building occupancy classifications, and investigate and determine practical means of implementing that standard, as mandatory building code provisions. This shall be done for each of the seismic design categories applicable to the state.

(2)__Subsequent to development of the building code provisions pursuant to paragraph (1), the working group shall direct the commission to propose the appropriate building standards for consideration by the commission during the next regularly scheduled Triennial Adoption Cycle occurring after January 1, 2020.***

(e)__For purposes of this section, "functional recovery standard" means a set of enforceable building code provisions and regulations that provide specific design and construction requirements intended to result in a building for which post-earthquake structural and nonstructural capacity are maintained or can be restored to support the basic intended functions of the building's pre-earthquake use and occupancy within a maximum acceptable time, where the maximum acceptable time might differ for various uses or occupancies.

Source: "California Legislative Information." 2018. https://leginfo.legislature.ca.gov/faces/billTextClient.xhtml?bill_id=201720180AB1857. Accessed on April 19, 2018.

Assembly Bill 2681

Existing law establishes a program within all cities and all counties and portions thereof located within seismic zone 4, as defined, to identify all potentially hazardous buildings and to establish a mitigation program for these buildings. The mitigation program may include, among other things, the adoption by ordinance of a hazardous buildings program, measures to strengthen buildings, and the application of structural standards necessary to provide for life safety above current code requirements.

This bill would, upon the identification of funding by the Office of Emergency Services, require each building department of a city or county to create an inventory of potentially vulnerable buildings, as defined, within its jurisdiction, based on age and other publicly available information, and submit that inventory to the office, as specified. By increasing the duties of local officials, this bill would create a state-mandated local program. The bill would require the office to, among other things, maintain a statewide inventory, create a standard reporting form, identify funding mechanisms to offset costs to building departments and building owners in complying with these provisions, and report annually to the Legislature on the compliance of building departments with these provisions. The bill would require the owner of a building identified by a building department as a potentially vulnerable building to retain a licensed professional engineer to identify whether the building meets the definition of a potentially vulnerable building, and if it does, to complete the standard reporting form. The bill would specify the date by which each requirement must be met. The California Constitution requires the state to reimburse local agencies and school districts for certain costs mandated by the state. Statutory provisions establish procedures for making that reimbursement. This bill would provide that, if the Commission on State Mandates determines that the bill contains costs mandated by the state, reimbursement for those costs shall be made pursuant to the statutory provisions noted above.***

[The bill states the rationale for proposed changes it includes.]

Chapter 12.2.5. Earthquake Vulnerable Buildings
8875.100. The Legislature hereby finds and declares all of the following:

(a)__The devastation left by hurricanes Harvey, Irma, and Maria, and the September 2017 earthquakes in Mexico is a wake-up call for California.

(b)__The most recent California ShakeOut study estimates that a major quake along the San Andreas Fault could cause more than two hundred billion dollars ($200,000,000,000) in physical and economic damage, and could result in up to 1,800 or more deaths.

(c)__The chronic labor and affordable housing shortages from which most cities in California already suffer would be made dramatically worse for years to come following such an event.

(d)__California contains thousands of buildings that are known to present a heightened earthquake risk of death, injury, and damage based on their age, structural system, size, and location.

(e)__Protecting our state's economy, affordable housing stock, and social fabric from the long-lasting turmoil of earthquakes is of utmost importance, and the failure to do so could impact Californians' quality of life for decades.

(f)__Because the state represents the sixth largest economy in the world, the aftershocks of such an event would have national and even global impacts.***

Source: "California Legislative Information." 2018. https://leginfo.legislature.ca.gov/faces/billTextClient.xhtml?bill_id=201720180AB2681. Accessed on April 19, 2018.

International Tsunami Warning System (2018)

The International Tsunami Warning System (International Tsunami Information Center, ITIC) is a division of the UNESCO

Intergovernmental Oceanographic Commission. It was established in 1965 to provide advance warning to individuals and organizations in regions having high probabilities of tsunami events. It consists of four major divisions: the Pacific, Indian Ocean, Caribbean, and North-Eastern Atlantic and Mediterranean Tsunami Warning Systems. In addition, the National Oceanic and Atmospheric Administration (NOAA) operates a separate tsunami warning program, the U.S. National Tsunami Warning Center. The following selection provides an overview of the mission and work of the last of these divisions.

Background

The U.S. National Tsunami Warning Center (NTWC) is operated by the Alaska Region of the National Weather Service and is located in Palmer, Alaska. The Center collaborates with the Pacific Tsunami Warning Center to provide tsunami warning service, and mutual backup, to United States coastal regions and many other countries throughout the world.

To accomplish its mission of providing accurate and timely tsunami bulletins to its AOR, the Center detects, locates, sizes, and analyzes earthquakes throughout the world. Earthquakes that activate the center's alarm system initiate an earthquake and tsunami investigation which includes the following four basic steps: automatic locating and characterizing the earthquake; earthquake analysis and review; sea level data analysis and tsunami forecasting; and disseminating information to the appropriate emergency management officials.

In addition to its basic functions, the Center actively pursues developmental projects which enhance tsunami warning operations, and supports community preparedness activities intended to increase public awareness of the tsunami hazard.

The NTWC operates 24 hours every day with two watch-standers on duty.

Observational Networks

Tsunami bulletins are initially issued based solely on seismic data. Data from approximately 1000 seismic stations are recorded at the Center. Seismic networks which provide the data are operated and funded by many different agencies, including the United States Geological Survey (USGS), the Global Seismic Network, NOAA, various universities throughout the country, and foreign governments. Access to data is provided through dedicated circuits, private satellite networks, and the internet.

Once a significant earthquake has occurred, the nearest sea level gages are monitored to confirm the existence or nonexistence of a tsunami, and its degree of severity. If a tsunami has been generated, the sea level data are critical for use in calibrating forecast models. The Center has access to approximately 1000 tide gage sites and 50 deep ocean tsunami detectors (DARTs). Many of these sites are maintained by NOAA's National Ocean Survey (NOS). In addition to the NOS sites, other international agencies provide sea level information to the Center. The NTWC also operates several gages in Alaska. . . .

Section 4: Messages . . .

Based on seismic data analysis or forecasted amplitude (dependent on whether the Center has obtained sea level data), NTWC will issue the appropriate message. Warnings and Advisories suggest that action be taken. Watches are issued to provide an early alert for areas that are distant from the wave front, but may have danger. Once the danger level is determined, the watch is upgraded to a warning or advisory, or canceled. The full definition of each message is given below:

Tsunami Warning—A tsunami warning is issued when a tsunami with the potential to generate widespread inundation is imminent, expected, or occurring. Warnings alert the public that dangerous coastal flooding accompanied by powerful currents is possible and may continue for several hours after initial arrival. Warnings alert emergency management officials to take action for the entire tsunami hazard zone. Appropriate actions to be taken by local officials may include the evacuation of low-lying coastal areas, and the repositioning of ships to deep waters when there is time to safely do so. Warnings may be updated, adjusted geographically, downgraded, or canceled. To provide the earliest possible alert, initial warnings are normally based only on seismic information.

Tsunami Advisory—A tsunami advisory is issued when a tsunami with the potential to generate strong currents or waves dangerous to those in or very near the water is imminent, expected, or occurring. The threat may continue for several hours after initial arrival, but significant inundation is not expected for areas under an advisory. Appropriate actions to be taken by local officials may include closing beaches, evacuating harbors and marinas, and the repositioning of ships to deep waters when there is time to safely do so. Advisories are normally updated to continue the advisory, expand/contract affected areas, upgrade to a warning, or cancel the advisory.

Tsunami Watch—A tsunami watch is issued to alert emergency management officials and the public of an event which may later impact the watch area. The watch area may be upgraded to a warning or advisory—or canceled—based on updated information and analysis. Therefore, emergency management officials and the public should prepare to take action. Watches are normally issued based on seismic information without confirmation that a destructive tsunami is underway.

Tsunami Information Statement—A tsunami information statement is issued to inform that an earthquake has occurred, or that a tsunami warning, watch or advisory has been issued for another section of the ocean. In most cases, information statements are issued to indicate there is no threat of a destructive basin wide tsunami and to prevent unnecessary evacuations as the earthquake may have been felt in coastal areas. Information statements may indicate for distant regions that a large event is being evaluated and could be upgraded to a warning, advisory, or watch.

For tsunami warnings, advisories, and watches, the Center issues three messages. One type, WEPA41 (Pacific) or WEXX20

(Atlantic), are segmented messages which are designed for automated systems. This type of message includes NWS universal generic codes (UGCs) and valid time event code (VTEC). The other, WEAK51/61 (Pacific) or WEXX30/40 (Atlantic), are intended for public consumption.

The NTWC also issues monthly communication tests over its primary dissemination paths. Each month a Pacific AOR and an Atlantic AOR test are conducted. As tsunamis are uncommon events, this testing is critical to ensure robust message dissemination.

Source: "User's Guide for the Tsunami Warning System in the U.S. National Tsunami Warning Center Area-of-Responsibility." 2017. NOAA/NWS/NTWC. http://wcatwc.arh.noaa.gov/op erations/opsmanual.pdf, 5, 13–14. Accessed on June 12, 2018.

National Landslide Preparedness Act (2017–2018)

Legislation involving natural disasters is relatively sparse at the state, federal, and local levels. One reason, of course, is that governmental bodies cannot "prohibit" such events from taking place. They can, however, develop programs for planning for hurricanes, tornadoes, landslides, and the like, and/or dealing with such events after they have occurred. An example of such legislation is H.R. 1675, the National Landslide Preparedness Act, introduced by Rep. Suzan K. DelBene (D-WA) in March 2017. The provisions of that bill have been summarized, as follows:

This bill: (1) directs the U.S. Geological Survey (USGS) to establish a National Landslide Hazards Reduction Program to identify and understand landslide hazards and risks, reduce losses from landslides, protect communities at risk of landslide hazards, and help improve communication and emergency preparedness; and (2) establishes the Interagency Coordinating Committee on Landslide Hazards to oversee the program.

The USGS shall:

- develop and publish a national strategy for landslide hazards and risk reduction in the United States;
- develop and maintain a publicly accessible national landslide hazard and risk inventory database;
- disseminate landslide planning and risk reduction materials;
- expand the early warning system for flash floods and debris flow;
- establish emergency response procedures for the rapid deployment of federal scientists, equipment, and services to areas impacted by a significant landslide event;
- support emergency response efforts and improve the safety of emergency responders;
- establish the Advisory Committee on Landslides; and
- support the identification, mapping, research, and monitoring of subsidence and groundwater resource accounting.

The USGS may provide competitive grants to state, local, and tribal governments to research, map, assess, and collect data on landslide hazards.

The National Science Foundation shall ensure that landslide research grants are provided on a competitive basis to advance the goals and priorities of the national strategy.

The USGS shall establish the 3D Elevation Program and the 3D Elevation Federal Interagency Coordinating Committee. The program shall:

- provide 3D elevation data coverage for the United States;
- coordinate and facilitate the collection, dissemination, and use of 3D elevation data among federal agencies and non-federal entities;
- produce standard, publicly accessible 3D elevation data products for the United States; and

- promote the collection, dissemination, and use of 3D elevation data among federal, state, local, and tribal governments, communities, institutions of higher education, and the private sector.

The USGS may make grants and enter into cooperative agreements to facilitate the improvement of nationwide coverage of 3D elevation data.

[*The term 3-D, as used in this bill, means* "high-resolution data obtained using lidar, ifsar, or other methods over the United States (including territories)" *and includes* "terrestrial and bathymetric elevation data."]

Source: "H.R.1675—National Landslide Preparedness Act." 2018. Congress.gov. https://www.congress.gov/bill/115th-congress/house-bill/1675. Accessed on June 16, 2018. For full text of the bill, see https://www.congress.gov/bill/115th-congress/house-bill/1675/text.

Measurement Scales (current)

Over the years, researchers have invented a number of systems for expressing the severity of a natural disaster. Among the most widely used of these scales are the Beaufort and Fujita (wind speeds), Richter and Mercalli (earth movements), and Saffir–Simpson (hurricane) scales. The currently most popular of these scales are shown.

Beaufort Scale (1805)

			Wind Effects	
Force	Wind Speed*	WMO Category**	On Water	On Land
0	<1	Calm	Sea surface smooth and mirror-like	Calm, smoke rises vertically
1	1–3	Light air	Scaly ripples, no foam crests	Smoke drift indicates wind direction, still wind vanes

(Continued)

			Wind Effects	
Force	Wind Speed*	WMO Category**	On Water	On Land
2	4–6	Light breeze	Small wavelets, crests glassy, no breaking	Wind felt on face, leaves rustle, vanes begin to move
3	7–10	Gentle breeze	Large wavelets, crests begin to break, scattered whitecaps	Leaves and small twigs constantly moving, light flags extended
4	11–16	Moderate breeze	Small waves 1–4 feet, becoming longer, numerous whitecaps	Dust leaves, and loose paper lifted, small tree branches move
5	17–21	Fresh breeze	Moderate waves 4–8 feet, taking longer form, many whitecaps, some spray	Small trees in leaf begin to sway
6	22–27	Strong breeze	Larger waves 8–13 feet, whitecaps common, more spray	Larger tree branches moving, whistling in wires
7	28–33	Near gale	Sea heaps up, waves 13–19 feet, white foam streaks off breakers	Whole trees moving, resistance felt walking against wind
8	34–40	Gale	Moderately high (18–25 feet) waves of greater length, edges of crests begin to break into spindrift, foam blown in streaks	Twigs breaking off trees, generally impedes progress
9	41–47	Strong gale	High waves (23–32 feet), sea begins to roll, dense streaks of foam, spray may reduce visibility	Slight structural damage occurs, slate blows off roofs
10	48–55	Storm	Very high waves (29–41 feet) with overhanging crests, sea white with densely blown foam, heavy rolling, lowered visibility	Seldom experienced on land, trees broken or uprooted, "considerable structural damage"

			Wind Effects	
Force	Wind Speed*	WMO Category**	On Water	On Land
11	56–63	Violent storm	Exceptionally high (37–52 feet) waves, foam patches cover sea, visibility more reduced	–
12	64+	Hurricane	Air filled with foam, waves over 45 feet, sea completely white with driving spray, visibility greatly reduced	–

Source: "Beaufort Wind Scale." 2018. Storm Prediction Center. NOAA. http://www.spc.noaa.gov/faq/tornado/beaufort.html. Accessed on June 10, 2018.

*In knots.

**World Meteorological Organization.

Enhanced Fujita Wind Scale (2007)

Fujita Scale (in mph)			Operational EF Scale (in mph)	
F Number	Fastest 1/4 mph Wind	3 Second Gust	EF Number	3 Second Gust
0	40–72	45–78	0	65–85
1	73–112	79–117	1	86–110
2	113–157	118–161	2	111–135
3	158–207	162–209	3	136–165
4	208–260	210–261	4	166–200
5	261–318	262–317	5	Over 200

Source: "Enhanced F Scale for Tornado Damage." 2018. Storm Prediction Center. NOAA. http://www.spc.noaa.gov/faq/tornado/ef-scale.html. Accessed on June 10, 2018 (contains link to original Fujita tornado scale).

Saffir–Simpson Hurricane Scale (1971)

Category	Sustained Winds (mph)	Types of Damage
1	74–95	Very dangerous winds will produce some damage: well-constructed frame homes could have damage to roof, shingles, vinyl siding, and gutters. Large branches of trees will snap, and shallowly rooted trees may be toppled. Extensive damage to power lines and poles likely will result in power outages that could last a few to several days.
2	96–110	Extremely dangerous winds will cause extensive damage: well-constructed frame homes could sustain major roof and siding damage. Many shallowly rooted trees will be snapped or uprooted and block numerous roads. Near-total power loss is expected with outages that could last from several days to weeks.
3	111–129	Devastating damage will occur: well-built framed homes may incur major damage or removal of roof decking and gable ends. Many trees will be snapped or uprooted, blocking numerous roads. Electricity and water will be unavailable for several days to weeks after the storm passes.
4	130–156	Catastrophic damage will occur: well-built framed homes can sustain severe damage with loss of most of the roof structure and/or some exterior walls. Most trees will be snapped or uprooted and power poles downed. Fallen trees and power poles will isolate residential areas. Power outages will last weeks to possibly months. Most of the area will be uninhabitable for weeks or months.
5	157 or greater	Catastrophic damage will occur: a high percentage of framed homes will be destroyed, with total roof failure and wall collapse. Fallen trees and power poles will isolate residential areas. Power outages will last for weeks to possibly months. Most of the area will be uninhabitable for weeks or months.

Source: "Saffir–Simpson Hurricane Wind Scale." 2018. National Hurricane Center. https://www.nhc.noaa.gov/aboutsshws.php. Accessed on June 11, 2018.

Modified Mercalli Scale (1931)

Intensity	Shaking	Description/Damage
I	Not felt	Not felt except by a very few under especially favorable conditions.
II	Weak	Felt only by a few persons at rest, especially on upper floors of buildings.
III	Weak	Felt quite noticeably by persons indoors, especially on upper floors of buildings. Many people do not recognize it as an earthquake. Standing motor cars may rock slightly; vibrations similar to the passing of a truck; duration estimated.
IV	Light	Felt indoors by many, outdoors by few during the day; at night, some awakened; dishes, windows, doors disturbed; walls make cracking sound; sensation like heavy truck striking building. Standing motor cars rocked noticeably.
V	Moderate	Felt by nearly everyone; many awakened; some dishes, windows broken; unstable objects overturned. Pendulum clocks may stop.
VI	Strong	Felt by all, many frightened; some heavy furniture moved; a few instances of fallen plaster; damage slight.
VII	Very strong	Damage negligible in buildings of goo construction; slight to moderate in well-built ordinary structures; considerable damage in poorly built or badly designed structures; some chimneys broken.
VIII	Severe	Damage slight in specially designed structures; considerable damage in ordinary substantial buildings with partial collapse; damage great in poorly built structures; fall of chimneys, factory stacks, columns, monuments, walls; heavy furniture overturned.
IX	Violent	Damage considerable in specially designed structures; well-designed frame structures thrown out of plumb; damage great in substantial buildings, with partial collapse; buildings shifted off foundations.
X	Extreme	Some well-built wooden structures destroyed; most masonry and frame structures destroyed with foundations; rails bent.

Source: "The Modified Mercalli Intensity Scale." 2018. USGS. https://earthquake.usgs.gov/learn/topics/mercalli.php. Accessed on June 11, 2018.

Summary of the California Emergency Services Act (2018)

Some utility companies have regarded the standard in the California constitution as unnecessarily harsh. They have pushed for a more lenient range of liability in case of a fire. In Senate Bill No. 1088, that result is achieved by requiring that utilities properly maintain their equipment so that the risk of fires is reduced. The portion of the bill dealing with this issue follows.

Under existing law, the Public Utilities Commission has regulatory authority over public utilities, including electrical corporations and gas corporations. Existing law authorizes the commission, after a hearing, to require every public utility to construct, maintain, and operate its line, plant, system, equipment, apparatus, tracks, and premises in a manner so as to promote and safeguard the health and safety of its employees, passengers, customers, and the public. Existing law requires electrical corporations to annually prepare and submit a wildfire mitigation plan to the commission for review. Existing law requires the commission to establish standards for disaster and emergency preparedness plans, as specified, and requires an electrical corporation to develop, adopt, and update an emergency and disaster preparedness plan, as specified.

The California Emergency Services Act, among other things, establishes the Office of Emergency Services for the purpose of mitigating the effects of natural, manmade, or war-caused emergencies and makes findings and declarations relating to ensuring that preparation within the state will be adequate to deal with those emergencies.

This bill would require the office, in consultation with specified public entities, by September 30, 2019, to adopt standards for reducing risks from a major event, as defined. The bill would require those standards to include model policies that may be undertaken by local governments regarding, among other things, defensible space, and actions that may be undertaken by an electrical or gas corporation, a local publicly owned electric or gas utility, or a water utility to reduce the risk of fire occurring during a major event. The bill would require the office to update the standards at least once every 2 years.

This bill would require an electrical or gas corporation, on or before July 1, 2019, and every July 1 every two years thereafter, to submit to the commission an application for review and approval of a safety, reliability, and resiliency plan that includes certain elements. The bill would require the commission, no more than 18 months after the submission of the plan, to approve the plan with or without modification.

The bill would require the commission to authorize recovery of the costs of implementing the plan through rates, as provided. The bill would require the commission to conduct an annual proceeding to review each electrical corporation's and gas corporation's compliance with its plan, as provided. If, after completing the compliance review, the commission determines that an electrical corporation or gas corporation is in substantial compliance with its plan, the bill would authorize the commission to find the performance, operations, management, and investment addressed in the plan to be reasonable and prudent, as specified. The bill would require the commission to assess a penalty on an electrical corporation or gas corporation for non-compliance with its plan. The bill would, except as provided, prohibit an electrical corporation from delegating, transferring, or contracting out any of its distribution system safety or reliability performance obligations, except as specified.

Source: "SB-1088 Safety, Reliability, and Resiliency Planning: General Rate Case Cycle." 2018. California Legislative Information. https://leginfo.legislature.ca.gov/faces/billTextClient .xhtml?bill_id=201720180SB1088. Accessed on June 13, 2018.

For a more detailed account of the dispute over this bill, see Pettersson, Edvard, Joel Rosenblatt, and Mark Chediak. 2018 "Edison, PG&E Seek Mercy from Courts over Doomsday Fire Payouts." Bloomberg. https://www.bloomberg.com/news/ar ticles/2018-04-23/edison-pg-e-seek-mercy-from-courts-over-doomsday-fire-payouts. Accessed on June 13, 2018.

TSUNAMI HAZARD ZONE
IN CASE OF EARTHQUAKE GO TO HIGH GROUND OR INLAND
BIKE ROUTE
SHARE THE ROAD

6   Resources

Introduction

The subject of natural disasters is a very large topic, to which many thousands of books, articles, web pages, and other sources have been devoted. Any review of this literature must, of necessity, provide no more than an overview of the topic. In some cases, an item in this list of references may occur in more than one form, such as a print article and a website reprint of the article. Items of this kind in this bibliography are so indicated in the annotation.

The topic of *natural disasters* encompasses so many important subtopics (e.g., earthquakes, tsunamis, volcanic eruptions, forest fires, landslides) that this bibliography cannot possibly adequately cover even the most important of the publications on these individual subjects. The bibliography focuses, therefore, to a large extent on items dealing primarily with the subject of natural disasters in general. Mention of some important works on individual topics is, however, included where possible in terms of space availability.

A short section at the conclusion of the main body of references lists a small number of books that focus specifically on earthquakes, vulcanism, flooding, and other major types of natural disasters.

A tsunami warning sign points out the evacuation route at Venice Beach in Los Angeles, California, 2018. (Pablo Hidalgo/Dreamstime.com)

Books

Abbott, Patrick L. 2017. *Natural Disasters*, 10th ed. New York: McGraw-Hill.

> This very popular textbook covers all essential aspects of natural disasters, including earthquakes and seismology, volcanic eruptions, tsunamis, tornadoes, hurricanes, extreme heat and cold events, floods, mass movements, impact with space objects, and climate change.

Allahdadi, Joseph N., and Joseph N. Pelton, eds. 2015. *Handbook of Cosmic Hazards and Planetary Defense*. Cham, Switzerland: Springer International.

> The 51 essays in this book explore virtually every conceivable natural disaster that could occur on Earth as a result of extraterrestrial events, such as those associated with asteroids, comets, bolides, meteors, solar flares and coronal mass ejections, cosmic radiation, and other events.

Arendt, Lucy A., and Daniel J. Alesch. 2015. *Long-Term Community Recovery from Natural Disasters*. Boca Raton, FL: CRC Press.

> "Recovery efforts" for most natural disasters tend to consist primarily of rebuilding housing and infrastructure. Arendt and Alesch point out, however, that other types of "recovery" are almost always needed but ignored in the real world. Their book focuses on the kinds of nonphysical problems that may remain after a natural disaster and the steps that may be necessary to deal with such problems. Sample chapters include "Communities as Complex, Open, and Self-Organizing Social Systems," "Postdisruption: Real Problems for Real People in Real Places," "Impacts on Local Government," and "Facilitating Recovery."

Banholzer, Sandra, James Kossin, and Simon Donner. 2014. "The Impact of Climate Change on Natural Disasters." In Ashbindu Singh and Zinta Zommers, eds. *Reducing Disaster: Early*

Warning Systems for Climate Change. Dordrecht: Springer, Chapter 2. Available online at https://www.ssec.wisc.edu/~kossin/articles/Chapter_2.pdf. Accessed on August 11, 2018.

> This chapter discusses past instances of the impact of human activities on natural disasters and likely prospects for such events in the future. It provides a very good introduction to the field of attribution science.

Birkmann, Jörn, ed. 2006. *Measuring Vulnerability to Natural Hazards: Towards Disaster Resilient Societies*. Shibuya-ku, Japan: United Nations University Press.

> The theme of this book is that natural disasters have become such a destructive force in human society today that more attention needs to be paid to the conditions in which such events may occur and the steps that could be taken to prevent a natural disaster. Some of the topics include ways of measuring vulnerability to natural disasters, global risk projects, disaster risk hot spots, development of a Human Risk Index, and issues relating to vulnerability at the local level.

Boulter, Sarah, et al. 2018. *Natural Disasters and Adaptation to Climate Change*. 2013. Cambridge, UK: Cambridge University Press.

> The authors explore specific natural disasters for which some connection with climate change has been claimed. The four sections include examples from North America, Australia, Europe, and the developing world. A final section provides a synthesis gained from studying these specific examples.

Bronski, Roger, and Roger Hill. 2018. *Hunting Nature's Fury: A Storm Chaser's Obsession with Tornadoes, Hurricanes, and Other Natural Disasters*. Berkeley, CA: Wilderness Press.

> This book tells the stories of Hill's pursuit of (primarily) severe storms, along with other natural disasters, for most

of his adult life. Eight pages of color photographs illustrate some of his experiences.

Carmichael, Robert S. 2017. *Notable Natural Disasters.* Ipswich, MA: Salem Press.

This book provides detailed accounts of more than 100 of the worst natural disasters to have occurred in history, including avalanches; heat waves; blizzards; ice storms; hail; hurricanes; typhoons and cyclones; droughts; dust storms and sandstorms; landslides, mudslides, and rockslides; earthquakes; lightning strikes; meteorites and comets; tornadoes; tsunamis; fires; volcanic eruptions; and floods.

Caron, David D., Michael J. Kelly, and Anastasia Tekesetsky. 2016. *International Law of Disaster Relief.* New York: Cambridge University Press.

The essays in this anthology are grouped into five major parts: The Legal Theory of International Disaster Relief, The Law of International Disaster Relief, The Right of Access to International Disaster Relief, Disaster Prevention/Relief, and Disaster Prevention and Relief. They analyze the legal basis of existing and proposed approaches to disaster relief for a variety of types of events and geographic locations.

A Citizen's Guide to Disaster Assistance. 2003. FEMA. Available online at http://www.disastercenter.com/agency.htm. Accessed on July 28, 2018.

This book has been reprinted by nongovernmental publishers on a number of occasions since its first appearance in 1999. It is classified as Independent Study IS-7, consisting of a pretest, five instructional units, a glossary, and a list of resources. It is helpful for someone wanting to learn about the topic, although obviously dated in specific information.

Companion, Michèle, and Miriam S. Chaiken, eds. 2917. *Responses to Disasters and Climate Change: Understanding Vulnerability and Fostering Resilience.* Boca Raton, FL: CRC Press.
The majority of the essays in this book focus on specific natural disasters or other events that can serve as models for developing responses to such events in a world experiencing climate change. Some topics included are "Vulnerability and Resilience to Climate Change in a Rural Coastal Community," "Youth Based Learning in Disaster Risk Reduction Education," "The Shared Vulnerability and Resiliency of Fukushima Animals and Their Rescuers," "Gender Dimensions in Disaster Management," "Best Family Rwanda: A Case Study on Religion Sources of Resilience," and "Grassroots and Guerillas: Radical and Insurgent Responses for Community Resilience."

DeVecchio, Duane E., and Edward A. Keller. 2019. *Natural Hazards: Earth's Processes as Hazards, Disasters, and Catastrophes*, 5th ed. New York: Routledge.
Each unit in this textbook on natural disasters begins with the discussion of a specific event: the Alberta floods of 2013, the 1998 ice storm, Hurricane Katrina, Harris Meisner's farm by the sea, and wildfires in British Columbia in 2003.

Dixon, Timothy H. 2017. *Curbing Catastrophe: Natural Hazards and Risk Reduction in the Modern World.* Cambridge, UK: Cambridge University Press.
The author discusses a number of particular natural disasters and attempts to find some common themes among these events. He focuses on common scientific, economic, political, and environmental issues that run through a variety of disaster events.

Gasparini, Paolo, Domenico Asprone, and Gaetano Manfredi, eds. 2014. *Resilience and Sustainability in Relation to Natural*

Disasters: A Challenge for Future Cities. Cham, Switzerland: Springer International Publishing.

 The essays in this anthology explore the issues faced by cities of the future in developing and maintaining resilience and sustainability in the light of inevitable natural disasters.

Golnaraghi, Maryam. 2012. *Institutional Partnerships in Multi-Hazard Early Warning Systems: A Compilation of Seven National Good Practices and Guiding Principles*. Berlin; New York: Springer.

 A number of countries have developed early warning systems for severe weather events. This book contains detailed descriptions of such systems in Bangladesh, China, Cuba, France, Germany, Japan, and the United States.

Griggs, Gary B. 2017. *Coasts in Crisis: A Global Challenge*. Oakland, CA: University of California Press.

 This book explores the special risks posed for coastal areas around the world from natural storms, human activities, and climate change.

Hallegatte, Stéphane. 2016. *Natural Disasters and Climate Change*. Cham, Switzerland: Springer International Publishing.

 The author explores the evidence for a connection between natural disasters and climate change and some consequences of this new relationship in today's world. Some of the topics considered are the meaning of a disaster from an economic point of view, what is the evidence for the concept of a "disaster risk," what are the general trends in the effects of climate change on natural disasters, methodologies for managing natural disasters in the light of climate change, and elements of decision making about natural disasters in a changing world.

Hinga, Bethany D. Rinard. 2015. *Ring of Fire: An Encyclopedia of the Pacific Rim's Earthquakes, Tsunamis, and Volcanoes*. Santa Barbara, CA: ABC-CLIO.

This book contains about 100 entries dealing with natural disasters that occur in the most seismically active part of the world, the so-called Ring of Fire surrounding the Pacific Ocean. Each entry contains a description and explanation of the event, along with helpful additional reading suggestions for the topic.

Hobson, Christopher, Paul Bacon, and Robin Cameron, eds. *Human Security and Natural Disasters*. New York: Routledge.
The papers in this anthology draw on specific natural disasters and their consequences for human security. Some of the topics covered include "Human Security after the Shock: Vulnerability and Empowerment," "Human Security and Disasters: What a Gender Lens Offers," "The Ethics of Disaster and Hurricane Katrina," "Responding to Chronic Disease Needs Following Disasters," and "State Negligence before and after Natural Disasters as Human Rights Violations."

Hyndman, Donald W., and David W. Hyndman. 2017. *Natural Hazards and Disasters*. Boston, MA: Cengage Learning.
This textbook contains chapters on the conventional topics in the field of natural disasters, such as earthquakes, volcanic eruptions, tsunamis, landslides, sinkholes, flooding, and wildfires, along with two chapters on the role of climate change in natural disasters.

Ismail-Zadeh, Alike, et al., eds. 2014. *Extreme Natural Hazards, Disaster Risks and Societal Implications*. Cambridge, UK: Cambridge University Press.
The essays that make up this book focus largely on specific earthquakes, hurricanes, tsunamis, landslides, and other major disasters in various parts of the world. In addition to describing the events themselves, the essays, as well as Parts II and VII, consider the social implications of such events.

Johnson, Edward A., and Kiyoko Miyanishi, eds. 2007. *Plant Disturbance Ecology: The Process and the Response*. Burlington, MA: Academic Press.

The essays in this book discuss the ways in which a variety of natural disasters may have beneficial effects on an ecosystem. Some of the disasters discussed include windstorms, abnormal heat or cold, forest fires, and flooding.

Jones, Lucy. 2018. *BIG ONES: How Natural Disasters Have Shaped Us (And What We Can Do about Them)*. New York: Icon; Doubleday.

The author selects a dozen major natural disasters from history, ranging from the eruption of Mount Vesuvius in 79 CE to the Great East Japan Earthquake of 2011, to discuss ways in which these events influenced human society in the areas of economics, politics, social structures, technology, and other fields. She then draws on this analysis to suggest ways in which humans can better deal with natural disasters "sometime in the future."

Kelman, Ilan, Jessica Mercer, and Jean-Christophe Gaillard, eds. 2017. *The Routledge Handbook of Disaster Risk Reduction Including Climate Change Adaptation*. London; New York: Routledge.

This volume contains 46 essays on various aspects of natural disaster risk reduction and climate change. Some topics include "Vulnerability and Resilience," "Violent Conflict and Disaster Risk Reduction," "Ethics for Disaster Risk Reduction," "Education and Training for Disaster Risk Reduction," "International Organizations for Doing Disaster Risk Reduction," and "Insurance for Disaster Risk Reduction."

Madry, Scott. 2015. *Space Systems for Disaster Warning, Response, and Recovery*. New York: Springer.

A variety of systems are now available for monitoring Earth for possible natural disasters. Such systems can report on conditions prior to, during, and following such events. The 11 chapters in this book deal with topics such as "Organizing for Disasters," "Space Systems for Disaster Management," "Geographic Information Systems," and "Major International and Regional Players."

Montz, Burrell E., Graham A. Tobin, and Ronald R. Hagelman III. 2017. *Natural Hazards: Explanation and Integration*. New York: The Guilford Press.

The authors take a somewhat different approach to the topic of natural disasters than found in most books, focusing less on specific types of disasters (e.g., hurricanes and tsunamis) and instead discussing common aspects of such events. Individual chapters deal with topics such as "Physical Dimensions of Natural Hazards," "Perception Studies: The Individual in Natural Hazards," "Behavioral Studies: Community Attitudes and Adjustment," "Public Policy and Natural Hazards," "The Economic Impacts of Hazards and Disasters," and "Risk Assessment."

Mutter, John C. 2015. *Disaster Profiteers: How Natural Disasters Make the Rich Richer and the Poor Even Poorer*. New York: Palgrave Macmillan.

The author argues that concerns about the effects of natural disasters are misplaced. He suggests that the most important consequence of such events is that the elite and rich prosper at the expense of the poor.

Nagel, Joane. 2016. *Gender and Climate Change: Impacts, Science, Policy*. New York: Routledge.

Nagel notes that some natural disasters affect all individuals, regardless of their genders. She observes that an increasing body of research indicates that such events *do* have different effects on different genders. She explores the relationships of gender and global warming, sea level rise, climate change science, the military–science complex, climate change skepticism, and climate change policy.

The Natural Disaster Survival Handbook. 2016. *Outdoor Life* magazine. San Francisco, CA: Weldon Owen Inc.

This convenient handbook provides general recommendations for preparing for, surviving, and recovering from natural disasters, in general, along with additional suggestions for specific types of natural disasters, such as heat and cold, high-wind advisories, seismic events, and wildfires.

Reice, Seth Robert. 2001. *The Silver Lining: The Benefits of Natural Disasters.* Princeton, NJ: Princeton University Press.

One quite naturally thinks of the devastating effects resulting from earthquakes, landslides, floods, and other natural disasters. But benefits can also accrue from such events, such as the regeneration of an ecosystem following a forest fire. The author takes note of benefits that may not always be appreciated from a range of natural disasters.

Sawyer, James, and Gerardo Huertas. 2018. *Animal Management and Welfare in Natural Disasters.* New York: Routledge.

The authors point out that natural disasters have devastating effects on animals, as well as on humans. They explore how animals are affected by specific types of disasters, what their emergency and subsequent welfare needs are, and appropriate interventions in such cases.

Scott, Alfred. 2015. *Encyclopedia of Disaster Management*, five volumes. Forest Hills, NY: Callisto Reference.

The five volumes in this series deal with different aspects of disasters, including assessment and impact, observations and implications, natural disasters, selected topics in natural disasters, and tsunamis.

Shearer, Peter M. 2014. *Introduction to Seismology*, 2nd ed. Cambridge, UK: Cambridge University Press. Available online at http://www.ndma.gov.pk/sep/books/Introduction-to-Seismo logy.pdf. Accessed on July 29, 2018.

> This book provides a technical introduction to the field of seismology, with an extensive amount of information understandable by the general reader. Of special interest is section 1.1, A Brief History of Seismology.

Singh, Ashbindu, and Zinta Zommers. 2014. *Reducing Disaster: Early Warning Systems for Climate Change*. Dordrecht: Springer.

> The papers in this book provide a nice melding of early warning systems currently available with new demands created by climate change. Some topics included deal with early warning systems for wildland fires, dust storms, floods, drought, and winter fog.

Siva Kumar, M. V. K., Raymond P. Motha, and Haripada P. Das, eds. 2005. *Natural Disasters and Extreme Events in Agriculture: Impacts and Mitigation*. Berlin; New York: Springer.

> The papers in this anthology explore the effects of drought, flooding, extreme storms, forest fires, and other natural disasters on various aspects of agriculture and silviculture. They also discuss ways of mitigating the impact of such events and positive results that may be associated with such events.

Skidmore, Mark, ed. 2017. *The Economics of Natural Disasters*. Cheltenham, UK: Edward Elgar.

> This volume brings together about four dozen reviews on important economic issues associated with natural disasters previously printed in scholarly journals. It includes chapters such as "Do Natural Disasters Promote Long-Run Growth?," "Catastrophic Natural Disasters and Economic Growth," "Natural Disasters as Creative Destruction?," "Small Island Developing States: Natural Disaster Vulnerability and Global Change," "Normalized

Hurricane Damage in the United States: 1900–2005," and "Mitigating Disaster Losses through Insurance."

Steinberg, Theodore. 2011. *Acts of God: The Unnatural History of Natural Disaster in America*, 2nd ed. Milton Keynes, UK: Lightning Source.
The author explores the ways in which so-called natural disasters may be influenced by human actions and inactions in a variety of fields, such as politics, economics, and science and engineering.

Thomas, Vinod. 2018. *Climate Change and Natural Disasters: Transforming Economies and Policies for a Sustainable Future*. New York: Routledge.
This book deals with various aspect of the relationship between climate change and natural disasters. Some of the topics considered include the anthropogenic link between climate change and natural disasters, the rising threat of such events to various parts of the world, methods of climate change mitigation, and adaptation to a changing climate and management of anthropogenic natural disaster events.

Vinitsky, Maya, and Hirmer Verlag. 2017. *3.5 Square Meters: Constructive Responses to Natural Disasters*. Tel Aviv-Jaffa: Tel Aviv Museum of Art; München: Hirmer.
This highly imaginative and creative book argues that traditional methods for responding to natural disasters are too slow to be effective in dealing with some of the worst consequences of such events. The authors suggest a number of simple, but effective, procedures by which individuals and communities can respond to such events.

Watson, Ronald R., et al., eds. 2015. *Handbook of Public Health in Natural Disasters: Nutrition, Food, Remediation and Preparation*. Wageningen, Netherlands: Wageningen Academic Publishers.

This book contains sections on the implications of natural disasters for public health policy and practices, as well as individual events, such as floods, droughts, and hurricanes and earthquakes and volcanoes; health considerations, such as epidemics and diseases during disasters; and disease, food, and malnutrition during disasters.

White, Robert S. 2014. *Who Is to Blame?: Disasters, Nature and Acts of God*. Oxford, UK: Monarch Books.
This book illustrates the way in which some religious individuals attempt to explain "acts of God." The author draws on numerous biblical teachings to explain how God allows (or makes possible) all types of natural disasters.

Wood, Robert Muir. 2016. *The Cure for Catastrophe: How We Can Stop Manufacturing Natural Disasters*. London: Oneworld Publications.
Wood argues that many/most so-called natural disasters are not, in fact, *natural*, in that they are caused by human decisions and actions. Construction within floodplains and using brick to build in earthquake zones are examples. Wood then goes on to describe the ways in which humans can act to reduce or eliminate the risk of certain types of "natural" disasters.

Journals and Articles

A number of print and online journals are devoted at least in part to the topic of natural disasters. Those journals include the following:

Disaster Prevention and Management: ISSN: 0965-3562.
Geomatics, Natural Hazards and Risk: ISSN: 19475705, 19475713.
International Journal of Disaster Risk Reduction: ISSN: 2212-4209.

International Journal of Disaster Risk Science: Print ISSN: 2095-0055; Online ISSN: 2192-6395.

Journal of Geography & Natural Disasters: (open access): ISSN: 2167-0587.

Journal of Natural Disaster Science: ISSN: 0388-4090.

Journal of Natural Disasters: ISSN: 10044574.

Natural Hazards: Print ISSN: 0921-030X; Online ISSN: 1573-0840.

Natural Hazards and Earth System Sciences: Print ISSN: 1561-8633; Online ISSN: 1684-9981.

Natural Hazards Review: Print ISSN: 1527-6988; Online ISSN: 1527-6996.

Risk Management: Print ISSN: 1460-3799; Online ISSN: 1743-4637.

Albrecht, Frederike. 2018. "Natural Hazard Events and Social Capital: The Social Impact of Natural Disasters." *Disasters.* 42(2): 336–360.

> This paper discusses the extent to which natural disasters affect social trust, defined as "a belief in the honesty, integrity and reliability of others." The author finds that the answer to that question depends on the number of deaths involved in the disaster and the extent of the damage produced by the event.

Bailey, Nicholas J., et al. 2010. "Global Vulnerability to Near-Earth Object Impact." *Risk Management.* 12(1): 31–53.

> The authors provide a somewhat technical analysis of the risks posed by asteroids and meteorites to life on Earth. They describe a computer program called NEOImpactor that can be used to estimate the social and economic consequences of such events on land and water.

Banerjee, Ananya, et al. 2016. "Towards a Collaborative Disaster Management Service Framework Using Mobile and Web

Applications: A Survey and Future Scope." *International Journal of Information Systems for Crisis Response and Management.* 8(1): 65–84. Available online at https://itra.medialabasia.in/ data/Documents/DISARM/publications/2017_03_01_11_1 8FA1P8I-Towards%20a%20Collaborative%20Disaster.pdf. Accessed on August 13, 2018.

> Mobile and web platforms are now being used to deal with issues surrounding natural disasters. They can be used to assess damage, coordinate relief operations, and offer location-based services to affected communities. The authors review specific examples of such programs and recommend a role for them in future such events.

Bao, Xuewei, and David W. Eaton. 2016. "Fault Activation by Hydraulic Fracturing in Western Canada." *Science.* 354(6318): 1406–1409. doi:10.1126/science.aag2583. Accessed on July 30, 2018.

> This article provides evidence for a hypothesis that has long been regarded as largely incorrect, namely that the process of fracking in and of itself, not the deep well injection of fluids used in the process, can cause earthquakes.

Bealt, Jennifer, and S. Afshin Mansouri. 2018. "From Disaster to Development: A Systematic Review of Community-Driven Humanitarian Logistics." *Disasters.* 42(2): 124–148. Available online at https://www.researchgate.net/publica tion/316573921_From_disaster_to_development_A_system atic_review_of_community-driven_humanitarian_logistics. Accessed on August 9, 2018.

> Aid for survivors of natural disasters commonly comes from agencies outside of the communities affected by the events. The prevailing wisdom has been that organizations within those communities are unable to take any effective actions to recover from a disaster. The authors of this paper argue that (1) dependence on outside agencies is often inadequate for dealing with disaster-related issues

and, in some cases, may actually exist only "on paper" and not in concrete actions, and (2) community organizations that may be highly effective at moving toward recovery in both short- and long-term ways already exist.

Ben-Menahem, Ari. 1995. "A Concise History of Mainstream Seismology: Origins, Legacy, and Perspectives." *Bulletin of the Seismological Society of America.* 85(4): 1202–1225. Available online at https://engineering.purdue.edu/~ce597m/Handouts/ConciseHistory_BenMenahem.pdf. Accessed on August 5, 2018.

Although said to be "concise," this paper actually provides a superb overview of the development of the science of seismology from the fourth century BCE to 1992. Written as a timeline with a helpful introduction and summary, the paper will be of interest to anyone interested in the history of seismology.

Bogue, Robert. 2012. "Monitoring and Predicting Natural Hazards in the Environment." *Sensor Review.* 32(1): 4–11. Available online at https://www.researchgate.net/publication/241700096_Monitoring_and_predicting_natural_hazards_in_the_environment. Accessed on August 4, 2018.

This paper reviews the systems that are available for monitoring and predicting possible natural disasters. Radar and satellite imaging are among the most common types of systems used for these purposes.

Cawood, Michael, Chas Keys, and Christopher Wright. 2018. "The Total Flood Warning System: What Have We Learnt since 1990 and Where Are the Gaps." *Australian Journal of Emergency Management.* 33(2): 47–52. Available online at https://knowledge.aidr.org.au/media/5507/ajem-33-2-18.pdf. Accessed on August 10, 2018.

In response to a series of severe floods in eastern Australia in the 1960s, the federal government appointed a committee to develop a warning system for such events.

The report produced by that committee has been updated a number of times, a history that is the focus of this article. Although drawn from the experiences in a single country, the concept of flood warning systems has applicability to many other countries.

Chapman, Clark R. 2015. "Facing a Hypervelocity Asteroid Impact Disaster: To Deflect or Evacuate?" *Procedia Engineering.* 103: 68–72. Available online at https://doi.org/10.1016/j.proeng.2015.04.010. Accessed on August 10, 2018.

> Researchers have long been aware of the possibility of a near-Earth object, such as a meteorite, colliding with Earth's surface. The probability of such an event is very low, but the consequences of a collision could be catastrophic. Chapman reviews the history of such research and poses some issues that would be associated with future events of this kind.

Costanza, Robert, and Joshua Farley, eds. 2007. "Ecological Economics of Coastal Disasters." *Ecological Economids.* 63(2–3): 249–636.

> This special issue of the journal focuses on the rise of coastal disasters, the role played by natural and human forces, the economic consequences of such events, and steps that can be taken to moderate the effects of these events.

Day, Ashleigh M. 2017. "Companion Animals and Natural Disasters: A Systematic Review of Literature." *International Journal of Disaster Risk Reduction.* 24: 81–90.

> In recent years, greater attention has been paid to issues dealing with pets, both during and following a natural disaster. Research asks not only how communities deal with the survival of pets themselves but also how animals can play a supportive role in the recovery from a natural disaster. This article reviews the literature on that topic.

Easterling, David R., et al. 2016. "Detection and Attribution of Climate Extremes in the Observed Record." *Weather and Climate Extremes*. 11: 17–27. Available online at https://doi .org/10.1016/j.wace.2016.01.001. Accessed on August 11, 2018.

This somewhat technical article provides a superb review of the development of attribution science and the contributions it has made to our current understanding of human influences on natural disasters.

Faure, Michael, Liu Jing, and Andri G. Wibisana. 2015. "Industrial Accidents, Natural Disasters and 'Act of God.' " *Georgia Journal of International and Comparative Law*. 43(2): 383–450. Available online at http://digitalcommons.law.uga .edu/cgi/viewcontent.cgi?article=2108&context=gjicl. Accessed on August 1, 2018.

This article explores the legal issues involved in dealing with technological (human-made) and natural disasters. The authors point out the complexity of these issues based on the fact that human actions often have a significant impact on the nature and consequences of a "natural" disaster.

Gill, Joel C., and Bruce D. Malamud. 2017. "Anthropogenic Processes, Natural Hazards, and Interactions in a Multi-Hazard Framework." *Earth-Science Reviews*. 166: 246–269. Available online at https://doi.org/10.1016/j.earscirev.2017.01.002. Accessed on August 10, 2018.

The effects of human activities on the probability and severity of natural disasters are an important theme of this book. In this article, the authors provide a basic introduction to the topic, along with an assessment of the effects of anthropogenic natural disasters.

Grigoli, F., et al. 2018. "The November 2017 Mw 5.5 Pohang Earthquake: A Possible Case of Induced Seismicity in South

Korea." *Science*. 360(6392): 1003–1006. doi:10.1126/science
.aat2010. Accessed on July 29, 2018.

> The authors explore any possible connections between the
> construction of a new geothermal plant in South Korea
> and a large earthquake appearing in the region at about
> the same time.

Hallegatte, Stéphane, and Valentin Przyluski. 2010. "The
Economics of Natural Disasters: Concepts and Methods."
The World Bank. http://documents.worldbank.org/curated/
en/255791468339901668/pdf/WPS5507.pdf. Accessed on
August 1, 2018.

> The authors of this paper discuss the concept of the eco-
> nomic costs of natural disasters. They suggest that tradi-
> tional methods for measuring this variable—the direct costs
> of an event—do not adequately express the real and com-
> plete cost of the event. They outline other ways by which
> such costs can be determined and why they are a better way
> of determining the economic costs of a natural disaster.

Hassol, Susan Joy, et al. 2016. "(Un)Natural Disasters: Communicating Linkages between Extreme Events and Climate
Change." World Meteorological Organization. *Bulletin*. 65(2):
2–9. Available online at https://public.wmo.int/en/resources/
bulletin/unnatural-disasters-communicating-linkages-between-
extreme-events-and-climate. Accessed on July 29, 2018.

> The authors discuss the problems with current efforts to
> connect individual earthquakes, tsunamis, forest fires, or
> other natural disasters with climate change. They point
> out the importance of developing methods of commu-
> nicating these results both to the general public and to
> experts in the field.

Huang, Huang, et al. 2016. "Web3DGIS-Based System for
Reservoir Landslide Monitoring and Early Warning." *Applied*

Sciences. 6(2): 44. doi:10.3390/app6020044. Accessed on August 10, 2018.

> Landslides are the most frequent type of natural disaster, with often catastrophic effects in terms of lives and property loss. This article describes a system developed for use in predicting landslides in the Danjiangkou Reservoir area of China, where the largest lake in Asia is located.

Klomp, Jeroen. 2016. "Economic Development and Natural Disasters: A Satellite Data Analysis." *Global Environmental Change.* 36(1): 67–88.

> The author attempts to measure the economic effects of natural disasters from data collected by Earth-orbiting satellites. The research is based on the assumption that the light intensity of a region is an accurate measure of its economic development.

Kousky, Carolyn. 2016. "Impacts of Natural Disasters on Children." *Future of Children.* 26(1): 73–92. Available online at https://files.eric.ed.gov/fulltext/EJ1101425.pdf. Accessed on August 9, 2018.

> Children can be affected disproportionately by a natural disaster in three ways: damage to their physical health and mental health, as well as experiencing interruptions to their education. The author discusses a number of steps that can be taken to reduce these effects on children.

Kuchment, Anna. 2016. "Drilling for Earthquakes." *Scientific American.* 315(1): 46–53. Available online at https://www.pbs.org/newshour/science/drilling-induced-earthquakes-may-endanger-millions-in-2016-usgs-says. Accessed on July 29, 2018.

> This article, written at the height of concerns about the risks posed by human-induced earthquakes in the U.S. Midwest, provides an excellent general introduction to the issue.

McPhillips, Lauren E., et al. 2018. "Defining Extreme Events: A Cross-Disciplinary Review." *Earth's Future.* 6(3): 441–455.

Natural disasters are a topic of interest to scholars from a wide variety of fields, including climatology, earth sciences, ecology, engineering, hydrology, and social science. The ways in which members of various fields talk about natural disasters, however, can be very different, making it difficult to study and discuss such events. The authors point out the importance of developing a common vocabulary and method of discussing natural disasters in order to better prepare for and work toward the recovery from such events.

Miao, Qing, Yilin Hou, and Michael Abrigo. 2018. "Measuring the Financial Shocks of Natural Disasters: A Panel Study of U.S. States." *National Tax Journal.* 71(1): 11–44. Available online at https://doi.org/10.17310/ntj.2018.1.01. Accessed on August 2, 2018.

This technical paper attempts to assess the cost of dealing with natural disasters for each of the 50 states. It confirms the presumption that the cost to various states differs to a large degree on the basis of the type of disaster concerned.

Mulargia, Francesco, and Andrea Bizzarri. 2015. "Anthropogenic Triggering of Large Earthquakes." *Scientific Reports.* 4(1): Article number 6100. Available online at https://www.nature.com/articles/srep06100. Accessed on July 30, 2018.

The authors review existing evidence on the connection between large earthquakes and possible human activities in the regions surrounding such events. The article is quite technical but provides good information for the general reader.

Nelson, Peter L., and Stephen P. Grand. 2018. "New Evidence for Plume beneath Yellowstone National Park." *Nature Geoscience.* 11(4): 280–284.

The authors report on their most recent research on the Yellowstone caldera and the supervolcanoes from which it was formed.

Noy, Ilan. 2016. "Natural Disasters in the Pacific Island Countries: New Measurements of Impacts." *Natural Hazards.* 84(1): 7–18. Available online at http://researcharchive.vuw.ac.nz/bitstream/handle/10063/4200/Working%20paper.pdf. Accessed on August 1, 2018.

The author asks how accurate the risk analysis for natural disasters is for the Pacific Islands. He finds that the currently accepted analysis "greatly underestimates the burden of disasters" for those islands. Specifically, he compares the risk for natural disasters for this region of the world to be significantly greater than it is for Caribbean islands.

Phalkey, R. K., and V. R. Louis. 2016. "Two Hot to Handle: How Do We Manage the Simultaneous Impacts of Climate Change and Natural Disasters on Human Health?" *European Physical Journal: Special Topics.* 225(3): 443–457.

The authors take note of the fact that there is now abundant evidence about the effects of natural disasters and of climate change on public health issues. They also point out the new issues posed by the interaction of these two forces to produce even more serious health problems. They also show that public health issues resulting from these forces are likely to affect developing nations to a much greater extent than developed nations. They discuss the planning issues posed by this combination of factors.

Sant'Anna, André Albuquerque. 2018. "Not So Natural: Unequal Effects of Public Policies on the Occurrence of Disasters." *Ecological Economics.* 152(10): 273–281. Available online at https://doi.org/10.1016/j.ecolecon.2018.06.011. Accessed on August 1, 2018.

Based on his study of evidence available from Brazilian events, the author asks the question of the extent to which, if any, a government's policies can affect the probability that certain "natural" disasters are likely to occur. He concludes that such policies may have "an important role for urban infrastructure, as proper sewage and waste collection, and forest cover in reducing the impacts of extreme rainfall."

Schmitt, Axel K., et al. 2014. "Identifying the Volcanic Eruption Depicted in a Neolithic Painting at Çatalhöyük, Central Anatolia, Turkey." *PLOS ONE*. Available online at https://doi.org/10.1371/journal.pone.0084711. Accessed on July 29, 2018.

The authors describe their research on cave paintings at Çatalhöyük, Turkey, that may depict the first earthquake recorded in human history. They are able to connect that event with specific mountains in the region.

Simmons, Krystal T., and Denika Y. Douglas. 2018. "After the Storm: Helping Children Cope with Trauma after Natural Disasters." *Communique*. 46(5): 23–25.

The authors point out that the individuals with the greatest likelihood of developing post-traumatic stress disorder (PTSD) are children and that special programs need to be developing for supporting children after a natural disaster.

Stults, Missy. 2017. "Integrating Climate Change into Hazard Mitigation Planning: Opportunities and Examples in Practice." *Climate Risk Management*. 17: 21–34. Available online at https://doi.org/10.1016/j.crm.2017.06.004. Accessed on August 9, 2018.

The author summarizes her research on the extent to which state governments have incorporated FEMA recommendations for including climate change in their disaster management plans. She finds that 23 of 35 states' studies have indicated a commitment to FEMA's recommendations, although they have, in general, not yet developed specific actions that would result in specific preparedness programs or actions.

"Symposium: A Worldwide Response: An Examination of International Law Frameworks in the Aftermath of Natural Disasters." 2011. *Emory International Law Review*. 25(3): whole. Available online at http://law.emory.edu/eilr/content/volume-25/issue-3/symposium/index.html. Accessed on August 9, 2018.

In the light of the devastating 2010 earthquake in Haiti, this journal sponsored a symposium to consider the contribution that international legal systems can contribute to the recovery from such events. Papers reprinted here discuss the experiences of the U.S. Agency for International Development following the event, what existing legal resources can contribute to disaster mitigation, the effect of the earthquake on women in Haiti, and focusing on children's rights in the aftermath of the event.

Urbatsch, R. 2016. "Judgement Days: Moral Attitudes in the Wake of Local Disasters." *Disasters*. 40(1): 26–44.

Some people with strong moral beliefs sometimes blame the occurrence of a natural disaster on moral failings of a nation, state, or region that permit certain types of immoral behaviors. (In 2017, for example, a leading Houston minister suggested that Hurricane Harvey was God's retribution on the city for electing a "very, very aggressively pro-homosexual mayor.") Urbatsch investigates this type of belief among a geographical region that had recently experienced a natural disaster. He found "increased antipathy" toward gay men and lesbians, who were blamed for the event. The pattern tended to disappear over time, however.

Urlainis, Alon, et al. 2014. "Damage in Critical Infrastructures Due to Natural and Man-Made Events—A Critical Review." *Procedia Engineering*. 85: 529–535. Available online at https://doi.org/10.1016/j.proeng.2014.10.580. Accessed on August 9, 2018.

Critical infrastructures (CIs), such as complex transportation and communication systems, continue to grow in number and complexity. The authors ask to what extent the development of these CIs has been accompanied by greater attention to possible damage from natural and man-made disasters. They explore some major events of recent years to answer that question. They find that there is a "mismatch between the actual risk to the CIs and between the investments that were made by decision makers for their preparedness."

Wen, Jun, and Chun-Ping Chang. 2015. "Government Ideology and the Natural Disasters: A Global Investigation." *Natural Hazards*. 78(3): 1481–1490.

The authors explore the question as to whether the ideology of a national government has an effect on the number of natural disasters that occur in a country. They find that the answer is "yes," and such events are less likely to occur in right-wing governments than in other types of government. They attempt to provide a possible explanation for this finding.

Witze, Alexandra. 2009. "Seismology: The Sleeping Dragon." *Nature*. 459(7244): 153–157. Available online at https://www.nature.com/news/2009/090513/full/459153a.html. Accessed on July 30, 2018.

Witze reviews the events surrounding the Great Sichuan Earthquake of May 12, 2008, and the debate that arose as to its possible connection with the construction of the Zipingpu Dam in that area.

"A Worldwide Response: An Examination of International Law Frameworks in the Aftermath of Natural Disasters." *Emory International Law Review*. 25(3): whole. Available online at http://law.emory.edu/eilr/content/volume-25/issue-3/symposium/index.html. Accessed on August 1, 2018.

This special edition of the journal includes papers on the legal, political, economic, and social issues related to natural disasters. A number of the papers draw on the experiences of the 2010 earthquake in Haiti.

Wynn, Stephanie T. 2017. "Natural Disasters Planning for Psychological First Aid." *Journal of Christian Nursing.* 34(1): 24–28. Wynn points out the psychological problems that can be associated with natural disasters and argues that providing so-called psychological first aid should be an important feature of pre-disaster planning.

Xie, Lili, and Zhe Qu. 2018. "On Civil Engineering Disasters and Their Mitigation." *Earthquake Engineering and Engineering Vibration.* 17(1): 1–10. The authors point out the significance of infrastructure in natural disasters and argue that the worst consequences of such events are often the result of poor planning in the construction of buildings and other structures. They suggest improvements that can be made in the training and monitoring of civil engineers to deal with this problem.

Zhou, Lei, et al. 2018. "Emergency Decision Making for Natural Disasters: An Overview." *International Journal of Disaster Risk Reduction.* 27: 567–576. Available online at https://doi .org/10.1016/j.ijdrr.2017.09.037. Accessed on August 2, 2018. The authors introduce the concept of emergency disaster managements (EDM), explain circumstances in which it is used, and how it is to be put into practice. They conclude with a discussion of the ways in which an EDM center can be set up and put into operation.

Zimmer, Adrienne. 2017. "Winds of Destruction: Law Enforcement Use Social Media and Emergency Notification Systems to Decrease Response Times and Increase Safety before, during and after Natural Disasters Strike." *Law Enforcement Technology.* 44(5). https://www.officer.com/training-careers/ article/12325848/law-enforcement-officers-as-first-respond ers-in-natural-disaster-emergency-response. Accessed on August 2, 2018.

This article provides an interesting insight into the use of social media by law enforcement agencies to keep citizens informed about the status of potential natural disasters.

Reports

"Attribution of Extreme Weather Events in the Context of Climate Change." 2016. National Academies of Sciences, Engineering, and Medicine. Washington, DC: The National Academies Press. https://doi.org/10.17226/21852. Accessed on August 7, 2018.

This report explores the extent to which individual natural disasters can be correlated with climate change. The authors conclude that such connections can now be made with a reasonable level of confidence for some natural disasters, such as heat waves, drought, and heavy precipitation. The evidence for such correlations for other disasters is still less convincing, although suggestive of such connections.

"Billion-Dollar Weather and Climate Disasters." 2018. National Centers for Environmental Information. https://www.ncdc.noaa.gov/billions/. Accessed on August 3, 2018.

This annual report provides basic data on the most extreme weather events in the United States. It includes maps that show the locations of such events, summary statistics, historical trends in severe weather events from 1980 to the present day, and a table of all events covered in the report.

"Disaster Resilience: A National Imperative." 2012. Committee on Increasing National Resilience to Hazards and Disasters; Committee on Science, Engineering, and Public Policy. Washington, DC: National Academies Press. https://www.nap.edu/catalog/13457/disaster-resilience-a-national-imperative. Accessed on August 3, 2018.

This report reviews the challenges posed by a host of disasters, including natural disasters, to the American people. It suggests that the best way of dealing with increasing threats from disasters due to climate change is improved programs of resilience, making it possible for communities to "spring back" from disasters as quickly and efficiently as possible.

Field, Christopher B., et al. 2012. "Managing the Risks of Extreme Events and Disasters to Advance Climate Change Adaptation. Special Report of the Intergovernmental Panel on Climate Change." Intergovernmental Panel on Climate Change. Cambridge, UK: Cambridge University Press. https://www.ipcc.ch/site/assets/uploads/2018/03/SREX_Full_Report-1.pdf. Accessed on February 18, 2019.

This special report from the IPCC focuses on the relationship between extreme weather events and climate change. Its major subdivisions deal with "Climate Change: New Dimensions in Disaster Risk, Exposure, Vulnerability, and Resilience"; "Determinants of Risk: Exposure and Vulnerability"; "Changes in Climate Extremes and Their Impacts on the Natural Physical Environment"; "Changes in Impacts of Climate Extremes: Human Systems and Ecosystems"; "Managing the Risks from Climate Extremes at the Local Level"; "National Systems for Managing the Risks from Climate Extremes and Disasters"; "Managing the Risks: International Level and Integration across Scales"; "Toward a Sustainable and Resilient Future"; and "Case Studies."

Guha-Sapir, Debarati, et al. 2017. "Annual Disaster Statistical Review: Numbers and Trends. 2016." Institut De Recherche Santé et Societé. Catholic University of Louvain. https://reliefweb.int/sites/reliefweb.int/files/resources/adsr_2016.pdf. Accessed on August 3, 2018.

This annual publication summarizes major statistical data about natural disasters throughout the world in the preceding year. Categories of data include an overall summary of disaster data, comparisons of the current year with previous years, and regional analysis for five major parts of the world.

Herring, Stephanie C., et al. 2018. "Explaining Extreme Events of 2016 from a Climate Perspective." Special Supplement to the *Bulletin of the American Meteorological Society.* 99(1). http://www.ametsoc.net/eee/2016/2016_bams_eee_low_res.pdf. Accessed on August 3, 2018.

> This report is the sixth annual report by the AMS about the influence of climate change on certain types of natural disasters. Thirty papers in the report examine detailed and technical aspects of specific events, such as those involving ocean heat waves, forest fires, snowstorms, and frost, heavy precipitation, drought, and extreme heat and cold events over land. Reports from previous years are available at https://www.ametsoc.org/ams/index.cfm/publications/bulletin-of-the-american-meteorological-society-bams/explaining-extreme-events-from-a-climate-perspective/. Accessed on August 11, 2018.

"The Human Cost of Weather-Related Disasters 1995–2015." 2015. United Nations Office for Disaster Risk Reduction; Centre for Research on the Epidemiology of Disasters. https://www.unisdr.org/files/46796_cop21weatherdisastersreport2015.pdf. Accessed on August 3, 2018.

> This report makes the assumption that much of the weather-related disasters that have occurred in the 20-year period covered is a result of climate change. Chapters of the report deal with statistical and descriptive information about weather-related disasters, the human costs of such events, the impacts of weather-related disasters on specific countries, weather-related disasters and national income, and the economic costs of such disasters.

"The Impact of Disasters on Agriculture: Addressing the Information Gap." 2017. Food and Agriculture Organization of the United Nations. https://reliefweb.int/sites/reliefweb.int/files/resources/a-i7279e.pdf. Access on August 9, 2018.

> Agricultural operations, especially in developing countries, are hard-hit by natural disasters. This report summarizes

a range of data and statistical information about the type and extent of such damages in developing nations of the world.

"The Impact of Disasters on Agriculture and Food Security." 2015. Food and Agriculture Organization of the United Nations. https://reliefweb.int/sites/reliefweb.int/files/resources/a-i5128e.pdf. Accessed on August 9, 2018.

The number, severity, and cost of natural disasters have risen dramatically in the past decade. Yet relatively little is known about the specific effects of these events on agricultural systems. This report was prepared to summarize and discuss the data that are available on the question. Individual chapters deal with the scope of disasters on agriculture, quantifying production losses and other economic harm, drought in sub-Saharan Africa as a special case of the trends, and a summary of core findings and recommendations.

Multihazard Mitigation Council. 2017. "Natural Hazard Mitigation Saves 2017 Interim Report: An Independent Study." Washington, DC: National Institute of Building Sciences. http://www.wbdg.org/files/pdfs/MS2_2017Interim%20Report.pdf. Accessed on August 12, 2018.

Questions sometimes arise as to whether and/or to what extent a variety of federal funding programs affect the recovery from major natural disasters. This report is the latest in a series of studies on this question. The most important finding reported here is that every dollar spent by the U.S. government on resiliency projects produces a savings of $6 on future costs of a disaster.

"Natural Hazards Mitigation." 2017. WBDG Secure/Safe Committee. https://www.wbdg.org/design-objectives/secure-safe/natural-hazards-mitigation. Accessed on August 9, 2018.

This website provides an overview of natural disasters and recommendations for their mitigation from the National

Institute of Building Sciences. The report covers virtually all types of natural disasters, with suggestions for reducing the damage caused by disasters for each type. The web page also contains a valuable guide to relevant codes and standards and additional resources on the topic.

Nicholson, Craig, and R. L. Wesson. 1990. "Earthquake Hazard Associated with Deep Well Injection: A Report to the U.S. Environmental Protection Agency." U.S. Geological Survey. Washington, DC: U.S. Government Printing Office.

This report reviews circumstances under which fluid injection operations can trigger earthquakes, some examples of those events, and conditions under which they may occur.

Parker, Miles. 2016. "The Impact of Disasters on Inflation." European Central Bank. https://www.ecb.europa.eu/pub/pdf/scpwps/ecbwp1982.en.pdf?9ec610060c1ba201946fa4602a9bb544. Accessed on August 9, 2018.

The author notes that the study of the ways in which natural disasters affect inflation is "one of the main remaining gaps in our understanding of the impact of disasters." His review of research on the topic finds that the impact of a natural disaster on a nation's rate of inflation depends on its economic condition (developed countries suffer relatively mild effects, while developing countries may experience devastating consequences) and the type of disaster involved.

Petersen, Mark D., et al. 2018. "One Year Seismic Hazard Forecast for the Central and Eastern United States from Induced and Natural Earthquakes." *Seismological Research Letters.* 89(3): 1049–1061. https://doi.org/10.1785/0220180005.

The authors review data for induced earthquakes in the United States since 2005, noting a large increase in such events between 2008 and 2015 but a steady decline from 2015 to the time of the report (2018).

Safaie, Sashar. 2017. "National Disaster Risk Assessment. Words into Action Guidelines. Governance System, Methodologies, and Use of Results." Geneva: United Nations Office for Disaster Risk Reduction. https://www.preventionweb.net/files/52828_nationaldisasterriskassessmentwiagu.pdf. Accessed on August 13, 2018.

> The first priority of the Sendai Framework for Disaster Risk Reduction 2015–2030 (see entry) was to promote the understanding of natural disasters as the basis for developing national policies about such events. This report is an attempt to "change words into actions" by outlining specific activities that can be taken by international, regional, and national agencies to achieve this goal. The three primary parts of the report deal with suggestions for policy, special topics (e.g., Health Aspect in Disaster Risk Assessment), and hazard-specific risk assessment (e.g., earthquakes and tsunamis).

Sanderson, David, and Anshu Sharma, eds. 2016. International Federation of Red Cross and Red Crescent Societies. https://www.ifrc.org/Global/Documents/Secretariat/201610/WDR%202016-FINAL_web.pdf. Accessed on August 3, 2018.

> This report attempts to make the argument for "a different approach to humanitarian action [in dealing with natural disasters], one that strives to strengthen the resilience of vulnerable and at-risk communities." The key to this approach is *resilience*, the ability of individuals and communities to recover from natural disasters as quickly as possible. The report outlines in detail the elements needed to assist communities in developing the infrastructure, technology, attitudes, and skills needed to improve their resilience to natural disasters. An especially useful part of the report is the annex, which contains 13 tables of data about natural disasters throughout the world.

"Sendai Framework for Disaster Risk Reduction 2015–2030." 2015. Geneva: United Nations Office for Disaster Risk Reduction.

https://www.unisdr.org/files/43291_sendaiframeworkfordr
ren.pdf. Accessed on August 3, 2018.

This document outlines the steps that need to be taken to "prevent new and reduce existing disaster risks." The program involves four major elements: understanding disaster risk; strengthening disaster risk governance to manage disaster risk; investing in disaster reduction for resilience; and enhancing disaster preparedness for effective response. The report lists seven targets and four priorities for achieving this objective. (For an important preliminary report prepared for the Sendai conference, see https://www.preventionweb.net/english/hyogo/gar/2015/en/gar-pdf/GAR2015_EN.pdf.)

"Tsunami Glossary, 3rd ed." 2015. Intergovernmental Oceanographic Commission. Technical Series 85. http://itic.ioc-unesco
.org/images/stories/about_tsunamis/tsunami_glossary/
309_16_Tsunami%20Glossary%20E_errata_20160907.pdf.
Accessed on July 29, 2018.

This publication provides an excellent general introduction to tsunamis, going far beyond the definition of terms used in the field. It also discusses tsunami classification, surveys and measurements, tides and mareographs, tsunami warning systems, and organizations and acronyms.

Ward, Sarah, Alison Hemberger, and Sasha Muench. 2017. "Driving Resilience: Market Approaches to Disaster Recovery." Mercy Corps. https://www.mercycorps.org/sites/default/files/
Market-Approaches-disaster-recovery-september-2017-Mercy-
Corps-JPMorgan.pdf. Accessed on August 11, 2018.

Although providing aid to individuals affected by a natural disaster is of paramount importance, efforts should be made to help the community recover also. This report discusses the ways in which that goal can be achieved by actions such as "injecting cash into the local economy, improving access to finance, providing economic opportunities for affected individuals, and protecting local networks and social capital."

"When Catastrophe Strikes: Responses to Natural Disasters in Indian Country." 2015. Hearing before the Committee on Indian Affairs, United States Senate, One Hundred Thirteenth Congress, Second Session, July 30, 2014. United States Senate. Committee on Indian Affairs. Washington, DC: U.S. Government Printing Office.

This hearing focuses on special concerns among Native Americans who are victims of a natural disaster, current policies and resources available to them for such events, and needed changes to improve resiliency and recovery in the face of future disasters.

Willis, Henry H., et al. 2016. "Current and Future Exposure of Infrastructure in the United States to Natural Hazards." Santa Monica, CA: Rand Corporation. https://www.rand.org/content/dam/rand/pubs/research_reports/RR1400/RR1453/RAND_RR1453.pdf. Accessed on August 7, 2018.

This report was produced in response to a request by the Department of Homeland Security's National Preparedness and Programs Directorate's Office of Infrastructure Protection to analyze the type of exposures to which national infrastructure systems are exposed by natural hazards and how these exposures are expected to change in response to climate change. Two major findings of the research are that "infrastructure exposure to natural hazards is expected to increase—and, in some cases, increase substantially—across the continental United States" and that "infrastructure in some areas of the country currently faces disproportionate exposure to natural hazards, and this exposure is likely to increase in the future as a result of climate change."

Internet

Adeboyejo, Bodé. 2018. "Natural Disaster: An Act of God or Man?" The Lord's Quill. http://www.lordsquill.com/Articles/Reformational/Natural_Disaster.htm. Accessed on August 12, 2018.

Adeboyejo is a "Christian freelance writer" who attempts to explain God's role in the occurrence of natural disasters, concluding that human actions contribute to the appearance of such events, although they are ultimately a reflection of God's will.

Aldrich, Daniel P. 2017. "Recovering from Disasters: Social Networks Matter More Than Bottled Water and Batteries." The Conversation. https://theconversation.com/recovering-from-disasters-social-networks-matter-more-than-bottled-water-and-batteries-69611. Accessed on August 11, 2018.

As the title suggests, the author believes that functioning social institutions are at least as important as, and probably more important than, individual humanitarian and physical aid. The article contains links to two research papers that discuss his findings on this issue in more detail.

"Attribution of the 2018 Heat in Northern Europe." 2018. World Weather Attribution. https://www.worldweatherattribution.org/analyses/attribution-of-the-2018-heat-in-northern-europe/. Accessed on July 31, 2018.

This study, done in real-time analysis of weather patterns in Northern Europe in 2018, concludes that "the probability of such a heatwave to occur has increased everywhere in this region due to anthropogenic climate change" and that "the probability to have such a heat or higher is generally more than two times higher today than if human activities had not altered climate."

Barnes, Kent B., John M. Morgan III, and Martin C. Roberge. 2002. "Impervious Surfaces and the Quality of Natural and Built Environments." Department of Geography and Environmental Planning. Towson University. http://citeseerx.ist.psu.edu/viewdoc/download?doi=10.1.1.477.2834&rep=rep1&type=pdf. Accessed on July 29, 2018.

The authors explain the ways in which an increase in impervious surfaces from greater construction in urban areas has affected the natural environment, including increases in annual average temperatures and greater flooding in an area.

Boccard, Nicolas. 2018. "Natural Disasters Trends." SSRN. http://dx.doi.org/10.2139/ssrn.3116231 or https://ssrn.com/abstract=3116231. Accessed on August 2, 2018.

The author attempts to assess trends in the occurrence of natural disasters based on a variety of factors, such as financial costs and loss of life. He notes that the risks to developing nations is about three times as great as it is for developed nations.

"Browse K-12 STEM Curriculum." 2018. Teach Engineering. https://www.teachengineering.org/curriculum/browse?q=natural+disasters. Accessed on August 4, 2018.

This website offers more than 80 well-developed teaching units, lessons, and other activities for students from kindergarten through 12th grade on various aspects of engineering issues associated with natural disasters. Some examples include "Engineering to Prevent Natural Disasters: Save Our City!"; "Natural Disasters: Earthquakes, Volcanoes, Tornadoes & More"; "A Closer Look at Natural Disasters Using GIS"; "Naturally Disastrous"; "Earthquakes Living Lab: Designing for Disaster"; "Mini-Landslide"; and "Survive That Tsunami! Testing Model Villages in Big Waves."

"Contingency Planning for Natural Disasters." 2018. Relief Web. https://reliefweb.int/sites/reliefweb.int/files/resources/5 9D109D27B44E277C1256C7C0040C6DB-unicef-contin gency-2000.pdf. Accessed on August 7, 2018.

This website provides a thorough listing of the steps one can take to increase survival odds before, during, and after an earthquake, tsunami, volcanic eruption, or other natural disaster event.

"Deep-Ocean Assessment and Reporting of Tsunamis (DART)." 2018. Pacific Marine Environmental Laboratory. NOAA Center for Tsunami Research. https://nctr.pmel.noaa .gov/Dart/dart_home.html. Accessed on July 29, 2018.

> DART is NOAA's system for forecasting tsunamis. This web page explains how that mission is carried out, with technical information and references, a history of the system and of individual components, and real-time data on possible events.

"The Disaster Center." 2018. http://www.disastercenter.com/. Accessed on July 28, 2018.

> This website provides a somewhat confusing list of links to various specific topics in the area of natural disasters, such as 7 Day Wildfire Forecast, National Fire News, FEMA Daily Situation Report, Ocean Prediction Center, and 6 to 10 Day Temperature Outlook.

"Disaster Relief Agencies." 2018. Disaster Center. http://www .disastercenter.com/agency.htm. Accessed on July 28, 2018.

> This web page contains a somewhat disorganized and religious-group-focused list of agencies that provide assistance in a wide range of natural disasters.

"Disaster Risk Management." 2018. The World Bank. https:// www.worldbank.org/en/topic/disasterriskmanagement. Accessed on August 12, 2018.

> The term *disaster risk management* has been defined as the development of policies and practices "to prevent new disaster risks, reduce existing disaster risks, and manage residual risks" from natural disasters. This website provides an overview of the World Bank's efforts in this area, with links to reports on the topic for six major regions of the world. The reports include reviews of disaster risk management programs in all countries within each region.

Edwards, Chris. 2014. "The Federal Emergency Management Agency: Floods, Failures, and Federalism." Policy Analysis. The Cato Institute. Number 764. https://object.cato.org/sites/cato .org/files/pubs/pdf/pa764_1.pdf. Accessed on August 11, 2018.
    The author discusses in detail the role the federal government has played in disaster recovery, primarily in the areas of hurricanes and floods. He concludes that federal laws, policies, and other actions have significantly contributed to the worsening of these events and helped to only a modest extent in helping communities recover from them. He makes recommendations for changing the government's role in helping regions recover from natural disasters.

Ferris, Elizabeth. 2010. "Natural Disasters, Conflict, and Human Rights: Tracing the Connections." The Brookings Institution. https://www.brookings.edu/wp-content/uploads/2016/06/ 0303_natural_disasters_ferris.pdf. Accessed on August 9, 2018.
    Natural disasters are often followed by actions that affect the human rights of survivors. This paper examines how this process happens and what its consequences are, based in part on the study of three major disasters: the 2004 tsunamis in Asia, Hurricane Katrina in 2005, and the earthquake in Haiti in 2010.

"Focus on Floods." 2018. The Nurture Nature Center. http:// focusonfloods.org/. Accessed on July 29, 2018.
    This web page provides an excellent general overview of flooding issues, including flood alerts, flood plans, flood history, flood zones, and flood insurance.

"Global Risk Data Platform." 2013. United Nations Environment Programme. http://preview.grid.unep.ch/index.php? preview=home&lang=eng. Accessed on August 2, 2018.
    This interactive website provides information on the risk of natural disasters occurring in every country in the world. Users can search by past events, current risk, exposure, and hazards, along with basic background information for every country.

"Grants & Assistance Programs for Individuals." 2017. FEMA. https://www.fema.gov/grants-assistance-programs-individuals. Accessed on July 28, 2018.

> The federal government provides aid of various kinds for individuals who have been affected by various types of natural disasters. This website provides links to all of the resources available for this purpose.

Guarino, Mark. 2012. "Fear the Almighty Wrath: Five Natural Disasters 'Caused' by Gays." Salon. https://www.salon.com/2012/10/30/fear_the_almighty_wrath_five_natural_disasters_caused_by_gays/. Accessed on August 2, 2018.

> This article reviews some of the natural disasters of recent years that have been attributed to gay acts or acts of governments that have permitted gay activities. It reflects a theme that has run through explanations of natural disasters since at least the times of the biblical flood.

"Heavy Weather: Tracking the Fingerprints of Climate Change, Two Years after the Paris Summit." 2017. Energy & Climate Intelligence Unit. https://eciu.net/assets/Reports/ECIU_Climate_Attribution-report-Dec-2017.pdf. Accessed on July 29, 2018.

> In recent years, researchers have become increasingly interested in efforts to connect specific disaster events with climate change. This article summarizes the results of a search for articles of this type in the two-year period following the Paris summit on climate change in 2015.

Isidore, Kouadio Koffi, et al. 2012. "Preventing and Controlling Infectious Diseases after Natural Disasters." United Nations University. https://unu.edu/publications/articles/preventing-and-controlling-infectious-diseases-after-natural-disasters.html#info. Accessed on August 4, 2018.

> Human effects of natural disasters often include human deaths and injuries. The authors point out, however, the more long-term effects can include epidemics of infectious

diseases. They discuss examples of such events and suggest steps that can be taken to reduce the risk of disaster-related diseases.

Kirschenbaum, Alan, and Carmit Rapaport. 2018. "Informal Social Networks as Generic Contingency Plans." *Journal of Contingencies and Crisis Management.* https://doi.org/10.1111/1468-5973.12222.
  The authors suggest that formal mitigation programs and protocols for natural disasters may often be inadequate for dealing with the rapid, unpredictable changes that occur during such events. They explore the possibility of making greater use of informal social networks for providing information and guidance during a natural disaster.

"The Landslide Guidebook—A Guide to Understanding Landslides." 2008. U.S. Geological Survey. https://pubs.usgs.gov/circ/1325/pdf/C1325_508.pdf. Accessed on July 28, 2018.
  This publication provides basic information about landslides, such as types of landslides, where they occur, what causes a landslide, the effects and consequences of landslides, and the relationship of landslides with other types of natural disasters.

"Mass Wasting." 2018. California State University Long Beach. https://web.csulb.edu/depts/geology/facultypages/bperry/Mass%20Wasting/Types_of_Mass_Wasting.htm. Accessed on July 29, 2018.
  This web page provides an excellent overview of mass wasting, its causes, and methods of prevention.

McClendon, Russell. 2013. "A Timeline of the Distant, Disturbing Future." Mother Nature Network. https://www.mnn.com/earth-matters/space/blogs/a-timeline-of-the-distant-disturbing-future. Accessed on August 12, 2018.
  Predicting the future is always a chancy enterprise, especially as one moves further into the future. McClendon

attempts to do so for natural disasters with predictions ranging from about 100 years (with some degree of dependability) to $10^{10^{10^{76.66}}}$ years (with only some general expectation of accuracy) into the future.

"Natural Catastrophes and Man-Made Disasters in 2017: A Year of Record-Breaking Losses." 2018. Swiss Re Institute. http://media.swissre.com/documents/sigma1_2018_en.pdf. Accessed on July 28, 2018.

This report by one of the world's leading reinsurers provides a fascinating detailed review of the natural and human-made disasters in one specific recent year, with a host of helpful tables, charts, and graphs.

"Natural Disaster News." 2018. Science Daily. https://www .sciencedaily.com/news/earth_climate/natural_disasters/. Accessed on August 4, 2018.

There is probably no better resource for the latest research and news on natural disasters of all kinds in all parts of the world. The articles cover events even with the last few hours before posting.

"Natural Disasters." 2018. Fact Monster. https://www.fact monster.com/world/natural-disasters. Accessed on August 12, 2018.

This website provides an excellent summary of natural disasters in human history. The list of these events is divided, first of all, by topic (21 items) and then by event within each topic chronologically arranged.

"Natural Disasters." 2018. govtrack. https://www.govtrack.us/ congress/bills/subjects/natural_disasters/6020#current_status[]= 28&congress=__ALL__. Accessed on August 13, 2018.

This website is a searchable tool for all bills that have been introduced, acted upon, and passed from 2009 to 2019. More than 500 such bills were introduced, 59 of which were passed and signed by the president.

"Natural Disasters or 'Acts of God'?" 2013. *New York Times.* https://www.nytimes.com/roomfordebate/2013/11/18/natu ral-disasters-or-acts-of-god. Accessed on August 12, 2018.

In November 2013, the *Times* ran an Opinion Page on the question as to how, if at all and to what extent, the concept of God is involved in natural disasters. The question is discussed by six individuals, a theologian, professor of law, professor of religion and environmental studies, and three authors of books on the topic. The complete, long debate is available on the website, along with numerous comments from readers in response to each commentator's remarks.

"Natural Disasters or Divine Punishment?" 2018. Understanding Islam. https://free-islamic-course.org/articles-on-topical-issues/natural-disasters-divine-punishment.html. Accessed on August 2, 2018.

This article explains when and why natural disasters occur as a punishment by God for immoral behaviors.

"Natural Disasters Timeline." 2018. World History Project. https://worldhistoryproject.org/topics/natural-disasters/page/1. Accessed on August 12, 2018.

This excellent website lists and describes a number of natural disasters ranging from the Minoan Eruption of Mount Thera during the period 1650–1450 BCE to the Lushan (China) earthquake of 2013.

"Natural Hazards." 2018. U.S. Geological Survey. https://www.usgs.gov/science/mission-areas/natural-hazards?qt-mis sion_areas_l2_landing_page_ta=0#qt-mission_areas_l2_land ing_page_ta. Accessed on August 4, 2018.

The USGS is a primary resource for information about many aspects of all natural disasters. This web page has sections on the science of natural disasters, data and tools, maps, USGS publications, multimedia resources, and recent news of events.

"Natural Hazards and Disasters." 2013. Washington, DC: U.S. Army Corps of Engineers. https://www.usace.army.mil/Portals/2/docs/STEM/STEM_ED_Curriculum2015.pdf. Accessed on August 4, 2018.

The U.S. Army Corps of Engineers, along with the Department of Defense Education Activity, has developed a series of lessons for middle school students on STEM (science, technology, education, and math) applications of natural hazards and disasters. The program involves cooperation between military and civilian scientists and engineers working with teachers and students on units for each of seven kinds of major disasters.

Nelson, Stephen A. 2018. "Natural Hazards and Natural Disasters." Tulane University. https://www.tulane.edu/~sanelson/Natural_Disasters/introduction.htm. Accessed on August 4, 2018.

This web page provides an excellent general overview about the nature of natural disasters, covering all relevant aspects of the topic.

Plumer, Brad. 2017. "Trump Ignores Climate Change. That's Very Bad for Disaster Planners." *New York Times*. https://www.nytimes.com/2017/11/09/climate/fema-flooding-trump.html. Accessed on August 7, 2018.

In a reflection of the administration of President Donald Trump's skepticism about climate change, FEMA's 2018–2022 Strategic Plan ignores any possible effects of climate change on the occurrence and/or severity of natural disasters. For one contrarian review of this action, see Scata, Joel. 2018. "FEMA's Disaster Preparedness Plan Is a Disaster for the U.S." Natural Resources Defense Council. https://www.nrdc.org/experts/joel-scata/femas-disaster-preparedness-plan-disaster-us. Accessed on August 7, 2018.

Roser, Max, and Hannah Ritchie. 2018. "Natural Catastrophes." Our World in Data. https://ourworldindata.org/natural-catastrophes. Accessed on August 4, 2018.

> This website provides a wealth of data on natural disasters in general (e.g., the number of people left homeless by natural disasters) as well as specific types of natural disasters (e.g., hurricanes, tornadoes, and cyclones).

"So Many People Yelling for Help." 2014. *Seattle Times*. http://old.seattletimes.com/flatpages/local/oso-mudslide-coverage.html. Accessed on July 29, 2018.

> This web page provides a collection of articles from the *Seattle Times* dealing with the Snohomish County landslide of March 22, 2014. The articles deal with all aspects of the event, including warnings about its dangers, the science of the slide, and recovering from the incident.

"Tsunami." 2018. National Oceanic and Atmospheric Administration. https://www.tsunami.noaa.gov/warnings_forecasts.html. Accessed on August 10, 2018.

> This website provides links to more than a dozen resources that provide additional detailed information about the Pacific Northwest tsunami warning system.

"What Is NIDIS?" 2018. Drought.gov. https://www.drought.gov/drought/what-nidis. Accessed on August 10, 2018.

> The National Integrated Drought Information Service was created in 2006 to, among other goals, develop a method for predicting the possibility of drought in nine regions of the United States. This website provides detailed information about that program. For an excellent illustrated PowerPoint presentation on the topic, see https://www.drought.gov/drought/sites/drought.gov.drought/files/media/regions/rdews/PacificNW/pre_05042015_PNWInland Outlook_Marrs.pdf. Accessed on August 10, 2018.

"What Is UN-SPIDER?" 2017. Knowledge Portal. Space-Based Information for Disaster Management and Emergency Response. http://www.un-spider.org/about/what-is-un-spider. Accessed on August 12, 2018.

In December 2006, the United Nations General Assembly adopted a resolution calling for the creation of an agency (UN-SPIDER) to ensure that all countries and regional groups have access to information about possible natural disasters, their effects, and recovery programs. This website provides a brief history of the organization, along with links to papers, reports, and other documents that have been produced by the agency since its founding.

"Wildland Fire Operations." 2018. Fire and Aviation Management. https://www.nps.gov/fire/wildland-fire/learning-center/fireside-chats/history-timeline/wildland-fire-operations.cfm. Accessed on July 29, 2018.

This web page provides a timeline of important events in the history of wildland fires in the United States, dating from the diaries of the Lewis and Clark expedition in 1804 to Smokey Bear's 60th anniversary in 2004.

"Wildland Fire Policy." 2018. Office of Wildland Fire. U.S. Department of the Interior. https://www.doi.gov/wildlandfire/fire-policy. Accessed on July 29, 2018.

This web page provides links to many issues associated with federal wildland policy, including manuals, policy memoranda, fire handbooks, standards for firefighting, with links to other federal agencies with wildland fire responsibilities.

Williams, Mary. 2018. "First Aid and Health Safety for Disasters." CPR Certified. https://www.cprcertified.com/blog/first-aid-and-health-safety-for-disasters. Accessed on August 4, 2018.

The author, a registered nurse and doctor of chiropractic, provides a detailed description of the major types of natural disasters, what risks are associated with each, how to prepare for a disaster, and what to do during and after the event.

Books on Specific Natural Disasters

Ahrens, C. Donald, and Perry J. Samson. 2011. *Extreme Weather and Climate*. Belmont, MA: Brooks and Cole.

Ahrens, Marty. 2013. *Brush, Grass, and Forest Fires*. Quincy, MA: National Fire Protection Association, Fire Analysis and Research Division. Available online at https://www.nfpa.org/-/media/Files/News-and-Research/Fire-statistics/Brush-grass-and-forest-fires/osbrushgrassforest.ashx?la=en. Accessed on August 8, 2018.

Brumbaugh, David S. 2010. *Earthquakes: Science and Society*, 2nd ed. Upper Saddle River, NJ: Pearson Education.

Clague, John J., and Douglas Stead. 2018. *Landslides: Types, Mechanisms and Modeling*. Cambridge, UK; New York: Cambridge University Press.

Cook, Ben. 2019. *Drought: An Interdisciplinary Perspective*. New York: Columbia University Press.

Decker, Robert, and Barbara Decker. 2006. *Volcanoes*, 4th ed. New York: W. H. Freeman.

Highfield, Samuel D., Wesley E. Kang, and Jung Eun Broday. 2018. *Rising Waters: The Causes and Consequences of Flooding in the United States*. Cambridge, UK; New York: Cambridge University Press.

O'Meara, Donna. 2008. *Volcano: A Visual Guide*. Richmond Hill, OH: Firefly Books.

Rothery, David. 2016. *Volcanoes, Earthquakes and Tsunamis: A Complete Introduction*. London: Hodder Education.

Satake, Kanji, et al., eds. 2012. *Tsunamis in the World Ocean*, two volumes. Basel: Springer.

Waltham, Tony. 2010. *Sinkholes and Subsidence: Karst and Cavernous Rocks in Engineering and Construction*. Berlin: Springer.

Winchester, Simon. 2017. *When the Sky Breaks: Hurricanes, Tornadoes, and the Worst Weather in the World*. New York: Penguin.

7 Chronology

Natural disasters have made an impact on human life, as well as the natural environment, throughout the planet's history. This chapter lists some of the most important of those events, along with some of the actions humans have taken to prevent or ameliorate the effects of such disasters.

About 440 million years ago   The first evidence for wildfires is found in charcoal resulting from the burning of low-growing vegetation in the area of modern Wales.

About 66 million years ago   An asteroid 10–15 kilometers (6–9 miles) in diameter strikes Earth near the present-day town of Chicxulub, Mexico. The impact created a crater about 180 kilometers (110 miles) in diameter and resulted in the destruction of dinosaurs and many other forms of life on Earth.

About 6600 BCE   A wall painting found at the Neolithic site at Çatal Höyük in Anatolia, Turkey, appears to show a volcanic eruption from nearby Mount Hasan in Central Anatolia.

About 2000 BCE   A Sumerian legend marks perhaps the first rendering of the "biblical flood" story, in which a group of gods decide to unleash a huge flood that will destroy human civilization. One of the gods, Ea, relents and tells a man by the name of Utnapishtim of the forthcoming flood, making it possible

---

A sinkhole opens up in front of JR Hakata Station in Fukuoka, Japan, on November 8, 2016. The sinkhole was 30 meters long, 30 meters wide, and 15 meters deep, but water flowing into the hole from a drain raised the possibility that it could expand further. (The Asahi Shimbun/Getty Images)

for him to build a boat on which he and some other living creatures are able to survive the flood.

1831 BCE   An earthquake that strikes Mount Tai in China is regarded as the first-recorded event of its kind. The report occurs in the Chinese historical text, the *Bamboo Chronicles*.

About 1600 BCE   A giant earthquake, or series of earthquakes, strikes the Supe Valley, along the coast of Peru. The quake (or quakes) caused massive landslides and may have also produced a huge tsunami, both of which wiped out fishing regions and farmland in the valley, bringing to an end a civilization that has thrived in the region for at least 2,000 years.

About 1500 BCE   A volcanic eruption known as the Thera, or Santorini, eruption occurs on the island of the latter name. The eruption is one of the largest eruptions in recorded history. It destroyed the Minoan town of Arkotiri and much of the island itself. The island of Santorini today consists essentially of the remnants of that eruption.

373 BCE   An earthquake and tsunami strike and destroy the city of Helika in the ancient region of Achaea, Greece. The city and all of its inhabitants are said to have sunk in the sea. Legend also holds that rats, snakes, and other vermin disappeared from the region a few days before the earthquake struck.

226 BCE   An earthquake that strikes the Greek island of Rhodes results in the destruction of a famous statue of the Colussus. The statue breaks apart at the knees and lays on the surrounding ground for about 800 years. The event occurs only 56 years after construction of the statue, often listed among the Seven Wonders of the Ancient World.

17 CE   The first earthquake for which extensive records are available strikes the Lydian region of modern-day Turkey. As many as 15 cities and towns are destroyed by the disaster.

79 CE   The eruption of Mount Vesuvius near the Bay of Naples results in more than 2,000 deaths, leading to its occurrence as being "the worst volcanic eruption in recorded history."

132 CE   Chinese inventor Zhang Heng invents an early type of seismometer for the detection of earthquakes. The device is intended to warn of one of the many disastrous earthquakes that had devastated the country over previous centuries. (For an image, see https://ancient-code.com/this-ancient-chinese-earthquake-detector-predates-modern-devices-by-nearly-two-millennia/.)

365 CE   An estimated 50,000 people die in an earthquake whose epicenter is located in Crete. The quake also destroyed the cities of Alexandria in Egypt and Leptis Magna in modern-day Libya.

1201   An earthquake thought to be the most destructive in human history strikes lands bordering the Mediterranean Sea (probably Egypt and/or Syria) resulting in an estimated 1.1 million deaths. The deaths are attributed not only to the immediate effects of the earthquake but also to famine and disease that followed the event.

1556   An earthquake strikes the region of Shaanxi Province, China, on January 23, resulting in an estimated 800,000 deaths and the destruction of numerous towns and villages. The earthquake is thought to be the most destructive such event in history.

1596   Flemish mapmaker Abraham Ortelius notes that the coastlines of the continents appear to fit together, suggesting that the continents were once joined and then later torn apart by some unknown force.

1700   The earthquake with one of the two greatest magnitudes in American history (8.7–9.2), the so-called Cascadia earthquake, strikes the Pacific Northwest. No written records remain of the event in a largely undeveloped area, but details of the event can be constructed from Japanese records describing a tsunami created by the earthquake.

1755   The Lisbon Earthquake of 1755 almost completely destroys the capitol of the Kingdom of Portugal, as well as towns and cities as far away as Algiers, in modern Algeria.

1804   Members of the Lewis and Clark expedition make extensive and detailed records of wildfires that spread across the Great Plains, along with the source of those fires, the reasons for human-caused fires, and the ecological benefits provided by the fires.

1811–1812   A series of earthquakes, known as the New Madrid earthquakes, occur along the Mississippi River in modern-day Missouri. The quakes are the most powerful earthquakes to occur in the United States east of the Mississippi River.

1815   The eruption of Mount Tambora on Sumbawa Island in modern-day Indonesia results in an estimated 71,000 deaths and changes in weather patterns so severe that the following year is often referred to as "the year without a summer."

1841   The first volcanological observatory, the Vesuvius Observatory, is founded in the Kingdom of the Two Sicilies by King Fernando II. The primary purpose of the facility was to observe changes occurring in the volcanic systems adjacent to the Bay of Naples.

1849   The Smithsonian Institution initiates the collection and distribution of weather information in the United States, an activity that was to become formalized in the formation of the U.S. National Weather Service in 1870 (q.v.).

1869 (other dates are also given)   The first fire tower in the United States is built outside Helena, Montana, after a wildfire destroyed most of the city's downtown area. The tower was demolished in 2017.

1870   The U.S. Congress establishes the U.S. National Weather Service as an agency of the U.S. Army Signal Service's Division of Telegrams and Reports for the Benefit of Commerce. A major activity throughout the agency's existence has been the study and provision of information about severe storms in the United States.

1871   The worst-recorded forest fire in North America history occurs in the region around Peshtigo, Wisconsin, a disaster covering 1.2 million acres, in which 1,182 people were killed.

1879   The U.S. Geological Survey is established by an act of Congress. The agency is currently responsible for the collection and dissemination of information about many types of natural disasters, including earthquakes, volcanic eruptions, tsunamis, and landslides.

1881   A group of individuals led by American nurse Clara Barton establish the American Red Cross, an organization dedicated to providing relief for victims of war, natural disasters, and other forms of human suffering. The organization's first formal activity is the provision of aid to survivors of the Great Thumb of 1881, for which they provided clothes, household items, and money.

1886   Troop M of the 1st United States Cavalry arrive in Yellowstone National Park for the purpose of managing the administration and protection of the park. Within a few weeks, members of the troop are called to fight a wildfire in the park, the first confirmed use of paid firefighters to deal with forest fires.

1888   A blizzard covering much of the eastern United States drops as much as 50 inches of snow, making it the worst storm of its type in U.S. history.

1896   In terms of deaths, the worst heat wave in U.S. history strikes New York City, where 10 days of more than 90°F degree temperatures result in the death of about 1,500 people, most residents of tenement buildings where no heat relief systems were available.

1899   British geologist and mining engineer John Milne, recognizing the need for international data on earthquakes, begins collecting such data from 35 countries. His data are first published in 1918 as the International Seismological Summary. Publication was continued after 1964 as the International Seismological Centre Bulletin.

1900   The Great Hurricane of 1900 strikes the Galveston, Texas, area. The storm is generally considered one of the most devastating natural disasters ever to hit the United States. It results in an estimated 6,000–12,000 deaths, 10,000–12,000 injures, 30,000 homeless people, and property damages reaching about $30 million ($840 million in 2018 dollars).

1900 One of the earliest examples of human-induced earthquakes is a series of seismic events in the gold mine fields of Kolar, India. The earthquakes were caused by the collapse of mines that had become too large to support overhanging materials.

1901 A heat wave with temperatures reaching 109°F covers most of the eastern United States. Approximately 9,500 people (along with more than 200 horses) die from heat-related conditions during the months of June and July.

1906 An earthquake usually described as the most destructive in the history of the United States occurs in the San Francisco Bay area. Death toll is thought to be about 3,000, and an estimated 80 percent of the city is destroyed.

1906 Motivated by the San Francisco earthquake, Alexander McAdie of the San Francisco office of the United States Weather Bureau sends out a letter calling a meeting to consider organizing a seismological society. The first regular meeting of the society, the Seismological Society of America, is held on November 20 that year.

1908 A meteorite (sometimes referred to as the Great Siberian Meteorite) explodes an estimated 5–10 kilometers (3–6 miles) above the Stony Tunguska River in Yeniseysk Governorate (now Krasnoyarsk Krai), Russia. The force of the explosion flattens an estimated 2,000 square kilometers (770 square miles) of forests around the blast site. The event is said to have been the largest impact of an extraterrestrial object on Earth in recorded history.

1909 Serbian seismologist Andrija Mohorovičić reports on a boundary between Earth's crust and mantle layers because of a difference in velocities of seismic waves traveling through each layer.

1910 The worst avalanche in U.S. history is recorded in the small town of Wellington, Washington, when a slab of rock and snow, 10 feet high, half a mile long, and a quarter of a mile wide, broke off Windy Mountain and consumed much of the town. An estimated 96 people were killed in the event.

1912 German meteorologist Alfred Wegener hypothesizes that the continents were, at some time in the past, joined in a supercontinent that he called Pangea. His idea is largely ignored by geologists because Wegener could not suggest a force that could produce such a result.

1920 The worst landslide in recorded history takes place in the rural district of Haiyuan, China. More than 100,000 deaths are attributed to the event.

1922 The Colorado River Compact (also called *The Law of the River*) is signed by six of the seven states that historically have drawn much of their water resources from that source. The agreement is designed to ensure that all of those states will receive a "fair share" of the river's water in perpetuity. The compact suffered from a number of weaknesses and was amended and revised a number of times over the next century.

1925 The worst tornado in U.S. history, the Tri-State Tornado, travels the greatest distance in recorded history, 523 kilometers (327 miles) over the longest-recorded time (4 hours 29 minutes) with the greatest forward speed (120 kilometers per hour; 73 miles per hour).

1927 The first discussion of seismic issues in construction is included as an appendix to the Uniform Building Code, published by the International Conference of Building Officials. Suggestions for voluntary compliance with recommendations are provided in the appendix.

1927 The Great Mississippi Flood engulfs 70,000 square kilometers (27,000 square miles) of water to a depth of up to 9 meters (30 feet), making it the worst flood in U.S. history.

1929 British geologist Arthur Holmes proposes that convection of materials through the mantle is the driving force behind continental drift.

1930s Drought conditions in the American Plains states, along with poor soil management practices, result in numerous wind and dust storms that remove millions of acres of productive soil, essentially eliminating ways of making a living (especially farming and dairying) for millions of residents of the area. With a conservative estimate of 7,000 deaths, the event is generally regarded as the most serious drought in U.S. history.

1931 A series of floods strike China that result in probably the greatest loss of life in human history, estimated as being anywhere from 250,000 to 4 million in number.

1932 The first documented example of human-induced earthquakes resulting from the construction of a dam occurs near the town of Oued Fodda in Algeria. The earthquakes end a few years after the dam was completed, and no long-term consequences occurred.

1933 In response to the Long Beach earthquake of 1933, the city of Los Angeles enacts the first formal seismic building codes in the United States.

1935 American seismologist Charles Richter creates a scale, now known as the Richter scale, for measuring the size of an earthquake.

1935 The Aerial Fire Control Experimental Project was created to study the use of aircraft in locating, monitoring, and attacking forest fires. Progress is made on the first two of these objectives but not on the third.

1935 The worst group of storms to occur during the history of the Dust Bowl in the U.S. Midwest occurs. During the so-called Black Sunday, an estimated 300 million tons of topsoil was blown away. Overall, the Dust Bowl resulted in the largest migration in U.S. history, with an estimated 3.5 million people leaving the Plains states to find new homes in states to the west, primarily California.

1939 The Intermountain Region of the National Forest Service begins trials on the use of firefighters' (smoke jumpers) being air-dropped into area of fires. The first successful smoke-jump occurs a year later.

1941   American seismologists Charles Richter and Beno Gutenberg publish *Seismicity of the Earth and Associated Phenomena*, which explains some fundamental features of seismicity, along with a discussion of the way earthquakes are concentrated in certain specific narrow zones around the planet.

1946   The United Nations creates the United Nations International Children's Emergency Fund (now UNICEF) to provide assistance to children whose lives were devastated by World War II and its aftermath. The organization later expands its mission to include individuals suffering from the effects of natural disasters such as hurricanes, floods, earthquakes, and tsunamis.

1947   A collaborative effort of the U.S. Forest Service and the U.S. Air Force provides the best existing test of the use of aircraft for the release of water and fire retardants as a way of controlling a forest fire. The results of the test become the basis for a new and effective means of dealing with such fires.

1948   The U.S. Coast and Geodetic Survey publishes its first earthquake hazard map, showing four locations in the United States where seismic events are most likely to occur. Such maps have continued to be produced since that date, currently under the auspices of the U.S. Geological Survey, known as *earthquake* or *seismic hazard maps*. (For current maps, see https://www.fema.gov/earthquake-hazard-maps.)

1949   Motivated by the devastating tsunami associated with the 1946 Aleutian Islands earthquake, the Pacific Tsunami Warning Center (PTWC) is established at 'Ewa beach in Oahu, Hawaii. The center monitors potential earthquake/tsunami action. PTWC currently provides warnings to Hawaii, Guam, American Samoa, Wake Island, Johnston Island, Northern Mariana Islands, and all other U.S. interests in the Pacific region.

1957   A task force of the U.S. Forest Service develops Ten Standard Firefighting Orders, guiding principles for fighting a forest fire. The principles were revised in the late 1980s and then returned to their original form in 2002. They are still used to guide firefighting practices in many circumstances.

1958   A landslide along the shore of Lituya Bay, Alaska, triggers the largest tsunami in recorded history, with a height of 524 meters (1,720 feet).

1959–1961   An extended drought in China leads to what is generally regarded as the worst famine in human history. Authorities differ about the total number of deaths during the period, with estimates ranging from more than 15 million to more than 45 million people.

1962–1971   A group of more than 1,500 earthquakes (an "earthquake swarm") occur in the region near Denver, Colorado. The series of events is found to be caused by the injection of chemical wastes into empty wells in the area.

1964   The second largest earthquake in the United States (after the 1700 Cascadia earthquake) strikes Alaska with a force of 9.2 on the Richter scale. One hundred forty-three lives are lost in the event.

1964   The Wilderness Act of 1964 introduces a change in national policy for dealing with forest fires. It permits and encourages a policy of allowing forest fires to run their natural course as long as they can be contained within specific boundaries. The policy is a sharp change from a longstanding policy of fighting *all* forest fires in *all* circumstances on federal lands.

1967   The National Tsunami Warning Center (NTWC) is established in Palmer, Alaska. It currently provides tsunami warnings to all coastal regions of Canada and the United States, except Hawaii, the Caribbean, and the Gulf of Mexico.

1968   The Smithsonian Institution's Global Volcanism Project is established at the Department of Mineral Sciences and the National Museum of Natural History. The purpose of the program is to develop a "better understanding of Earth's active volcanoes and their eruptions during the last 10,000 years."

1968   The research vessel *Glomar Challenger* discovers that rocks along the Mid-Atlantic Ridge are younger than rocks around them, from which they conclude that upwelling of materials from the mantle is bringing new materials to Earth's surface. The discovery provides important evidence in support of Holmes's theory of convection in the mantle, 1929.

1968   Columbia University researchers Bryan Isacks, Jack Oliver, and Lynn R. Sykes publish a famous paper in which they describe "the new global tectonics" and provide evidence in support of Wegener's hypothesis from 1912. The paper is often taken as the turning point in the debate over the possibility of plate tectonics. (The paper is available at http://www.mantleplumes.org/WebDocuments/Isacks1968.pdf.)

1968   The U.S. Congress creates the National Flood Insurance Program to provide a way for citizens to buy affordable flood insurance guaranteed by the U.S. government. The program remains in existence today.

1969   The state of Florida passes legislation providing reinsurance ("backup" insurance) for sinkhole damage. The legislation is shortly declared "obsolete" by the state because few policyholders purchased the option. New sinkhole legislation is not adopted for more than a decade (see **1981**).

1970   The world's worst-recorded avalanche occurs on Mount Huascarán, completely burying the towns of Yungay and Ranrahirca. An estimated 20,000 people are killed in the incident.

1970   The National Oceanic and Atmospheric Administration (NOAA) is founded within the U.S. Department of Commerce, with one of its missions being to provide "better protection of life and property from natural hazards . . . [and] for a better understanding of the total environment." It is currently the primary source for information about hurricanes in the United States. A subsidiary of NOAA, the National

Weather Service, is also involved in both hurricane and tornado education, awareness, preparedness, and related issues.

1970   President Richard M. Nixon signs the Disaster Relief Act of 1970. The act "establishes a permanent, comprehensive program to extend emergency relief and necessary assistance to individuals, organizations, businesses, and States and local communities suffering from major disasters." It includes federal authority to repair or replace damaged public facilities, programs for providing loans to affected individuals, and authority to aid state and local governments for the prevention or amelioration of possible natural disaster. The act was amended in 1974 and 1988, the latter by the Stafford Disaster Relief and Emergency Assistance Act (q.v.).

1971   A group of French doctors create an organization, Médecins Sans Frontières/Doctors Without Borders (MSF), to aid victims of wars and natural disasters. As of 2019, MSF remains one of the preeminent organizations for assisting individuals affected by such events.

1971   American civil engineer Herbert Saffir and meteorologist Robert Simpson devise a numerical scale for representing the intensity of tropical storms.

1972   The worst blizzard in recorded history struck more than 200 villages in Iran with as much as 26 feet of snow. More than 4,000 deaths were reported.

1976   The National Wildfire Coordinating Group is created by a conglomerate of six cabinet-level agencies, the International Association of Fire Chiefs, Intertribal Timber Council, and National Association of State Foresters. The mission of the organization is to coordinate the firefighting efforts of many different groups and prevent duplication of efforts in fighting wildfires.

1977   Congress establishes the National Earthquake Hazard Reduction Program (NEHRP) to reduce the risks to life and property from future earthquakes in the United States and its territories. The goals of the legislation are carried out in the creation of the NEHRP within the U.S. Geological Survey.

1978   As one part of the Presidential Reorganization Plan No. 3 of 1978, the Federal Emergency Management Agency (FEMA) is created. The mission of the new agency is to co-ordinate the response to a disaster in the United States that overwhelms the resources of local and state authorities. In 2002, FEMA became part of the newly created Department of Homeland Security.

1980   Hurricane Allen strikes the Florida Keys with the strongest winds ever recorded for a hurricane reaching the United States, 305 kilometers per hour, or 195 miles per hour.

1980   American physicist Luis Alvarez and his son, Walter, coauthor a paper in which they hypothesize that the Chicxulub Crater in Mexico was created by the impact of an asteroid on Earth about 66 million years ago.

1980   An earthquake at Mount St. Helens, in Washington State, sets off the first limnic eruption occurred in Cameroon at Lake Monoun in 1984, causing asphyxiation and death of 37 people living nearby. A second, deadlier eruption happened at neighboring Lake Nyos in 1986, this time releasing over 80 million cubic meters of CO_2, killing around 1,700 people and 3,500 livestock, again by asphyxiation, said to be the largest in U.S. (and, perhaps, world) history. The dislocated material traveled at speeds of 70–150 miles per hour and removed an estimated 3.7 billion cubic yards (0.67 cubic miles) of material from the mountain.

1981   The state of Florida adopts legislation requiring insurance companies to offer coverage for damage resulting from sinkholes.

1982   Largely through the efforts of American businessman Robert Macauley and Pope John Paul II, the organization Americares is formed to provide aid to victims of natural disasters and other destructive events. Since that time, the organization has provided assistance to a host of events, including the drought in South Sudan beginning in 2013, 2011 floods in Pakistan, 2013 typhoon Haiyan in the Philippines, 2010 Haiti earthquake, 2011 earthquake and tsunami in Japan, and hurricanes Katrine (2005) and Sandy (2012) in the United States.

1982   Chris Newhall of the U.S. Geological Survey and Stephen Self at the University of Hawaii invent a Volcanic Explosivity Index, a measure of the relative severity of volcanic eruptions. The index ranges from 0 (effusive, negligible, and/or no release of material into the atmosphere) to 8 (mega-colossal, with vast release of material into the atmosphere).

1984/1986   Limnic eruptions occur at Lake Monoun (1984) and Lake Nyos (1986), both in Cameroon, causing the death of 37 and more than 1,700 people, respectively, living near the two lakes. The two events are the only known historical events of this kind.

1985   A heavy rainstorm and burst water pipe in the town of Mameyes, Puerto Rico, result in the deadliest mudslide in North American history, with an estimated death toll between 130 and 300.

1986   A sinkhole opens up in the Ural Mountains of Russia over the site of a potash mine. The sinkhole continues to grow larger to the present day (2018), with the likelihood that it will eventually consumer the entire city.

1986   A working group of the U.S. Geological Survey develops a landslide warning system that consists of three states: advisory, watch, and warning.

1988   The U.S. Congress passes the Robert T. Stafford Disaster Relief and Emergency Assistance Act, an amended version of the Disaster Relief Act of 1974. It was designed to outline and provide for an orderly and systematic system for providing aid to state and local communities devastated by a natural disaster. The act provides the framework still used today for the federal government's mechanisms for dealing with natural disasters. Among the services provided for survivors of natural disaster are unemployment assistance, crisis counseling assistance and training, community disaster loans, relocation assistance, and legal services. (For the act in its entirety, see https://www.fema.gov/media-library-data/151 9395888776-af5f95a1a9237302af7e3fd5b0d07d71/Stafford Act.pdf.)

1988   The Intergovernmental Panel on Climate Change is established by the World Meteorological Organization and the United Nations Environment Programme for the purpose of providing the world with an objective, scientific view of climate change and its political and economic impacts.

1989   The most devastating tornado in recorded history strikes the Manikganj district of Bangladesh. The storm destroys the towns of Saturia and Manikgank Sadar, causes damage over an area of about 150 square kilometers (60 square miles), kills an estimated 1,300 people, injures more than 12,000, and leaves about 80,000 people homeless.

1989   The United Nations adopts a resolution designating the 1990s as the International Decade for Natural Disaster Reduction. The purpose of the action is to decrease the loss of life; property destruction; and social and economic disruption caused by natural disasters, such as earthquakes, tsunamis, volcanic eruptions, floods, landslides, droughts, and other types of natural disasters.

1990   Iranian American investment banker founds Relief International, initially for the purpose of providing relief services to survivors of the 7.7-magnitude Manjil–Rudbar earthquake in northwestern Iran. The organization sent and distributed food, shelter, blankets, and other emergency items to earthquake survivors.

1992   Representatives from multiple fire protection agencies create Firewise, a program designed to recommend practical steps that individuals and communities can take to reduce their vulnerability to wildfire.

1993   In response to the Great Flood of 1993 on the Mississippi and Missouri rivers, financial planner Steve Lear founded NECHAMA, the Jewish Response to Disasters, for the purpose of providing direct aid to the survivors of floods, hurricanes, tornadoes, and other natural disasters.

1996   The Departments of Agriculture and Interior combine to produce a Federal Wildland Fire Management Policy and Program Review that recommends overall policy for the handling of forest fires by the two departments. The report includes nine guiding principles to be followed in this effort. The plan is reviewed, revised, and updated in 2001 and 2009.

1999   As a follow-up on the International Decade for Natural Disaster Reduction, the United Nations creates the Office for Disaster Risk Reduction. The agency's charge is to carry out provisions of UN resolution 54/219, which outline the organization's continuing commitment to the reduction of damage caused by natural disasters. (The resolution can be found at http://www.un.org/ga/search/view_doc.asp?symbol=A/RES/54/219.)

1999   Heavy rains in the Vargas district of Venezuela result in the largest mudslides in history. A number of towns and cities are completely covered by debris, with death rates ranging from 10 percent to 100 percent in the region. No death count is possible because so many people were buried in the mudslide, although estimates range from 10,000 to 30,000.

1999   The Intergovernmental Panel on Climate Change (IPCC) issues its first Assessment Report, summarizing the best-available information on global warming, its causes, and its effect on the planet and its inhabitants. IPCC issues a supplement to this report in 1992, followed by second (1995), third (2001), fourth (2007), and fifth (2013–2014) assessment reports. Each report includes the best-available information on climate change at the time of the document's release.

2002 The Homeland Security Act of 2002 establishes a program for preventing, preparing for, responding to, and recovering from major catastrophes, such as terrorist attacks, major natural disasters, and other emergencies. The program is known as the National Response Framework.

2003 The worst forest fire in recorded history occurs in the taiga forests of eastern Siberia. An estimated 47 million acres of forests is destroyed, six times more than the second worst fire in the world (2014 Northwestern Territories blaze).

2003 A heat wave covering the 30-day period from July 30 to August 30 sweeps through Europe, eventually resulting in the death of more than 70,000 people. Heat conditions are made worse by stagnant air that holds toxic chemicals in place over most of the continent.

2004 A 9.1 earthquake off the western coast of the island of Sumatra in Indonesia generates the most destructive tsunami in recorded history. The tsunami results in the death of more than 225,000 people and property damage estimated at about $19.9 billion ($26.6 billion in 2018 dollars).

2005 Inspired by the devastating tsunami triggered by a 2004 earthquake in the Indian Ocean, a special meeting of the United Nations in Kobe, Japan, creates the Indian Ocean Tsunami Warning System to provide advance notice of residents in the area of potential tsunami threats.

2006 President George W. Bush issues Executive Order 13411, "Improving Assistance for Disaster Victims." The order is designed to ensure that anyone who is the "subject of an emergency or major disaster declaration" "have prompt and efficient access to Federal disaster assistance, as well as information regarding assistance available from State and local government and private sector sources." The provisions of this order are carried out, in part, by the creation of the Disaster Assistance Improvement Program (DAIP), which remains in effect today. Resources available to such individuals

can now be traced through DAIP's website at https://www
.disasterassistance.gov/.

2008   An earthquake generally regarded as the most disastrous such event resulting from human dam-building activities
occurs in Sichuan Province, China. In the months following
completion of the dam, a number of earthquakes occurred
resulting in an estimated 461,751 deaths and injuries, about
45 million homes destroyed, and economic losses of an estimated $150 million.

2011   The number of earthquakes, apparently as the result of
human actions, begins to increase rapidly. The trend continues
for at least the next five years.

2011   FEMA releases the National Disaster Recovery Framework (NDRF), a companion document to the National Response Framework, outlining policies and practices for dealing
with major natural and human-caused disasters.

2013   An asteroid about 18 meters (59 feet) in diameter with
a mass of about 9,100 metric tons (10,000 short tons) enters
Earth's atmosphere with a speed of about 19.3 kilometers per
second (40,000–42,900 miles per hour). It explodes a few meters above ground with the release of a burst of light equal to
that of the sun, visible at a distance of up to 100 kilometers
(60 miles).

2014   California governor Jerry Brown signs the Sustainable
Groundwater Management Act (SGMA), a group of three bills
designed to provide a framework for sustainable groundwater
management in the state.

2016   The largest sinkhole in Florida (and U.S.) history opens
in Polk County, at the site of a potash mine. The hole is 40 feet
wide and more than 100 feet deep. Its collapse released into the
surrounding aquifer a mix of toxic and radioactive materials.

2016   The National Academies of Science, Engineering, and
Medicine releases a report, "Attribution of Extreme Weather
Events in the Context of Climate Change," that explores the
current state of research, in terms of the ability to correlate

individual examples of a natural disaster with climate change. It concludes that research of that type is becoming a new field of research in its own right, with many examples of successful efforts to achieve just this objective.

2017   A series of seismic shocks in the vicinity of Pohang, South Korea, is thought to be associated with the construction of a new geothermal plant in the region.

2017   A summary of recent research on natural disasters and climate change issued by the Energy & Climate Intelligence Unit finds that substantial evidence exists for a positive connection between the two phenomena in 41 of 59 cases studied. The greatest number of effects is observed for extreme heat (15 cases), followed by drought and rainfall and flooding (9 cases each), wildfires (4 cases), storms (3 cases), and extreme cold (1 case).

2018   The state of California adopts a new legislation requiring both urban and agricultural suppliers of water in the state to set specific standards for the sustainable use of water.

2018   The federal government releases a report, the *National Near-Earth Object Preparedness Strategy and Action Plan*, reviewing the possible risks from meteorite impacts on Earth, the consequences of such events, and steps that can be taken to reduce the harm resulting from an impact. The report notes that the probability of such events is very low, but their consequences can be catastrophic.

2018   Hawaii's Mount Kilauea erupts with a magnitude of about 5.0. The eruption lasts from May 2018 to January 2019.

Glossary

This glossary includes both terms used in this book and some terms not found in the text. They are terms a person might come across during further research on a natural disasters topic. When a term is specific to a type of disaster, that disaster type is indicated in parentheses.

aftershock   An earthquake with an intensity relatively modest to that of a larger quake, after which it follows.

anthropogenic   Caused by human action.

aquifer   An underground layer of water-bearing permeable rock or unconsolidated materials, such as sand, silt, clay, or gravel, from which groundwater can be usefully extracted.

arrival time (tsunamis)   The time at which the first maximum tsunami waves arrive at some given point.

ash (volcanic)   Fine fragments (less than 2–4 millimeters in diameter) of volcanic rock formed by a volcanic explosion or ejection from a volcanic vent.

asthenosphere   The ductile (flexible) part of the earth in the upper mantle, just below the lithosphere.

attribution science   Research that attempts to find explicit connections between climate change as a general trend and specific examples of natural disasters.

backfire   A fire set to consume fuel in the path of a wildfire and/or change the direction of the fire.

buffer zone   An area of reduced vegetation that separates wildlands from residential or business developments.

caldera   A large basin-shaped depression with a diameter many times larger than included volcanic vents.

cell (weather)   The smallest unit of a storm system, consisting of an air mass that contains up and down drafts that move and react as a single entity; also known as a *storm cell*.

cenote   A sinkhole with exposed rocky edges containing groundwater, most commonly found in the Yucatan Peninsula of Mexico.

climate   The average weather over an area over an extended period of time, typically about 30 years.

climate model   A set of mathematical equations that attempt, based on past weather and climate records, to predict climate patterns at some point in the future.

cold front   An area in which a cold air mass is advancing toward a warm air mass.

confluence   A pattern of wind flow in which air flows inward toward an axis oriented parallel to the general direction of flow. *Also see* **difluence**.

cost/benefit analysis   A method for determining the relative benefits and costs of carrying out some activity on a piece of land, as an aid to determining whether that project should go forward.

cyclone   In general, a storm system in which winds rotate around a center of low atmospheric pressure. Rotation is in a clockwise direction in the Southern Hemisphere and a counterclockwise direction in the Northern Hemisphere; also used as a term for tropical storms that occur in the Indian Ocean.

difluence   A pattern of wind flow in which air flows outward away from an axis oriented parallel to the general direction of flow. *Also see* **confluence**.

disturbance ecology   The study of distinct events that disrupt the functioning of an ecosystem.

Doppler radar   Radar that measures speed and direction of a moving object, such as wind.

downburst   A column of air that sinks downward to the ground and then spreads out in all directions from the center of the column.

drought index   A system developed to indicate the dryness of an area with numbers that represent the net effect of evaporation, transpiration, and precipitation on the land.

earthquake   A sudden and violent shaking of the earth, caused by volcanic action of subsurface movement of tectonic plates.

earthquake swarm   *See* **seismic swarm**.

effusive eruption   The release of magma onto the earth's surface at a slow and steady pace.

ejecta   Any type of material expelled during a volcanic eruption.

El Niño   A weather phenomenon that occurs in the eastern and central equatorial Pacific Ocean, during which the area's winds weaken and sea temperatures rise.

epicenter   The point on Earth's surface that is directly above the focus of an earthquake. *Also see* **focus**.

expansive soils   Types of soil that shrink or swell as the moisture content decreases or increases, thereby causing cracking, breaking, and shifting that may lead to a landslide.

extreme event attribution   Determination of the extent to which some specific type of natural disaster can, with confidence, be attributed to climate change.

eye   The roughly circular area of comparatively light winds that occurs at the center of a hurricane or other severe tropical cyclone.

eyewall   An organized ring of cumulonimbus clouds that surround the eye of a tropical cyclone; also known as a *wall cloud*.

fault   A fracture in Earth's crust in which two blocks of crust on either side of the fault have moved relative to one another.

fire break   A natural or constructed barrier used to stop or check fires or to provide a control line from which to work.

flash flood   A flood caused by heavy or excessive rainfall in a short period of time, generally less than six hours, characterized by raging torrents after heavy rains that rip through river beds, urban streets, or mountain canyons.

flood   An overflow of water onto normally dry land, often caused by rising water in an existing waterway, such as a river, stream, or drainage ditch.

flood basin   A region of land submerged during the highest-known flood in that region.

flood stage   The level at which a body of water begins to flow over its banks onto dry land, usually expressed in feet above sea level.

focus   The region beneath Earth's surface at which an earthquake is generated; also known as the **hypocenter**.

foreshock   Relatively small earthquakes that precede a larger earthquake in a series.

fuel (forest fires)   Combustible material from which a forest fire begins and which allows the fire to continue. Fuels include materials such as grass, leaves, ground litter, plants, shrubs, and trees.

fumarole   Vents from which volcanic gases escape into the atmosphere.

funnel cloud   A rotating mass of air, often at the core of a tornado or hurricane, that reaches from the base of a cloud to a point above (but not touching) Earth's surface.

groundwater   Water that occurs underground, usually in the fractures in rocks and/or in the pores between rocky particles.

high   An area of high atmospheric pressure; also called an *anticyclone*.

hot spot   A region of a wildfire that is especially active.

100-year flood   Floods that are expected to occur, on average, about once in a century. Such floods, then, have a 100 to 1 chance of occurring in any single year.

hydrologic cycle   The natural series of reactions by which water circulates throughout the environment.

hypocenter   *See* **focus**.

induced earthquake   An earthquake that results at least in part as the result of some type of human activity.

intensity (of an earthquake)   A number (written as a Roman numeral) that indicates the severity of an earthquake, in terms of its effects on humans and physical properties.

interstitial water   Water that occurs underground in the empty spaces between rocky material; also known as **pore water**.

inundation distance   The maximum horizontal distance a tsunami reaches upshore from the shoreline.

inundation height   The maximum elevation of a tsunami wave about sea level at the wave's inundation distance.

karst topography   A landform in which underground formations consist of caves caused by the erosion of soluble bedrock, such as limestone or dolomite.

landfall   The point at which the center of a tropical cyclone makes contact with the shoreline.

landslide dam   An artificial, earthen dam created when a landslide completely blocks a stream or river.

lava   Magma (q.v.) that flows to the earth's surface during a volcanic event.

liquefaction   A process that occurs when vibrations in the ground, water pressure, or some other force within a mass of soil cause the soil particles to lose contact with one another, causing the soil to act as a liquid rather than a solid. The soil may then begin to flow downhill.

low   An area of low atmospheric pressure; also known as a **cyclone**.

magma   Magma is molten rock that may be completely liquid or a mixture of liquid rock, dissolved gases, and crystals. Molten rock that flows out onto the earth's surface is called **lava**.

magma chamber   An underground source of magma.

maximum sustained surface wind   The standard measure of a tropical cyclone's intensity, defined as the highest 1-minute average wind at an elevation of 10 meters with an unobstructed exposure at a particular point in time.

Mercalli intensity scale   A system for measuring the effects of an earthquake that includes not only its intensity but also its effects on Earth's surface, humans, objects of nature, and man-made structures.

microburst   A downburst of less than 4 kilometers (2.5 miles) in diameter.

mitigation   Any activity taken to reduce or eliminate the probability that a disaster will occur and/or that eliminates or reduces the effects of a disaster after it actually occurs.

modified Sieberg sea-wave intensity scale   A system for measuring the observed intensity of a tsunami wave, ranging from 1, very light (so weak as to be measured only on recording devices), to 6, disastrous (partial or complete destruction of man-made structures for a significant distance from the shoreline).

mudflow   A process by which fine-grained earthy materials achieve a high degree of fluidity and begin to flow downhill. A more precise term for **mudslide**.

mudslide   *See* **mudflow**.

MYA   Scientific abbreviation for "million years ago."

percolation pond (tank)   A pond, usually constructed by humans, that captures and holds water at times of the year when rains or other water sources are abundant. During dry seasons, the water travels (percolates) back into the ground, recharging an area's aquifer.

pore water   *See* **interstitial water**.

prescribed fire   A fire that is set intentionally for some beneficial purpose, such as eliminating the fuel from which a forest fire might begin.

recession   A drawdown of sea level prior to tsunami flooding, when the ocean bottom may be exposed; a warning sign of an upcoming tsunami.

recharge   The process by which water flows from the earth's surface to underground repositories; the primary method by which water enters an aquifer; also known as *deep drainage* or *deep percolation*.

relative humidity   The ratio of the amount of moisture in the air to the maximum amount of moisture that air would contain if it were saturated.

resilience   The ability to resist and overcome the consequences of a natural disaster. A variety of more detailed and more complex definitions have also been given for this term.

retardant   A substance that reduces the flammability of a combustible material.

retention pond   An artificial pond constructed to manage stormwater runoff, thereby preventing flooding and downstream erosion; also called a *wet pond* or *wet detention basin*.

Ring of Fire   The zone surrounding the Pacific Ocean in which about 90 percent of the world's earthquakes occur.

rockburst (or rock burst)   A kind of induced earthquake caused by human activities, such as mining excavations.

seismic swarm   A series of earthquakes within a relatively small area resulting from a common cause, such as the injection of liquid wastes into wells.

seismicity   The occurrence of earthquakes caused by the fracturing of rocks in the earth's crust; also known as *seismic activity*.

seismograph   A device used to detect and record earthquakes. The term is often used as a synonym for **seismometer**.

seismometer   *See* **seismograph**.

slip   The relative motion of rock on either side of a fault with respect to the other side.

storm surge   The abnormal rise in seawater level during a storm, measured as the height of the water above the normal predicted astronomical tide, caused primarily by onshore winds associated with the storm.

subaqueous landslide   *See* **submarine landslide**.

subduction   The process by which portions of the lithosphere underlying the ocean collide with and descend beneath the continental lithosphere.

submarine landslide   A landslide that occurs beneath water; also known as **subaqueous landslide**.

subsidence   The downward movement of surface material as the result of natural or anthropogenic actions, normally caused by the removal of underground water or underground mining.

supercell   An unusually large storm cell that may spawn numerous thunderstorms and/or tornadoes.

tectonic plate   Large, thin, relatively rigid plates that move relative to one another on the outer surface of Earth.

tsunami   A large tidal wave caused by a seismic event, volcanic eruption, or other seabed event.

typhoon   A tropical cyclone with winds more than 74 miles per hour and located in the north Pacific, west of the international date line.

Volcanic Explosivity Index (VEI)   A numeric scale that measures the relative explosivity of historic eruptions, based on volume of products, eruption cloud height, and qualitative observations. Terms used to describe each of the eight categories in the index range from "gentle" to "mega-colossal."

warm front   An area where a warm air mass is advancing toward a cold air mass.

watershed   An area that drains into a lake, stream, or other body of water; also known as a *catchment area*.

wildland-urban interface (WUI)   The region in which houses come into contact with, or lie close to, undeveloped wildland vegetation.

wind shear   A difference in wind speed and/or direction over a relatively short distance in the atmosphere. Atmospheric wind shear may be described as either vertical or horizontal wind shear.

Index

Note: page numbers followed by the letters "t" and "f" in italics indicate tables and figures/photographs, respectively.

About the Author

David E. Newton holds an associate's degree in science from Grand Rapids (Michigan) Junior College, a BA in chemistry (with high distinction), an MA in education from the University of Michigan, and an EdD in science education from Harvard University. He is the author of more than 400 textbooks, encyclopedias, resource books, research manuals, laboratory manuals, trade books, and other educational materials. He taught mathematics, chemistry, and physical science in Grand Rapids, Michigan, for 13 years; was professor of chemistry and physics at Salem State College in Massachusetts for 15 years; and was adjunct professor in the College of Professional Studies at the University of San Francisco for 10 years.

The author's previous books for ABC-CLIO include *Global Warming* (1993), *Gay and Lesbian Rights* (1994, 2009), *The Ozone Dilemma* (1995), *Violence and the Media* (1996), *Environmental Justice* (1996, 2009), *Encyclopedia of Cryptology* (1997), *Social Issues in Science and Technology: An Encyclopedia* (1999), *DNA Technology* (2009, 2016), *Sexual Health* (2010), *The Animal Experimentation Debate* (2013), *Marijuana* (2013, 2017), *World Energy Crisis* (2012), *Steroids and Doping in Sports* (2014, 2018), *GMO Food* (2014), *Science and Political Controversy* (2014), *Wind Energy* (2015), *Fracking* (2015), *Solar Energy* (2015), *Youth Substance Abuse* (2016), *Global Water Crisis* (2016), *Same-Sex Marriage* (2011, 2016), *Sex and Gender* (2017), and *STDs in the United States* (2018). His other recent books include *Physics: Oryx Frontiers of Science Series* (2000), *Sick!* (four volumes) (2000), *Science, Technology, and Society: The Impact of*

Science in the 19th Century (two volumes, 2001), *Encyclopedia of Fire* (2002), *Molecular Nanotechnology: Oryx Frontiers of Science Series* (2002), *Encyclopedia of Water* (2003), *Encyclopedia of Air* (2004), *The New Chemistry* (six volumes, 2007), *Nuclear Power* (2005), *Stem Cell Research* (2006), *Latinos in the Sciences, Math, and Professions* (2007), and *DNA Evidence and Forensic Science* (2008). He has also been an updating and consulting editor on a number of books and reference works, including *Chemical Compounds* (2005), *Chemical Elements* (2006), *Encyclopedia of Endangered Species* (2006), *World of Mathematics* (2006), *World of Chemistry* (2006), *World of Health* (2006), *UXL Encyclopedia of Science* (2007), *Alternative Medicine* (2008), *Grzimek's Animal Life Encyclopedia* (2009), *Community Health* (2009), *Genetic Medicine* (2009), *The Gale Encyclopedia of Medicine* (2010–2011), *The Gale Encyclopedia of Alternative Medicine* (2013), *Discoveries in Modern Science: Exploration, Invention, and Technology* (2013–2014), and *Science in Context* (2013–2014).